Horse Lover's
DAILY COMPANION

QUARRY

Horse Lover's
DAILY COMPANION

....

365 Days
of Tips and Inspiration for Living a Joyful Life with Your Horse

Audrey Pavia

Principal Photography by Tom Sapp

QUARRY BOOKS

First published in the United States of America by
Quarry Books, a member of
Quayside Publishing Group
100 Cummings Center
Suite 406-L
Beverly, Massachusetts 01915-6101
Telephone: (978) 282-9590
Fax: (978) 283-2742
www.quarrybooks.com

Library of Congress Cataloging-in-Publication Data
Pavia, Audrey.
Horse lover's daily companion : 365 days of tips and inspiration for living a joyful life with your horse / Audrey Pavia ; photography by Tom Sapp.
p. cm.
Includes index.
ISBN-13: 978-1-59253-570-5
ISBN-10: 1-59253-570-4
1. Horses--Miscellanea. I. Title.
SF301.P347 2009
636.1--dc22

2009011809
CIP

ISBN-13: 978-1-59253-570-5
ISBN-10: 1-59253-570-4

10 9 8 7 6 5 4 3 2 1

Design: everlution design
Illustrations: Gayle Isabelle Ford

Printed in China

Horse Lover's Daily Companion contains a variety of tips and recommendations for your horse. While caution was taken to give safe recommendations, it is impossible to predict the outcome of each suggestion. Neither Audrey Pavia, Tom Sapp, nor the publisher, Quayside Publishing Group, accepts liability for any mental, financial, or physical harm that arises from following the advice or techniques, using the procedures in this book. Readers should use personal judgment when applying the recommendations of this text.

For Milagro, my gift from above

contents

Introduction: Equine Inspiration

Horses are beautiful and amazing creatures, and anyone who has spent time with these animals knows they were put here to provide us with both joy and the chance to discover ourselves. But sometimes life with horses can be challenging. They get sick and depress us, they misbehave and scare us, and they bleed our bank accounts. They need to be cared for and attended to regardless of the weather, no matter how we are feeling, and despite whatever we'd rather be doing.

If horses are your life's passion, it doesn't take long for you to get over whatever negative feelings have arisen at the moment and get back to enjoying your horse. But it sure helps to have a little inspiration. That's where this book comes in. The photos, which weave a story of their own, will inspire you as you peruse the pages.

In this tome, you will find rousing notions, activity suggestions, and novel details that will remind you of why you love horses. These pages will help you refocus on your horse and get you back to the place inside that brought you to horses to begin with.

The information in this book is organized based on the days of the week, and each day is assigned a source of equine inspiration and hands-on practice. It may feel like a calendar in some ways and a book of days in others. It's not meant to represent any particular season, location, or time. Instead, our intent is to give you a year's worth of day-by-day ideas and activities that will stoke your passion for horses and inspire you to spend as much time as you can in their presence.

Whether you need something to remind you of how incredible horses really are, or you are looking for some fresh ideas for how to spend quality time with your horse, this book will fit the bill.

—AUDREY PAVIA

How to Use This Book

This book is organized as a day minder, with entries creating a complete year's worth of information. Each of the year's fifty-two weeks has six entries.

You can start reading this book from the beginning, following the days of the week through the calendar year, reading one entry each day. You can also read from the middle of the book, the end, or skip around from week to week as inspiration strikes. The most important thing to remember is that you can use this book however you want. When you love a horse, every day is a surprise, and this book reflects that spirit. Turn to any page, and you will find another useful tip. Another (equally enjoyable) part of the horse–human relationship is the daily routine—whether it is your daily ride or favorite grooming habit. Likewise, you can come back time and time again to your favorite page.

What's next? Set aside some time and find a quiet place that is yours alone. Enjoy this book at your own pace and remember to have fun. You already know how special horses are. Now, with this book, you will have all the tips, history, and techniques you will need for living a rich life with your horse.

A Horse Lover's Year

 MONDAYS introduce the wide variety of horse breeds, from the Appaloosa to the Zorse.

 TUESDAYS detail equine activities, such as riding sidesaddle, herding cows, and driving.

 WEDNESDAYS are devoted to horses through the ages, from prehistory to modern equine heroes.

 THURSDAYS offer behind-the-scenes access to real life in the stable.

 FRIDAYS are devoted to health, wellness, and nutrition.

 WEEKENDS are reserved for bonding and relationship building, and planning special occasions.

The Colorful Appaloosa

THE APPALOOSA FIRST originated as an American breed in Idaho. Spotted horses were among the mounts of the Nez Perce tribe of Pacific Northwest when Lewis and Clark made their famous journey to the Oregon coast. In the 1940s, a group of American horsemen who appreciated the rugged nature and beautiful coat patterns of this breed formed the Appaloosa Horse Club. This organization still registers the breed today, and there are equivalent organizations in most countries worldwide.

Appaloosas are known for their gentle dispositions, their hardy constitutions, and their colorful coats. The breed comes in patterns that include leopard, blanket with spots, frosted hips, and snowflake. The color genetics of this breed are fascinating, and are regularly studied by researchers, who are striving to isolate the different coat pattern genes.

Appaloosas are used for just about every discipline, including trail, Western showing, cow work, hunter and jumper, and cross-country.

Appaloosa

Hitting the Trail

FEW ACTIVITIES ARE as relaxing as riding a well-trained horse down a beautiful woodland trail. Trail riding is the most popular pastime of horse owners, and if you've ever participated in this activity, you know why.

Although most trail riding is done in open, undeveloped, natural environments, horse owners in developed areas also take their mounts out on the trail. Bridle paths are a part of many equestrian communities in well-populated areas, and they pose special challenges to both horses and riders who must deal with distractions that rural horses rarely see, such as dogs on leashes, packs of pedestrians, and all-terrain vehicles

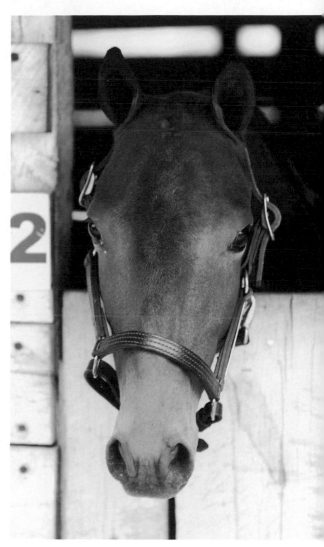

If you don't trail ride with your horse, you should start. Begin by getting your horse used to the idea. Take him out the first time with one or two very calm horses, and don't go too far. Horses that are used to working only in an arena can become worried when they leave the safety of the ring. By gradually accustoming your horse to the idea of being outside in the world, you'll find, in most cases, he will learn to like it.

Whenever you trail ride, take a buddy and a cell phone with you. Make sure your phone is attached to your body and not to the horse—just in case the two of you become separated. Know where you are going and how to get back, and always let someone know when you plan to return.

Remember to always wear a helmet when you are trail riding. Although it's romantic to feel the wind in your hair when you are riding, it's smarter to protect your gray matter with a helmet.

Alexander's Horse

ALEXANDER THE GREAT, the ancient Greek king of Macedonia who lived from 356 to 323 BC, was a great warrior and leader, but he was also a famous horseman. His black stallion, Bucephalus, is credited by some to have inspired Alexander to his role as conqueror.

Alexander met Bucephalus when the horse was three years old and Alexander was just a boy. The unruly colt did not allow anyone on his back until Alexander tamed him. This triumph sparked (or confirmed) Alexander's passion for dominance.

Bucephalus carried Alexander all the way from Macedonia to modern-day Afghanistan—a journey that took three years. Believed to be the offspring of a Barb stallion, Bucephalus was Alexander's mount until the Battle of the Hydaspes in 326 BC in what is now Pakistan. He is buried in Jalalpur Sharif, a small town just outside of Jhelum, Pakistan.

Stall Mucking, Anyone?

IT'S EVERY HORSE OWNER'S least favorite activity but one of the most frequently necessary. Who could possibly enjoy removing manure from a stall or paddock?

By cleaning out your horse's stall each day, you provide him with a more aesthetically pleasing environment, and also a healthier one. Horses who live in dirty stalls are prone to hoof disease, especially thrush, which is a nasty infection that can rot a horse's hoof from the inside out. Removing soiled bedding and manure from the stall also reduces the number of stable flies in the horse's world. Stable flies bite your horse until he bleeds, and they are carriers of disease.

A clean stall is also good for your horse's lungs. Horses that inhale ammonia vapors that accumulate from lingering urine can have compromised airways.

To help make your mucking job easier, apply the following tips:

- Invest in a good manure fork. A variety of different style forks are at your local feed store, including ones that are ergonomically designed.

- Provide your horse with bedding that is absorbent without being dusty, especially if you or your horse has allergies.

- Have manure hauled off your property often to cut down on odor and flies. If you decide to spread or compost your manure, check with your local officials. Depending on where you live, and whether you live in a horse community, environmental agencies may be strict about keeping waterways free of bacteria from animal waste. Spreading and composting of manure is no longer allowed in many areas.

Stay on top of your stall cleaning, and your job will be easier. Nothing is worse than tacking a stall that hasn't been cleaned for several days.

13

Coping with Colic

HORSE OWNERS DREAD DEALING WITH colic, and for good reason. In horses, colic produces a serious and unpleasant set of symptoms that can result in death or severe illness if not treated immediately.

Colic is basically stomach pain, which, in horses, can be extremely uncomfortable. Because of the way horses are built—they can't vomit, and they have many feet of intestine in their abdominal cavity—digestive issues can be difficult to resolve.

The symptoms of colic include pawing, rolling, sweating, and biting at the flanks. Any horse with these symptoms must be seen by a veterinarian immediately. Causes can range from something as simple as gas pain to a problem as severe as a ruptured intestine.

It's easier to prevent colic than to fix it. Feed your horse plenty of hay for roughage, as often as you can each day. Always have a plentiful amount of fresh drinking water on hand. Provide your horse with daily exercise to keep her digestive system functioning well, and make any changes to her diet as gradually as possible.

THE EQUINE DIGESTIVE SYSTEM

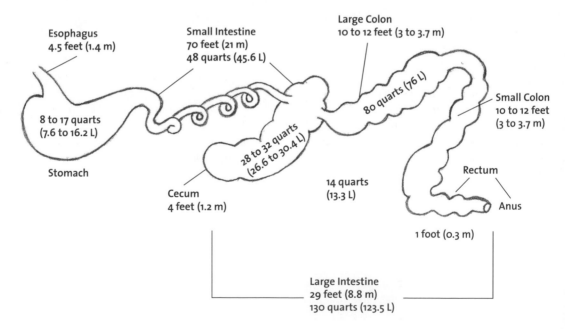

Esophagus
4.5 feet (1.4 m)

Small Intestine
70 feet (21 m)
48 quarts (45.6 L)

Large Colon
10 to 12 feet (3 to 3.7 m)

80 quarts (76 L)

Small Colon
10 to 12 feet
(3 to 3.7 m)

8 to 17 quarts
(7.6 to 16.2 L)

Stomach

28 to 32 quarts
(26.6 to 30.4 L)

Cecum
4 feet (1.2 m)

14 quarts
(13.3 L)

Rectum

Anus

1 foot (0.3 m)

Large Intestine
29 feet (8.8 m)
130 quarts (123.5 L)

Take a Walk with your Horse

MOST PEOPLE WHO OWN HORSES love to ride, and spend all their horse time sitting on their horse's back. You can do wonders to nurture the relationship between you and your horse by spending some time with your horse with your feet on the ground.

Taking a walk with your horse is a great way to spend time with him. Instead of mounting up, dress your horse only in his halter and go for a stroll. If you board your horse at a stable, cruise around the facilities with your horse at your side. If you live on a farm, survey your property with your horse as your walking companion. If you have access to a trail nearby, walk your horse into the great wide open.

EXERCISE

A casual hand walk is a good time to reinforce your horse's ground manners. Ask him to stop every now and then, and reward him when he follows your direction precisely. Do some turns with your horse, asking him to circle. Occasionally stop and ask him to back up. Reward him with plenty of praise and pats for his work.

As you stroll, talk to your horse and tell him about your day. Or describe the scenery around you and tell your horse what you like about it. The jury is out on whether your horse can really understand what you are trying to communicate, but he will pick up on the fact that you are enjoying spending time with him. And he'll reward you for it with a deeper bond.

The Spanish Mustang

WHEN THE SPANIARDS FIRST CAME to the New World, they brought more than swords and a lust for gold with them. They also brought horses.

Bred to carry soldiers for days on end through rugged terrain, the horses that came with the Spaniards to Mexico eventually found their way to what is today the southwestern United States. From there, wild horses slowly spread to the American Plains and the Pacific Northwest, where they flourished. By the mid-1800s, millions of wild horses roamed the continent, and they served as the mounts for Native Americans and anyone else who could capture and tame them.

After the Indian Wars (1823–1890), the populations of these rugged mustangs began to decline. As a result of deliberate cross-breeding and extermination, their numbers dwindled until, in the 1950s, only a handful of the original Spanish horses were left in remote areas of the western United States.

It was then that a few ranchers, hoping to save this horse from extinction, rounded them up and began breeding them in captivity.

Today, this breed is called the Spanish Mustang. Though small in stature and numbers, this horse is rich in history. The breed is also as hardy as its ancestors once were. Easily trained and full of personality, Spanish Mustangs are also among the most colorful horses in the world. They can be seen in dun, grulla, brindle, pinto, and Appaloosa colorings.

Although rare, the breed is slowly growing in numbers as horsemen around the world are discovering its rare and beautiful traits.

Spanish Mustang

Riding Sidesaddle

IT'S NOT A COMMON WAY TO RIDE, but it's a fun one: sidesaddle. There was a time when women only rode this way. It was considered unladylike to sit astride a horse, especially in a dress.

The sidesaddle was developed in the Middle Ages in Europe to allow women in fine dress to ride politely. The saddle has undergone changes over the millennia, and now features a second horn on the front of the saddle, which gives the rider more security.

Riding sidesaddle is a unique experience if you have only ever ridden astride. It feels odd to have both your legs on one side of the horse, and it takes skill and strength to keep your pelvis straight and centered in the saddle.

It's not common to see women riding sidesaddle anymore, but those who do are proficient in this discipline. Just about any discipline ridden astride can also be ridden aside. Jumping, barrel racing, dressage, and even cattle work can be done sidesaddle.

Although a horse needs some training to be ridden sidesaddle, just about any mount can be taught to accommodate this kind of saddle and riding style. The most difficult part of sidesaddle is finding a trainer who teaches it. The International Side Saddle Organization certifies instructors in this discipline and provides referrals for people wanting to learn this type of riding. (See "Resources" on page 316.)

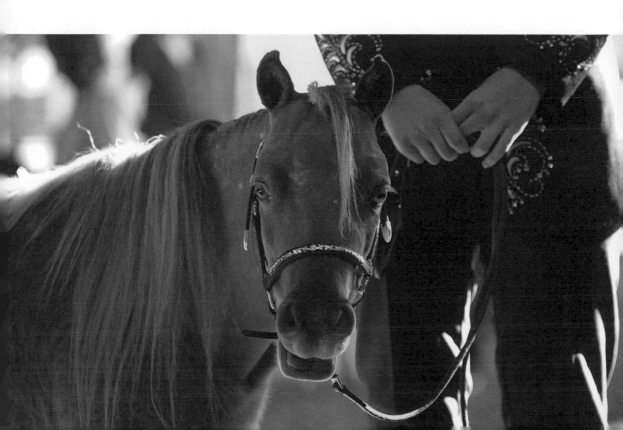

Life for Prehistoric Eohippus

IT IS HARD TO BELIEVE that the modern horse was once only the size of a fox. At least that is the consensus of scientists who have studied the evolution of the horse.

The horse has undergone incredible physical change over the past sixty million years. The very first horse was a creature called eohippus (also called hyracotherium). With four toes on the front feet and three in the back, eohippus grazed on the leaves of trees and brush, and occasionally ate fruits and nuts. Its feet were suited for walking on the soft, leafy ground of the forests. Carnivores preyed on this early horse, including cat- and dog-like beasts who also lived in the primeval jungle.

Scientists believe eohippus had a tawny coat with a spotted front and striped rear, making it harder for predators to see in the leafy forest. Its teeth were short in the crown and long in the root. This eventually changed as horses began to graze in the open instead of eating leaves in the forest.

Over millions of years, eohippus evolved from having four toes in the front and three in the back to having one toe on each leg. Vestiges of the original toes can still be seen on all horses in the form of splint bones, chestnuts, and ergots.

Imagining life for eohippus gives us insight into the minds of modern horses. Although protected from horse-eating predators, today's horses still retain the powerful instinct of wariness that enabled their ancestors to survive for eons.

When Horses Sleep

MANY PEOPLE THINK HORSES never lie down. This must mean they sleep standing up, right? The truth is that they do lie down, and yet they also sleep on their feet.

Unlike humans, horses don't need eight to ten hours of sleep a night. Because they are prey animals, nature designed them to be able to function well on very little sleep—only a few hours a day, in fact. After all, a sleeping prey animal is a vulnerable one.

Humans need about two hours of REM sleep per night, but horses only need fifteen minutes of this type of sleep in a twenty-four-hour day. To get this deep sleep, they must lie down. She either lies flat on her side or lounges in a recumbent position, her legs tucked to the side and her chin resting on the ground. The rest of sleep time can be standing up, thanks to a "stay apparatus" in the legs that allow her to lock her leg joints so she can doze without falling over.

For a horse to get the sleep she really needs, she has to feel safe and be completely relaxed. Most horses can't achieve this level of comfort without a buddy horse nearby to stand guard in case of predators. Researchers believe that horses living alone are often sleep deprived because they never feel secure enough to lie down for REM sleep.

Protection from West Nile Virus

NEARLY EVERYONE HAS HEARD OF West Nile Virus, a nasty disease spread by mosquitoes. Only two common animal species are profoundly affected by the virus: humans and horses.

Videos of horses suffering from the acute stages of this devastating disease are heartbreaking to watch. They stagger and fall repeatedly, or worse, they are unable to get up. Death ultimately results, and at this point, it is welcome.

As a horse owner, it's your responsibility to protect your equine companion from infection by West Nile Virus. The following steps are precautions everyone should take:

- Vaccinate your horse regularly against the disease. Frequency recommendations vary among veterinarians, but once or twice yearly is the norm.

- Keep mosquito populations down in your area. You can do this by eliminating standing water wherever you find it: rain gutters, barrels, buckets, and even puddles. Water leaks are a good source for pools of water that attract mosquitoes laying eggs.

- Stock your water trough with mosquito fish. These small, guppy-like critters will eat all the mosquito larvae they can find. Your local health department or vector control agency will probably provide them to you for free.

- Board your horse indoors at night to prevent contact with biting mosquitoes. Cover him up with a fly sheet that also blocks mosquitoes. Get your horse inside just before dusk, and wait until well after dawn to put him back outside.

If you notice your horse is showing any signs of West Nile infection—stumbling, loss of muscle coordination, muscle twitching, drooping head, lethargy, or falling asleep while eating—contact your veterinarian right away.

Planning a Portrait Session

YOU ARE PROUD of your horse and want to show her off. It's only natural. One way to do this is to keep photos of her in your wallet, on your desk at work, or on your computer desktop.

You don't need a professional photographer to get good photos of your horse. With the help of an assistant, you can take pretty good shots of your equine buddy.

PREPARATION FOR THE SHOOT

Bathe your horse thoroughly the day before you plan to shoot. This will give her natural oils time to come back into her coat, which will give her better shine in the photographs. Put a blanket or sheet on her overnight to keep her from getting dirty after you put her away. Braid her tail and wrap it in a tail bag to keep it silky and free from tangles before the photo session.

If you regularly **clip your horse's fetlocks, muzzle, and bridle path**, remember to do this too, either the day before the shoot or the morning of. You want her to look as neat and trim as possible.

Find your horse's nicest halter or a good bridle and dress her in it for the shoot. Be sure to clean it up before you put it on her. Remove the dust and dirt with a damp sponge. If it's made of leather, apply some leather conditioner and buff it so it shines.

THE DAY OF THE SESSION

If you are using a digital camera, set it to the highest quality setting. You can always reduce the size of your photo file if you want to email it, but you can't make the file larger once you have taken the photo.

Find a picturesque location for your horse to stand for the photo. Trees, bushes with colorful flowers, or a flat, natural landscape all make good backgrounds. Have your assistant position your horse so you see this attractive background behind your horse from where you plan to shoot. Make sure the sun is behind you so you aren't shooting into it. The sun should illuminate your horse. See if any part of your horse is in shadow. If so, change her position.

After you position your horse, be sure to **look through the lens** and make sure you don't see any cars, trailers, or barnyard junk in the background as this will distract from your horse.

Next, **decide if you want just a head shot** of your horse, or her entire body. Frame your horse so either her head or her body takes up most of what you see through the camera lens. Be careful not to cut off her ears or her hooves.

Now comes the hardest part: **get your horse's ears up so he looks alert!** Try kissing your lips toward your horse to see if she pricks her ears and looks toward you. Or ask a third person to stand behind you at an angle and make noises so the horse will look. You may also have this person wave a plastic bag or other object to get your horse to perk up. Be sure the person is standing far enough away from your horse that the horse doesn't spook.

Take as many different shots as you have time for. If you get one or two good ones out of a session of many photos, you are lucky. Professional photographers often take hundreds of pictures to get just a few that are worth publishing.

20

The Hardy Haflinger

THE HAFLINGER IS AN ATTRACTIVE little horse that hails from the Austrian and Italian Alps of Europe. Named after the Tyroleon mountain village of Hafling, these hardy mountain ponies lived in the Alps during the Middle Ages. They spent their lives among the winding, narrow paths of the steep mountains, plowing fields, pulling logs, and carrying alpine farmers through the rugged terrain.

Although most European farmers began using tractors and other motor vehicles for farm work by the early 1900s, the Haflinger remained the transportation of choice in the Alps. During World War II, the breed was also used as military packhorses in the mountains. Not long after the war ended, the Austrian government took control of the breeding of Haflingers.

In the 1960s, the first Haflingers were exported to the United States. One group of horses went to live in the state of Washington, the other in Illinois. Two registries formed to represent the breed in the United States, the Haflinger Registry of North America and the Halfinger Association of America. In 1998, these two registries combined to make the American Haflinger Registry, the group that registers the breed today. (See "Resources" on page 316.)

Today, Haflingers are used in a variety of disciplines. They are seen in different shades of chestnut, from light to dark. All Haflingers have a white or blond mane and tail, and they measure anywhere from 13.2 hands to 15 hands in height.

What Is a Hand?

In equine vernacular, a hand is a measurement used to describe the height of a horse. A hand is equivalent to 4 inches (10 cm). So a horse that is 60 inches (1.5 m) at the withers (where the neck joins the back) is 15 hands high. A horse that is 62 inches (1.5 m) at the withers, is considered 15.2 hands

22

Haflinger

Competitive Sport: Cutting Cows

THE SPORT OF CUTTING CATTLE is as colorful as its origins on the wild North American frontier. Cutting is the singling out of a designated cow from a herd of approximately thirty head of cattle. The horse and rider team separates the cow from the group and prevents it from returning to the other cows. Not as easy as it sounds!

Cutting is an exciting sport that really gets your adrenaline pumping. You need a horse with "cow sense" to participate in this sport, because the horse does most of the work on his own.

Quarter Horses, Paints, and Appaloosas are the breeds most often seen in cutting competitions, although Arabians and Morgans can also be good at it.

Cutting events require that a rider remove a cow from the herd and keep it away from the rest of the cows for a full two minutes. Horses are judged on their abilities to do the job without interference from the riders.

The Invention of the Stirrup

IF THERE IS ONE PIECE OF equipment modern riders take for granted, it's the stirrup. These days, every saddle uses stirrups, no matter what the style. But before 300 AD, stirrups didn't exist. Riders essentially rode either bareback or with a treeless saddle, and nothing to support the foot.

In India in 500 BC, a toe loop was used to stabilize the rider's foot. It wasn't until the Chinese invented the dual stirrup 800 years later that riding styles began to change.

With the invention of the stirrup, warfare on horseback became very different. Mounted warriors were no longer so easily cast from their horses during battle.

They were also able to use their weapons with more force because they were able to brace themselves against the stirrups as they plunged their swords toward the enemy.

Some scholars believe that the invention of the stirrup was as important as the development of the wheel. Its effect on civilization was profound because it made horses much more useful in the areas of warfare and transportation.

Stirrups never fell out of favor over the centuries, and they still remain a vital piece of equipment for riders of every discipline. Next time you mount up, think about this invention that literally changed the world.

23

Fly, Fly, Go Away

IT'S HARD TO FIND A HORSE PERSON whose love for horses isn't equalled by his or her hatred of flies. These pests are more than annoying. They inflict painful bites on horses (and humans) and spread disease.

At a glance, all flies seem to look alike. If you look closer at these insects and observe their behavior, you'll see that the flies that hang around horses are of several different species.

The most common horse-pestering insect is the stable fly. These flying parasites feed on the blood of horses and can be seen resting on the lower legs, where they prefer to bite. Stable flies lay eggs in manure and soiled bedding, and they multiply very quickly. One stable fly can produce 1,600 offspring in one month.

Another common pest is the face fly. These creatures feed on the secretions of the equine eye, and they gather in the corner of a horse's eye from sunrise to sunset, causing extreme irritation and spreading disease. These flies lay their eggs in cattle manure, and they are usually seen on horses that are stabled within a mile (1.6 km) or so from cows.

The horse fly may also bother horses, although not in the same numbers as stable and face flies. Horse flies are large black insects with white heads that land on a horse's withers or hindquarters and deliver painful bites. These flies reproduce in damp places, such as stagnant marshes and areas near drainage pipes.

Also common is the black fly (or no-see-ums), which are more like gnats and can be difficult to spot. Your horse has them if she's always shaking her head, especially around dawn or dusk when these insects are most active. Look closely, and you'll probably see the bugs crawling around on the inside of your horse's ears. These flies breed in dampness, and they are most prevalent when there is standing water nearby.

Getting rid of flies completely is impossible, but you can do a lot to manage them by employing an arsenal of different anti-fly weapons. Try these:

- Fly traps: Either baited traps or sticky traps or both

- Fly predators: Tiny parasitic wasps that feed on fly larvae

- Fly cover-ups: Fly sheets, fly masks, leg wraps, and ear covers come between the fly and the horse's skin

- Fly sprays and wipes: Products designed to kill and repel flies when they try to land on the horse

A combination of fly control products can help make your horse's life a little easier when it comes to dealing with these pesky insects.

Eating Hay—and Lots of It

HORSES EAT HAY, and with good reason. It's the most palatable and accessible type of forage available for the domestic horse.

The horse evolved over time as a grazer, which means nature designed her to consume large amounts of low-quality forage. In the wild, the horse had to eat a lot of plant material to maintain her body weight. The equine digestive system is an amazing machine that can pull nutrients from even the poorest quality grazing. The flipside of this is that the horse's body is meant to slowly absorb large amounts of roughage, over many hours per day. In fact, wild horses forage for around eighteen hours each day.

In domestic life, horses are often fed infrequently, usually only twice a day. They are often given large amounts of concentrated feed, such as grain or commercial horse food. They eat this food quickly and absorb its energy rapidly. This wreaks havoc with their natural digestive process—and their minds as well. After all, nature never intended them to eat in this way. Horses are supposed to chew, constantly—nearly all day—slowly ingesting low-energy roughage.

Unfortunately, most horse owners don't have the luxury of being able to graze their horses in pastures for many hours per day. Many horses live in paddocks, corrals, or even stalls, and they are dependent on their human caretakers to provide them with their meals.

Given this reality, the most natural way to feed horses is to provide them with hay, and plenty of it. Horses do best when fed at least three times a day—more often if possible. (Some experts even recommend access to hay twenty-four hours a day.) These meals should consist mostly of hays that are relatively low in protein, such as orchard grass, Bermuda grass, or timothy. Alfalfa hays are too high in calories and energy for most horses (it's a crop originally produced for cattle), and they should be used only in small amounts if at all. Grass hays most resemble the kind of feed horses evolved to eat.

Maintaining Beautiful Manes and Tails

LONG, FLOWING EQUINE LOCKS give a horse a wild and romantic look. The quality and quantity of a horse's mane and tail are largely the result of genetics, but you can do a lot to help things along while at the same time spending quality time with your horse.

EXERCISE

To get your horse's mane and tail in their best possible shape, start with a good washing. Use a shampoo that is made specifically for horses because the pH balance will be just right. Rinse thoroughly and follow with a mane and tail conditioner. You'll find many products in your local tack and feed store, or in horse supply catalogs and on the Internet. (If you aren't sure what brand to buy, ask other horse owners what they like or talk to the tack store staff for a recommendation.)

After washing and conditioning the mane and tail, let them air-dry thoroughly. Use your fingers to undo any tangles and follow by brushing them out with a body brush. Avoid the temptation to use a regular hairbrush or mane and tail comb. That would result in pulling out and breaking the hair.

Once the mane and tail are clean, dry, and silky, it's time to protect them. If your horse has a long mane and you have the time, braid it in sections. This will help keep the individual hairs from breaking and from tangling.

Plait your horse's tail in a single braid, secure the end with a rubber band, and wrap it in a tail bag, which you can buy at tack and feed stores. This will help keep it clean and further protect the hairs from breakage.

Every time you take your horse out for a ride, unwrap the tail braid and brush the tail out with a body brush. Then, before you put your horse back in his stall, braid his tail again and put it back into the tail bag. Whenever you bathe your horse, wash his mane and tail again and follow this same procedure. In six months, you'll be stunned at how long your horse's mane and tail have grown, and how great they look.

> All the time you spend working on your horse's mane and tail is time together bonding. Standing for this procedure also helps teach your horse patience when tied. These regular beautifying sessions will leave your horse looking great, and he'll also feel special for all the extra attention.

27

The Magnificent Morgan

ONE OF THE OLDEST American breeds of horses is the Morgan, a small animal with a powerful history.

The story began when a two-year-old colt was born in Springfield, Massachusetts, in 1789 and became the property of a Vermont farmer and music teacher named Justin Morgan. Morgan named the horse Figure and used him for riding and farm work. The young stallion soon became known throughout the region for his profound strength, speed, and willing temperament. Only 14 hands in height, he could drag more weight than far larger horses. He also beat taller horses in match races, and he was wiling to do anything asked of him.

Because of Figure's noteworthy prowess, he became a popular stallion with mare owners, who traveled many miles to breed their horses to him.

Figure's offspring were surprisingly similar to their sire in both strength and temperament, and Figure's prepotency became legend.

For good reason, Figure is considered the foundation sire of the Morgan horse breed. Figure's descendents went on to become vital in the development of the United States over the decades to come. They were among the mounts of the Civil War and the horses that carried the U.S. cavalry in the West.

Today, the Morgan horse remains a strong, willing mount, complete with a beautiful, graceful appearance and a tough constitution. These horses are seen vying in the show ring, working cattle in the West, and competing on the trail.

Morgan

Everyone Loves a Parade!

MOST PARADES FEATURE HORSES in various roles, and they are one of the most welcome, entertaining sights for parade-goers.

You don't have to have a fancy horse or an elaborate costume to be part of a parade. Plenty of small, local parades need horse and rider teams to participate, and their expectations are minor. As long as your horse is well groomed and your tack is clean, you may be eligible to be part of the parade.

Most equestrian parade exhibits represent horse clubs, such as a local breed club or a trail riding group. If you like the idea of riding in parades, look into joining a local riding club that participates in parades.

PREPARING FOR A PARADE

Once you find a group to join, start preparing your horse for the experience of his first parade. Horses often find parades extremely stimulating, and sometimes downright scary. Expose your horse to crowds whenever you can by taking him to horse shows—just to observe.

Ride him in groups with other equestrians so he gets used to being part of a "herd on horseback." Expose him to loud noises and strange-looking objects, too, since he'll see plenty of those along the parade route.

When you choose your first parade, try to pick one that is limited to horses only. This may be difficult, so you may have to settle for a parade that is very low-key to help your horse get acclimated. Horses are most afraid of loud marching bands, clowns and heavily costumed characters waving things around and making a lot of noise, and huge floats with moving parts.

Reminder: Make sure your horse listens to you well on the trail, as well as in the arena. His emotions will be high the first few times he goes in a parade, so you want to make sure he stays tuned into you.

Secretariat: The Greatest

NOT ALL GREAT HORSES IN HISTORY have centuries-long legacies. One of the most incredible equines of all time lived and died in the late twentieth century.

His name was Secretariat, and he was a 16.2-hand chestnut Thoroughbred stallion born in Doswell, Virginia. His sire was Bold Ruler, a well-known racehorse, and his dam a mare named Somethingroyal.

By the age of three, Secretariat had won fourteen out of eighteen races run. When Secretariat entered the Kentucky Derby, he was the favorite and won by 2½ lengths. He then took home the Preakness, beating the great racehorse Sham by 2½ lengths once again. But it was the Belmont Stakes that will forever be etched in the mind of racing fans and horse lovers around the world. Secretariat made the small field of four look like they were standing still as he broke the record for 1½ miles (2.4 km) by winning by 31 lengths.

Secretariat is clearly the greatest racehorse in modern times, and when he died in 1989 after suffering an acute bout of laminitis, he was mourned like the national hero that he was. (For more on laminitis, see Day 54.)

The Triple Crown

The prestigious Triple Crown of Thoroughbred horse racing consists of three races: the Kentucky Derby, the Preakness Stakes, and the Belmont Stakes. These three races are open to three-year-old colts and fillies, and each is more grueling than the last.

The Kentucky Derby, held in Louisville, Kentucky, the first Saturday of May, is 1¼ miles (2 km) long. The race has been held in Kentucky since 1875. Some of the most famous racehorses in U.S. history have won this race, including War Admiral, Count Fleet, and Seattle Slew.

The Preakness Stakes is in Baltimore, Maryland, on the third Saturday in May. Horses run 1³⁄₁₆ miles (1.9 km). The Preakness was first held in 1873. A number of horses that won the Kentucky Derby also won the Preakness, including War Emblem, Native Dancer, and Majestic Prince.

The toughest of the three races to win is the Belmont Stakes, held in Elmont, New York. It comes two weeks after the Preakness, giving Triple Crown contenders little time to recuperate from the previous two racing jewels, and it is also the longest race at 1½ miles (2.4 km).

The last horse to win the Triple Crown was Affirmed, who secured the title in 1978.

Organize Your Tack

SOME PEOPLE ARE NATURALLY organized, but if you are like most equestrians, your tack area could use a bit of straightening up. Getting your tack organized will cut down on the time you spend looking for hoof picks and lead ropes, and it will also help you discover what you no longer need to keep around.

Take inventory. Whether you keep your tack in a trunk or a tack room, start by taking a good look at all the equipment you have and decide how much of it you want to keep. Whatever is excess can go to a local tack consignment store, be donated to an equine rescue or handicapped riding program, or be put up for sale on the Internet.

Prioritize and discard. How do you know what to get rid of? If you have seven different bits when you only use two or three, the rest can probably be removed from your tack supply. The same goes for stuff you used on horses you no longer have, such as saddles that won't fit your current horse, or martingales that were a must on your old horse but aren't needed on the one you have now.

But don't be overzealous when discarding. Items such as bridles, halters, bell boots, and blankets can be kept around for use on current and future horses—even if they are extra. You never know when you might need an extra halter, for example. If one breaks, it's good to have a spare.

Plan an organizing system. Once you have narrowed down your equipment to what you want to keep, think about how to arrange it. If you have a tack box, use compartments to keep small items such as hoof picks and scissors, and delegate larger compartments for brushes and curry combs. For the room where you store your riding equipment, invest in bridle hooks to hang bridles and halters. Get one hook for each bridle or halter you own so you don't need to double up. If you don't have saddle racks attached to the wall, buy freestanding saddle stands rather than just setting your saddles on the floor.

Once you have finished organizing your tack, you'll feel a sense of accomplishment and control—a feeling that hopefully will extend into the time you spend with your horse.

The Magic of Psyllium

FOR HORSE OWNERS LIVING IN regions where the soil is sandy, worrying about sand colic is a fact of life. Sand colic is caused by accidentally ingesting sand during feeding, and it can be incredibly painful, expensive to treat, and even deadly.

Besides avoiding feeding your horse directly off the ground, the best way to avoid sand colic is to give your horse psyllium. This material, obtained from the seed coating of the Plantago plant species, becomes a gel-like substance when it makes contact with water. This substance attracts sand when it enters the horse's intestine, and it subsequently carries the sand out of the body during the digestive process.

Equine veterinarians recommend feeding psyllium to horses in sandy areas on a regular basis. Four ounces (114 g) per day for five days to a week is a commonly recommended regimen. You can mix the psyllium with your horse's grain or commercial feed. If you use the powdered version, your horse is more likely to eat it. Some vets believe the powdered form is more effective as well. Avoid the urge to add water to the grain/psyllium mixture since water will cause the psyllium to turn into a gel, and your horse may not eat it. To get it to stick to the grain, add a little corn oil.

Desensitizing Your Horse

HORSES ARE PREY ANIMALS: They are always on the lookout and always ready to take off at a moment's notice should danger loom. While this flight response is a great survival mechanism in the wild, it can be a hazard for riders who are simply hoping for a relaxing ride on the trail, or a winning day in the show ring.

Although you can never completely remove the flight instinct from your horse (Mother Nature has ingrained that in the horse's brain), you help your horse understand he has little to fear when you are around.

Help your horse get used to scary objects by introducing them to him where he lives. Horses feel secure in their home environment, whether it's a box stall, a paddock, or a pasture. This will help him learn to accept the object sooner than he would in an unfamiliar environment.

If particular things frighten him on the trail—such as white plastic grocery bags, garbage pails, or errant balloons—focus on these objects first. If you don't know what your horse is afraid of, experiment. Approach his stall with one of the above-mentioned objects and watch his reaction. If he tenses up, if his head goes up high, or if he spins and bolts, you'll have an answer.

EXERCISE

Introduce one object at a time to your horse. Start with a white plastic bag since most horses don't like these. Tie the bag to a fence where your horse lives, being careful not to pick a spot too close to his food and/or water. You don't want to keep him from eating or drinking.

Observe your horse's reaction. He may run away, snort and stare, or freeze up with his head held high. If your horse has a curious nature, he will soon approach the bag. Depending on how brave your horse is, it will take either minutes or days to start ignoring the bag. He may play with it and try to pull it of the fence, or he may just ignore it. If he starts to ignore it, you can then up the ante by using your hand to make the bag flap around while it's still tied to the fence. Your horse may act afraid all over again. Keep flapping the bag until your horse relaxes and understands he has nothing to fear.

Leave the bag hanging on his fence for a day or two, and don't remove it until he has completely lost interest in it.

Follow the same process with a different object. After a while, your horse will be desensitized to the objects you have placed on his stall. When he comes across them on the trail, his reaction is likely to be "Oh, that thing again," instead of "Oh no, get me out of here!"

35

Spooky Stuff

Horses have a knack for getting scared of the strangest things. One mare named Snickers was only afraid of kitchen appliances that somehow found their way onto the trail. Another horse, Sam, an Arabian, was terrified of large rocks. Garbage trucks sent an Appaloosa gelding named Bailey into a tailspin, while Gunner the mustang was frightened by children embarking from a school bus.

The Colossal Clydesdale

THE CLYDESDALE IS ONE OF THE most dramatic looking equines in the world. These massive horses with their white "feathered" legs and solid muscling are among the most well known of all horse breeds.

If you watch TV, you know the Clydesdales— those massive bay horses that pull the Budweiser beer wagon in those incredibly popular commercials. The most famous draft horse of all thanks to Budweiser, the Clydesdale is more than just a "spokeshorse" for a brew.

Descending from the warhorses of the Middle Ages, the Clydesdale has been working the fields of Scotland for centuries. The breed developed its distinctive look in the eighteenth century, and it was given its name in 1826, at the Glasgow Exhibition in honor of the Clyde River Valley from where the breed first came. Today, the Clydesdale is virtually the only draft horse seen in Scotland.

The Clydesdale eventually found its way to the United States and was in demand during the late 1800s for work in the field. The arrival of mechanized machinery seriously damaged the Clydesdale's popularity, along with that of the other draft breeds. Powerful workhorses were replaced on farms by motorized tractors, which did not have the same maintenance requirements as the big horse and could do a lot more work in less time.

As the need for Clydesdales lessened, the breed's numbers began to shrink. A handful of breeders dedicated to the breed hung on desperately, and they continued to keep the Clydesdale alive as a show and exhibition horse. This is a job that the Clydesdale continues to excel at today.

While Clydesdales are known for being big, sizes can vary within the breed. A Clydesdale can be anywhere from 16.2 hands to 18 hands, and their weight can vary from 1,600 to 2,200 pounds (725 to 997 kg).

Color and markings also vary within the breed. While most people think of the Clydesdale as bay with a white blaze and white stockings, not all Clydesdales fit this description. While bay is the most common color, Clydesdales also come in black, brown, and chestnut. Roans are seen in all of these colorations.

Today the Clydesdale is used for draft work, and they're used for riding, too. More and more equestrians are finding these big horses with their feathered feet to be great mounts for the trail.

Clydesdale

Join a Horse Club

PEOPLE SEEM TO HAVE NATURES similar to the animals they gravitate to. Horse people tend to be just like horses: They like to gather with their own kind.

Because horse people are sociable by nature— and bond quickly with other horse people— horse clubs are in no shortage around the world. You can find horse clubs for just about every breed and discipline, in just about every community or region.

Whether you show your horse or just like to trail ride, you can find a horse club that suits your interests. If you have a purebred horse, you can join a club that represents your breed. Many breed clubs have local chapters that sponsor activities, so this is a great way to meet people in your area who share your love for a particular breed.

Discipline clubs are popular, too. Whether you enjoy competing in gymkhana (see Day 44), chasing cows, or jumping, you can find a club filled with likeminded horse people.

Community equine organizations are among the best groups to join because they bring horse people together in a particular locale. These groups sponsor poker rides, organized trail rides, horse shows, clinics, and all kinds of fun events. You can make a lot of friends by joining a local horse club. Plus, as horses already know, there is safety in numbers. When horse people gather together, they can do wonders to help protect trails and the equestrian lifestyle in their communities.

The Horses of World War I

IMAGES OF WORLD WAR I often show soldiers fighting in the trenches, but what most people don't realize is that many horses gave their lives during this conflict. In fact, it is estimated that six million horses were used during World War I, most of which were killed in battle.

Many of the horses that fought on the battlefields of Europe came from the United States. The United States exported nearly one million horses to Europe for the war. Very few returned.

The equine population in the United States was depleted as a result, leaving a scant number of horses behind. In fact, horse populations were depleted all throughout Europe by the end of the war. Horse populations made a comeback in Europe during the decades that followed, only to be adversely affected again by World War II.

Water Ways

HORSES ONLY NEED ONE THING more than food to stay alive, and that's water. Without access to fresh, clean water, horses won't live more than a few days.

When providing that all-important water, you essentially have two options. The method you choose should be the one that best suits both you and your horse.

AUTOMATIC WATERER

The first choice of many horse owners is the automatic waterer. These types of water sources always provide the horse with clean, fresh water to drink. Available in bucket or bowl style, automatic waterers work using one of two systems. With the float system, as soon as the water level goes below a certain line, the float causes water to enter the bucket. With the bowl system, the horse presses on a lever that causes water to flow into the bowl.

The benefit of using automatic waterers is that you know your horse always has access to water, even if you aren't home. The downside is that sometimes these systems fail, and the horse can be without water without you even knowing it. Some horses don't like drinking from the bowl-type waterer, either, and will avoid drinking as much as they need to.

TROUGH METHOD

The other method of providing water is the old-fashioned trough method. You simply get a garden hose and fill up a trough or large basin with water. The horse has constant access to the water, which should always be clean and fresh.

The benefit of this method is that you know exactly how much water your horse is drinking because you control what goes into the trough. The downside is that your horse can run out of water if you don't fill the trough in a timely manner. You may also have a problem with mosquitoes if you use a water trough, although this can be remedied by keeping a small population of mosquito fish in the water to keep the mosquitoes under control. (See Day 12 for more on mosquito fish.)

Whatever method you choose, make sure your horse's water is a top priority.

The Eyes Have It

THEY SAY THE EYES ARE THE windows to the soul, and that is certainly true when it comes to horses. You can tell a lot about a horse's mood just by looking at her eyes.

Unfortunately, eye disease is all too common in horses, threatening the horses' overall well being in a variety of ways.

One of the most common eye problems in horses is corneal ulcers. Often the result of trauma to the eye, corneal ulcers start as a pin-prick-sized hole in the cornea and can develop into serious wounds if left untreated. In extreme cases, horses can lose their eyes to corneal ulcers.

Another eye ailment often seen in horses is equine recurrent uveitis. Most common in Appaloosas, this disease is somewhat mysterious in origins. Also called moonblindness, it results in periodic inflammation of the eye. Over time, this recurrent inflammation damages the interior of the eye, and results in blindness.

Cataracts can also affect horses, and they are most often seen in aged equines. These cloudy films over the lens affect a horse's vision.

Eye problems can go from mild to serious in a short period of time. For most equine veterinarians, a swollen, painful eye is considered an emergency. If your horse is holding his eye closed, has swelling around the eye and considerable discharge, or the eye has a cloudy appearance, contact your veterinarian immediately.

♥ Camping with Your Horse

IF YOU LIKE TO TRAIL RIDE, and you like to camp, you can easily combine the two by taking your horse camping with you. Horse camping is incredibly fun and rewarding, and all you need is your camping gear and a horse trailer.

Here's how it works: You trailer your horse to your campsite, tie your horse to the outside of your trailer or secure him in an available horse corral, pitch your tent and camp per usual. But instead of hiking, you trail ride!

First, find a horse-friendly campsite. Read the rules and regulations for the regional or state park where you plan to camp or the national forest where you'd like to go. Make sure horses are allowed and find out which campsites permit horse camping. Be sure to choose a campsite that is adjacent to trail heads that allow horses so you have someplace to ride.

Acclimate your horse to being tied. Of course before you embark on your first horse camping trip, you need to get your horse used to the idea. If your horse doesn't tie well—that is, he pulls back or paws the ground impatiently, he needs to work on learning how to stand. Start by tying him for periods of time to your trailer or to a hitching post. If he has a tendency to pull back, use a special elastic lead rope made for horses that pull back, or get a special slip tie-ring so he can't hurt himself. Once your horse is comfortable standing tied for at least an hour, he's ready for camping.

Pack for your horse, too. You know how to pack for yourself when you are camping, but packing for your horse is another thing. Bring all the hay you'll need to feed your horse, plus some extra. (Check the rules where you plan to camp. Some places don't allow hay to be brought it, only pelleted feed.) Also pack a light blanket for your horse since you'll want to cover him at night when he's tied. He'll need extra help staying warm because he can't move around to heat himself up when tied to the trailer.

Be sure to bring all your tack, plus brushes, hoof pick, and insect repellent. Only camp where water will be plentiful, and bring a water bucket or bin for your horse to drink from. Don't forget to bring a hay net and a roll of duct tape.

When you tie your horse to the trailer for the night, tie him high and so the clip that snaps onto his halter hangs about an inch (2.5 cm) from the ground before it is clipped on. This will give your horse enough slack so he can lie down if he wants to. Inspect the outside of your trailer for areas where the lead rope can get caught and cause an accident. Trailer door handles and wheel wells can be a problem. Use towels and duct tape to cover areas where the lead rope might snag.

Of course if the place you chose to camp has a horse corral, you don't have to worry about any of this. Simply put your horse in the corral after you have inspected it for safety, and relax!

Packing List for Camping with Your Horse

- Feed (enough for each day you'll be camping)

- Water (if none available at campsite)

- Tack (saddle, bridle, pad, etc.)

- Grooming tools and hoof pick

- Buckets for food and water

- Light horse blanket

- Insect repellent

Peruvian Treasure

IN THE FARMLANDS OF PERU, where land stretches out for miles and the majestic Andes rise in the distance, a breed of horse was created to help plantation owners survey their estates—the Peruvian Horse.

The history of the Peruvian Horse goes back to Spain in the time of the conquistadors. The Spaniards, who conquered the Peruvian Incas in the 1500s brought horses with them of Barb and Spanish Jennett blood. The Barb was hardy and trainable, while the Spanish Jennet had a ground-covering, four-beat gait.

When settlers came from Spain to Peru, they brought even more horses of Iberian breeding with them. These horses mixed with the Barb and the Jennett to create the Peruvian.

During the seventeenth century, the horses of Peru became isolated, enabling a distinct breed to develop. Eventually, wealthy Peruvian landowners bred these horses for specific characteristics, including a smooth, fast gait that would help them cover as much ground as possible.

Today, the Peruvian Horse has secured foothold in the United States, and thousands have been registered by the North American Peruvian Horse Association. The United States Peruvian Horse Association also registers Peruvian Horses.

Measuring no higher than 15 hands, Peruvian horses have a graceful, elegant look. Stallions show the thick, arched neck characteristic of their Iberian ancestors.

The breed comes in an assortment of basic solid colorations, including chestnut (sometimes with a flaxen mane and tail), black, brown, bay, gray, palomino, buckskin, and roan.

The Peruvian's gaits are distinctive and set it apart from other breeds. These horses are born with the ability to perform the paso llano and sobreandando gaits. Both have a four-beat movement that gives the rider a very smooth ride.

A trait called termino is also unique to the Peruvian Horse. The term refers to a specific action of the front legs that causes them to swing out as the leg rolls from the shoulder outward, forward, and then down.

Another characteristic unique to the Peruvian Horse is brio. Bred into the Peruvian horse for centuries, this trait is the ability to work for the rider with alertness and a willing attitude. Peruvian Horses who possess brio are sensitive without being hyper, and they have lots of energy but are easy to handle. For many people, brio is among the most important characteristics of the Peruvian breed.

Peruvian

Poker Rides

IF YOU BELONG TO A local equestrian group or live in a horsy community, you have probably heard of a poker ride. Poker rides have become popular ways for organizations to make money while getting members together to ride.

A poker ride is essentially a trail ride where riders play a horseback version of poker. Each rider gets five cards throughout the ride at designated stations along a trail route of anywhere from 5 to 10 miles (8 to 16 km). Riders can purchase as many hands as they want. The rider with the best poker hand of all the riders at the end of the ride wins the jackpot.

Poker rides are fun to put together and even more fun to participate in. They are good fundraisers for small organizations, and they bring riders together. Think about holding a poker ride for a local charity, or join in on a ride just to have fun.

The Horse with Wings

HE'S AS WHITE AS THE SNOW, as graceful as a swan, and as magical as they come. He's Pegasus, the winged stallion of Greek legend.

Pegasus came into existence when he sprang from the neck of the hideous Medusa, a deity of the underworld with hair of hissing snakes. Pegasus's birth occurred when Medusa was beheaded by the hero Perseus while she was pregnant by Poseidon, making Pegasus the son of the great sea god.

Pegasus had many adventures in Greek mythology, and every place he struck his hoof on Earth, a spring of water came forth. Eventually, Pegasus became the servant of the Muses. Zeus rewarded Pegasus for his service by making him a constellation. If you live in the Northern Hemisphere, you can still see Pegasus when you look at the night sky in late summer through the autumn.

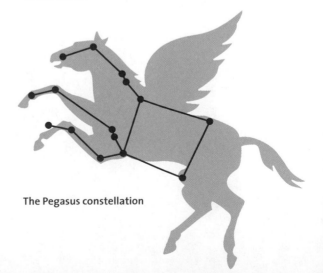

The Pegasus constellation

Trailer Maintenance

TODAY IS A GOOD DAY to check your trailer for maintenance needs. The safety and comfort of your horse depends on it.

Follow these steps to make sure your trailer is in good working order:

- Check tires to make sure they have at least ¼ inch (6 mm) of tread.

- Evaluate tires for proper inflation, including your spare.

- Make sure your jack and safety triangle are in good working order.

- Examine your floorboards and keep an eye out for weak spots or rotting.

- Check all screws, nails, and bolts to make sure they are secure.

- Verify that all lights are working. This includes the tail lights, brake lights, directional signals, marker lights, and interior and exterior lights.

- Inspect hitch welds, safety chain welds, and snaps

- Grease the hitch ball if it needs it.

Tying Up Syndrome

Also known as *azoturia* or *exertional rhabdomyolysis*, tying up syndrome is a systemic condition that results when horses are put through extreme exercise after several days of having little or no exercise and after eating grain or another high-carbohydrate feed. Some horses tie up simply because they aren't physically fit for the job they are being asked to do. Others tie up as a result of electrolyte imbalance, heat exhaustion, or a vitamin E deficiency.

The symptoms of tying up include sudden hind limb stiffness, lameness, muscle cramping, refusal to move, increased heart and respiratory rates, sweating, and colic.

The best way to avoid tying up syndrome is to warm your horse up well before hard work and to gradually condition the horse for exercise.

Feed her plenty of roughage and avoid high carbohydrate diets. Once a horse has experienced tying up, she is prone to it again. Your vet can tell you the best diet and exercise regimen for a horse that has experienced tying up.

45

Symptoms of Tying Up

- Sudden hind limb stiffness

- Lameness

- Refusal to move

- Increased heart and respiratory rates

- Sweating

- Colic

Teaching Tricks

Dogs do tricks all the time, so why not horses? Teaching tricks to your horse is a great way to deepen your bond, and it also gives you and your horse a way to entertain your friends.

Some of the tricks you can teach your horse include bowing, counting, drinking from a bottle, and sitting up. Let's work on one of the easiest tricks to teach: kissing.

EXERCISE

Cut up some carrots in small pieces and have them close by. Dress your horse in a halter and lead rope and work with him in his stall. Stand in front of him with a piece of carrot in your hand. Lift the carrot up to your cheek as you give the command "Gimme kiss!" Your horse will stick his nose up to your hand to get at the carrot.

As soon as your horse touches his nose to your cheek, open your hand and give him the carrot.

Perform this about ten times so your horse will be sure to get it. Then try it without the carrot. Instead of putting your hand up to your cheek, just raise your hand up near your face and say "Gimme kiss!" If your horse touches his nose to your face, make a big fuss over him while you give him a piece of carrot.

The secret to this trick—and all tricks—is repetition. You want your horse to understand the verbal cue and respond to it eventually without using a hand signal. Keep practicing, and start to slowly eliminate your hand from the trick. When your horse eventually responds only to your verbal command, he has officially learned the trick!

The Amazing Paint

IT'S HARD TO BELIEVE A TIME once existed when pinto-marked Quarter Horses were considered outcast, unloved and unwanted in the horse industry. That all changed in the 1960s when a group of horsemen decided to give official recognition to this colorful version of the Quarter Horse. They started a new breed called the Paint Horse.

Today, the Paint is the second most popular breed in the United States, after the Quarter Horse. Paints are seen in a variety of disciplines, including cattle classes, Western pleasure, trail, dressage, hunters, and driving. Their conformation is very much like their Quarter Horse cousins, only splashed with color.

Paint horses come in two general patterns: tobiano and overo. Tobianos have both white and a dark color on their bodies. This dark color can be black, bay, chestnut, buckskin, or palomino, and it usually covers one or both flanks. All four legs are usually white, at least below the hocks and knees. The patches in this pattern tend to be oval or round, and go down over the neck and chest. The face markings are the same as on a solid-colored horse.

Overos have a white and dark color on their bodies. The white does not cross the back of the horse between its withers and its tail. The white also tends to look scattered or splashed.

Paint

Gymkhana

ONE OF THE MOST EXCITING Western horseback sports is gymkhana, a rodeo-style sport that involves speed and precision.

Barrel racing and pole bending are the two most well-known and popular gymkhana activities. In barrel racing, barrels are set up in a pattern. The horse and rider team are expected to run the barrels in a clover or other type of pattern. Riders enter the arena one at a time and try to run the pattern in the fastest time.

In pole bending, a group of poles are set up in a straight line. Horse and rider weave through the poles at a gallop, hoping to beat the time of other riders who will perform the same task.

The best thing about gymkhana is that you don't need a fancy horse and expensive tack to participate. As long as your horse has been trained to make sharp turns and respond to your cues with precision, you can compete in gymkhana.

The Great War Horses

PAY A VISIT TO A HISTORY MUSEUM, and you'll see them in paintings, sculptures, and tapestry. The great war horses of the Middle Ages have been preserved for all time in these forms of art.

Who were these magnificent beasts who carried men wearing heavy armor and ran bravely into battle? Equine historians say these horses were called destriers, and they were specifically bred for this purpose. Always stallions, they weighed anywhere from 1,200 to 1,400 pounds (544 to 635 kg). Their bulk and might proved invaluable on the battlefield from 476 to 1450 AD, from the fall of the Roman Empire to the end of the Hundred Year War between France and England, giving more impact to the soldier's lance.

As methods of battle changed and soldiers began to fight more on foot to accommodate their new and improved weapons, the destriers fell into disuse. They remained popular as a status symbol, however, and they were the mounts of choice for knights embarking in displays of chivalry.

The Vice of Cribbing

CRIBBING IS ONE OF THE MOST distasteful of equine behaviors, and horses with this habit are often ruled out when prospective owners are looking for a horse to buy.

When a horse cribs, she grasps her front teeth on a horizontal object, tightens her neck muscles, and sucks in air with a grunt. A horse that cribs will usually do it anywhere, on any horizontal object she can hang her teeth on. This habit can wear down a horse's front teeth and drive her owner crazy.

Recent research has shown that there may be a link between digestive problems and cribbing. Evidence shows that a high carbohydrate diet can make a horse predisposed to develop the habit of cribbing. Pain in the gut may be the motivator, caused by high acidic levels in the stomach.

Once a horse starts cribbing, it's almost impossible to break the habit. Owners of cribbing horses will put anti-cribbing collars on their horses' necks in an effort to make the behavior uncomfortable. Some will even fit the horse with a muzzle to stop her from latching her teeth onto available surfaces. Others will hot-wire the horse's paddock to keep her away from fences where she can crib.

The best way to prevent cribbing is to give your horse plenty of roughage to eat, exercise, and companionship. Horses who are bored and stressed and not getting enough hay seem most prone to developing this habit.

EPM and Your Horse's Health

IN THE 1990s, A NASTY DISEASE caused by an organism called sarcocystitis neurona began gaining attention among horse owners. Called equine protozoal myeloencephalitis (EPM), the disease causes severe neurological damage in horses that can often become permanent, and it is the most common neurological disease in horses today. It is seen mostly in the United States, but it has also appeared in southern Canada and Central and South America.

The organism that causes EPM is a single-celled parasitic protozoa that is found in the muscles of contaminated birds. When these birds die and are eaten by a scavenging opossum, the parasite is excreted in the opossum's waste. If a horse eats or drinks where the opossum has defecated, the parasite is ingested and infects the horse.

When a horse is infected with the organism responsible for EPM, inflammation occurs in the central nervous system. Symptoms can include seizures, depression, blindness, deafness, facial paralysis, and lack of coordination.

Veterinarians treat EPM with drugs designed to kill the offending organism, with mixed results. Some horses recover completely while others are beyond help and die.

PREVENTING EPM

The best ways to prevent EPM is to keep your horse healthy, since a strong immune system can fight off the organism in the event of exposure. Keeping opossums off your property is also a good way to avoid exposure to EPM. Don't leave out pet food or garbage that will attract these scavengers. Keep your horse's grain securely covered and your hay behind closed doors, if possible. Make sure your horse's water source is clean and out of reach of opossums.

Keeping a Studbook

For centuries, people who breed horses have kept track of which stallions have been bred to which mares, using a studbook. A studbook is essentially a record of breedings. When a purebred stallion is bred to a pure mare of the same breed, the resulting offsprings is recorded in the studbook.

Some horse breeds, such as the Thoroughbred and the Arabian, have studbooks that go back to the eighteenth century, when the practice of keeping breeding records began in earnest.

Homemade Horse Treats

YOU DON'T NEED A SPECIAL OCCASION to make homemade treats for your horse. The time you spend putting together some recipes for your equine buddy is time well spent simply because your horse will love you more for the trouble you took.

EXERCISE

Make your horse a bowl of Cowboy Stew, from *The Original Book of Horse Treats*, by June V. Evers.

INGREDIENTS

3 pounds (1.36 kg) carrots, shredded

2 cups (160 g) sweet feed

2 cups (160 g) oats

1 flake of timothy alfalfa hay mix

In a blender, gradually blend the carrots, adding about ½ cup (125 ml) of water to help it blend. Place into a big bowl. Add the sweet feed and oats and mix thoroughly.

Put the flake of hay mix in a feed bucket and pour the mixture over the top as a garnish.

EXERCISE

Make your horse Toast Nuggets, also from *The Original Book of Horse Treats*.

INGREDIENTS

1 piece of white or wheat bread

Strawberry, raspberry, or grape jam

Sugar

Toast the bread until it is crispy. Then spread jam thickly onto toast and sprinkle about a tablespoon of sugar on top. Cut into quarters and feed cool. Your horse will love it!

The Aristocratic Arabian

NO ONE IS COMPLETELY CERTAIN of where the Arabian horse originated. His beginnings are mysterious, which is fitting given the romance behind the rest of the breed's history.

The first documented breeders of the Arabian horse were the Bedouins. These nomadic desert people of the Middle East valued the Arabian horse as their greatest possession. They relied on the Arabian for transportation and to carry them into battle.

The Arabian was more than just a beast of burden. The Bedouins saw their horses as friends, inviting them to sleep in the family tent on cold nights and escape the hot sun there during the day. As a result, Arabian horses developed a strong affinity for humans, which lingers to this day.

The Arabian is graced with a distinctive, delicate head with a concave face, called a dish. This classic head features large, widely set eyes, small curved ears, and a wide forehead.

The Arabian's back is shorter than that of most other breeds, and his croup is nearly flat. His neck is set on steeply sloping shoulders, giving him a high head carriage. Arabian horses are most commonly seen in gray, bay, chestnut, and black, and they have long, flowing manes and tails. They rarely grow taller than 15.3 hands.

Arabian

Drill Teams

GO TO JUST ABOUT ANY MAJOR horse event, and you'll see a drill team perform on horseback. Drill teams are usually twelve or more riders who perform as a group in a series of patterns, to music. Drill teams sometimes carry flags, and they always wear matching uniforms. Horses in a drill team may be the same breed or color, but they may also be a variety of breeds and colors.

Drill teams give exhibitions at equine events, ride in parades, and attend competitions. For a horse to be part of a drill team, she has to be well trained enough to perform reliably at the trot and canter, and be willing to work calmly around other horses.

Drilling on horseback is an enjoyable activity. You get to work as part of a team while teaching your horse to be more obedient. You also make new friends and learn a new sport.

Przewalski's Horse

WILD HORSES ROAMED the plains of North America and Europe during the last Ice Age, and became extinct some 30,000 years ago. But you can still get a glimpse of what that prehistoric equine looked like if you take a gander at Przewalski's Horse.

This endangered equine is actually extinct in the wild and can only be found in zoos and preserves. About the size of a pony, Przewalski's Horse comes in various shades of dun, and has a Mohawk-style mane and stripes on the legs. This ancient horse has sixty-six chromosomes instead of sixty-four, like a domestic horse.

They live in harem herds, which are made up of one dominant stallion and a group of mares, just like feral horses do.

Scientists have learned a lot about horse behavior by observing Przewalski's Horse, who most recently existed in the wild in Mongolia until its numbers were wiped out by hunting and loss of habitat. Przewalski's Horse exhibits the same vices as domestic horses when kept in confinement, such as pacing and cribbing, and it has the same type of social structure within the herd as feral horses do.

Hay Storage

KEEPING HORSES ON YOUR PROPERTY means storing bales of hay. The amount of hay you store at any one time depends on how many horses you have, and how much room you have to store.

The key when storing hay is to keep it dry. When water penetrates a bale of hay, mold quickly grows. This mold is toxic to horses and can make them very sick. Most horses will avoid eating it, but some don't seem to know any better—or are too hungry to care—and will ingest it anyway.

If storing hay outdoors, make sure it is well covered by a shelter or tarp. Take wind into account when you are covering your hay; rain rarely falls straight down.

Also, if you use a tarp, don't bother covering your hay if it gets wet before you have a chance to get out the tarp. Covering damp hay only encourages mold to grow. If you are storing square bales, wait until the rain stops and then open each bale, separating the flakes to let air in to dry. Get it up off the wet ground or pallets too, because mold will quickly grow underneath the hay.

When storing square bales on top of pallets, keep an eye out for rodents that may take up residence between the pallets and the ground. Keep the area under the hay cleaned out so they have fewer places to hide.

Laminitis

ALSO KNOWN AS FOUNDER, laminitis is one of the most dreaded lameness conditions for horse owners. A diagnosis of laminitis means a lifetime of possible lameness, or at the very least extensive management of the condition.

Laminitis results when the laminae—the tissue that surrounds the coffin bone within the hoof—become severely inflamed. The inflammation can disrupt the attachment of the coffin bone to the hoof, causing the coffin bone to rotate downward. This causes the horse tremendous pain, and serious lameness results.

The causes of laminitis are many, and they include use of corticosteroid medication, obesity, bedding with black walnut shavings, severe colic, poor or infrequent trimming and shoeing, retained placenta in mares, excessive exercise on hard surfaces, grazing on lush pasture without slow introduction, trailering long distances, any other hoof disease, high fever, and metabolic disease.

The best way to avoid laminitis is to practice good horse care, paying special attention to the areas of husbandry that can result in laminitis. Talk to your veterinarian about how you can best care for your horse without putting her at risk for this condition.

Causes of Laminitis

- Use of corticosteroid medication
- Obesity
- Bedding with black walnut shavings
- Severe colic
- Poor or infrequent trimming and shoeing
- Retained placenta in mares
- Excessive exercise on hard surfaces
- Grazing on lush pasture without slow introduction
- Trailering long distances
- Other hoof disease
- High fever
- Metabolic disease

♥ Crossing Water

IF YOU LIKE TO TRAIL RIDE, you are bound to face a water crossing at some point. In fact, perhaps you already have and lived to tell the tale!

Water crossing doesn't have to be traumatic for you and your horse, although tackling water is something you need to work on if you plan to ride your horse in the great wide open.

Different trainers have varied approaches for teaching a horse to cross water. If you have time and patience, the slow and steady approach is best because it helps your horse learn to trust you, and it keeps stress to a minimum.

EXERCISE

If your horse has never crossed water before, or if he refuses to do it when you are out on the trail, start working on this issue at home. Get a garden hose and place it in a spot where you can create a small stream. Let the water run slowly so the stream is flowing when you introduce your horse to it.

Hand-walk your horse up to the water and let him look at it. If he's water-phobic, he will probably act afraid to approach it. Let him stand for as long as he needs to relax. Once he seems calm and is no longer paying attention to the water, ask him to take a step forward. He will probably act worried again. If he does, praise him for having taken a step forward and let him stand until he relaxes again.

Repeat this over and over until you get to the point where your horse will step in the water. It may be days before you reach this point, or your horse may put his foot in it after only 10 or 15 minutes; it all depends on your horse. When your horse does finally step into the water, ask him to stand in it for a few minutes and praise him heartily.

When your horse gets to the stage where he will readily walk up to the water, stand in it, and then walk through it, you are ready to try the same thing under saddle. You may find you are back to square one once you get on since horses lose some of their courage when you are riding as opposed to leading. Be patient and work with him in the same way.

If you can get your horse to walk through water at home, he'll be more likely to negotiate this obstacle when out on the trail.

Shetland Pony

THE MOST FAMOUS OF all children's mounts is the Shetland pony, that diminutive equine who is responsible for giving most kids their first ride.

The Shetland pony got its start on the Shetland Isles, off the coast of Scotland. Breed aficionados say the Shetland first appeared on these islands at least 2,000 years ago, maybe earlier. Their hardy nature is a direct result of having survived for so long in a difficult environment, where the weather is cold and food hard to come by.

Today, Shetland ponies are seen all over the world. They come in two types: a heavier-boned draft-type pony and a lighter pony for riding. Their primary job is as a children's mount, but they are also popular in the show ring and for carriage driving.

Shetland ponies stand around 11 hands high and come in a wide variety of colors. They usually have profuse manes and tails, and they get quite fuzzy in the wintertime—a throwback to their centuries spent on the cold Shetland Isles.

Shetland Pony

Driving

MOST PEOPLE NO LONGER NEED horses to pull carriages for transportation in this modern world, yet this use for our equine friends is alive and well.

Driving is not as popular as riding, but it's still high on the list for many equestrians. This elegant discipline harkens back to a time when horses were the only way to get from one place to another, often in great style.

Driving is essentially a horse working in harness, pulling a cart, wagon, or carriage behind. Driving comes in many forms. Heavy draft horses pulling hay wagons or trolleys are at one end of the spectrum, while light, high-stepping carriage horses competing at shows are at the other.

Driving can have a practical purpose in rural areas, where some horses are still used to till the fields and bring fallen trees in from the forest. In many cases, driving is a competitive event, whether it's a small, elegant horse in light harness or a four-in-hand working through a combined driving course.

Horses must be trained to drive, of course, but they can learn it easily if they are already broke to ride. Carriages and wagons of every type are still for sale in the horse world, some antiques and others newly built. Driving is a rich discipline that deserves a look from every serious horse lover.

Pony Express

IN THE MID-1800s in the American West, frontier men and women needed a way to communicate with their families back East. A stagecoach route had been established between California and the East, but mail took a month or more to be delivered by this method—if the coach even made it at all. Westerners wanted a faster and more secure way to get mail, so in 1860, the Pony Express was born.

A freighting company called Russell, Majors & Waddell started the service, which delivered mail weekly on horseback from San Francisco to St. Joseph, Missouri. Horses and riders traveled 10 to 15 miles (16 to 24 km) at about 10 miles per hour (4.5 m/s), which is a gallop. Stations were located at these intervals, and riders would jump from their spent horses to fresh ones at each station, taking their 20-pound (9 kg) saddlebag of mail with them. Each rider rode for 75 to 100 miles (120 to 160 km) during his shift.

While the riders were important in the Pony Express (only young, healthy men of good character were sought), the horses were the life-blood of the system. The Pony Express mounts in the eastern sections of the route were mostly of Thoroughbred breeding, while the Western horses were usually Morgans and native mustangs. These 400 horses were carefully chosen for their endurance and speed, and they were highly valued and very well-cared for. Fed grain to help them outrun the mounts of potentially hostile Native Americans, the horses of the Pony Express were of an elite caliber. Their service provided a crucial communication link between the newly forming West and the established East until it was dismantled only a year and a half after it was started to make way for stagecoach mail delivery.

Escape Artists

IF YOU HAVE ONE OF THESE CREATURES, you know all about them: the escape artists. With dexterous lips and smarts beyond what their equine brains should possess, these Houdinis of the horse world manage to find a way to get out of being tied up or enclosed more times than not.

Escape artists have learned how to untie knots and unhook latches using their lips and teeth the way humans use their hands. To outsmart these wise guys, you need to use superhuman intelligence to out-think them.

If your horse has learned how to untie your usual knot, it's time to learn a new one. A few different safety knots are suitable for tying a horse, and with a little research, you can get a few under your belt. Ask other horse owners how they tie their horses and learn their methods.

Another approach is to double tie your horse with two lead ropes, so if she undoes one, she is still tied up with the other. Of course if both ropes have the same knot, it's only a matter of time before she turns herself loose completely.

Crossties are another option for horses adept at untying themselves. The top of the cross-tie clips high up on a rail, and the other end clips to your horse's halter. This way there are no knots for your wily beast to untie.

Horses who undo gate latches are a bit easier to foil. Simply secure your gates with a chain featuring a snap at the end. It's a rare horse who can unhook the snap on a chain, since this takes two hands even for a human. The trick is to remember to always latch the chain. If you forget to do it once, your horse will seize the moment.

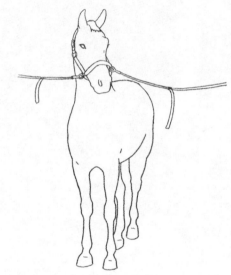

Crossties are a good option for horses that like to untie traditional knots.

Planning Vaccinations

WHEN IT COMES TO PROTECTING your horse's health, vaccinations should be at the top of your list. A number of very contagious and debilitating diseases regularly circulate throughout the equine population, and vaccines are the best way to stop them from hurting your horse.

The best way to determine which vaccines your horse should get is to discuss the matter with your veterinarian.

Horses are prone to different illness at different times of the year and in different regions, and your vet can make the best recommendations.

Regardless of where you live, your vet will likely recommend the following vaccines on a regular basis: tetanus, flu/rhino, West Nile Virus, and encephalitis.

Attend a Clinic

NOT EVERYONE HAS MONEY for a full-time trainer, but thanks to the many clinicians who travel around to teach horse owners, you don't need deep pockets to learn.

Attending a clinic is a great way to build your horsemanship skills and find new ways to solve problems with your horse. Clinics specific to certain disciplines can be found, as well as basic clinics that address horses of all breeds and disciplines. Some of the different types of clinics include training gaited horses, working in the round pen, good ground manners, and de-spooking.

Some clinics are one-day or one-weekend events. Others last for several days or even a week. The one you choose should depend on what you can afford, what you need to learn, and how much time you have to spend. In some cases, you can bring your horse to the clinic. Other times, you can just be a spectator. It's more expensive to participate in the clinic with your horse, and it can be hard to find a slot that is open. But you'll never have trouble finding a ticket as an auditor, which means you sit in the audience and observe.

If you can't find a clinic in your area, the next best thing is to order a training DVD from a clinician you like. Many good clinicians have DVDs for sale on their websites. These DVDs contain the same information you will learn in a clinic.

Here's how to find a clinic.

- Watch the calendar section in your local horse-friendly publication

- Get on the mailing list of clinicians you admire.

- If you don't know of any clinicians, search online for "horse" and "clinician." You'll find more choices than you might have imagined.

- Ask other equestrians in your area, your veterinarian, and the folks in charge of your riding club.

Born to Trot: The Standardbred

ALTHOUGH THOROUGHBRED RACING is the most watched equine sport, harness racing is a not-too-distant second in North America. The horses that pull the sulkies down the track, trotting or pacing at speeds up to 35 miles per hour (16 m/s), are Standardbreds.

The Standardbred was developed in colonial America, when people preferred their race horses pull carts. They also liked seeing horses that could race at the trot instead of at the gallop. The Standardbred was created to do both.

Thoroughbreds and Canadian Horses were used to develop the Standardbred breed. Some experts think a small horse called the Narragansett Pacer, which no longer exists, is also part of the Standardbred's early history.

Standardbreds resemble their Thoroughbred cousins in conformation, although Standardbreds tend to have a longer body and are more muscular. Their heads are usually bigger than a Thoroughbred's, and they have powerful thighs. They usually stand 15 to 16 hands, and they come in bay, chestnut, brown, gray, and black.

Retired Standardbreds face the same dilemma as retired Thoroughbreds: They often have nowhere to go. Many rescue-and-rehabilitation centers make it their mission to retrain Standardbreds for riding so they can be adopted out to good homes. Retired Standardbreds find new careers in Western classes, jumping, dressage, team penning, endurance, gymkhana, saddleseat, and trail.

Standardbred

Organized Trail Rides

As we have learned on Day 30, horse people are as social as horses. And what better way for horse people to socialize than on horseback?

The idea of having fun with your horse friends while you all go out for a ride led to the birth of the organized trail ride. Sponsored by riding clubs, equine community organizations, or just groups of horsy friends who want to spend a day together, organized trail rides enable riders to feel like they are part of something bigger as they head down the trail.

Organized trail rides can have as few as ten riders and as many as 400. The smaller the group, the easier it is to keep your horse under control and visit with people. Large group rides, while quite exciting, can also be cumbersome.

Before you sign up for an organized trail ride, do a little homework. Find out who is organizing the ride and what they have planned. If you are riding a horse that is green or doesn't have much experience in groups, pick a ride that is small. Find out how fast the leaders plan to go, and only participate if they plan to stay at a walk.

Rules to follow when on an organized trail ride include staying at the same gait as the rest of group (no trotting or galloping to get ahead of other riders), bringing only well-mannered horses on the ride, and being generally courteous of those around you. Make sure the group you are joining has rules in place This will ensure that your ride is a safe one.

Organized rides can be lots of fun, and they also offer a good training opportunity for your horse. Your horse will gain a new experience that will help him whenever he's out on the trail.

The White Horse of Uffington

Around 3,000 years ago, the figure of a white horse was carved into a chalk hillside in the British parish of Uffington, in the south of England, west of London. This simple yet stylized horse, white against a dark background, is visible from nearby high hillsides and from the air. It is also a subject of controversy today.

Although local residents maintain the figure is actually a dragon killed by Saint George, a legend that pre-dates Christianity, the 374-foot-long (114 m) figure has been referred to as a horse from at least the eleventh century.

A similar figure appears on pre-Roman British coinage of 1000 BC. Some experts believe the figure represents a local horse goddess, worshipped only in this region.

For centuries, the white horse was ritually scoured every seven years as part of a festival that included games, traditional cheese rolling, and wrestling. The celebration fell into obscurity 100 years ago, and the horse is now maintained by members of the English Heritage, an organization that safeguards historic English landmarks.

A Look at Bedding

IF YOUR HORSE SPENDS MUCH OF her time in a box stall or paddock, she needs bedding. Bedding provides a soft place to lie down, and also a spot where the horse's urine can be absorbed.

You'll find all kinds of bedding available on the market. The one you choose will depend on your budget and your personal preferences. Among the options, you'll most often see wood shavings, wood pellets, straw, and sawdust. Each has its advantages and disadvantages.

If you aren't sure what kind of bedding to get, ask the advice of your feed store representative or consult with your veterinarian. Always remember to use bedding that is specifically designated for horses. Some materials that are acceptable for other animals—such as black walnut shavings—are harmful to horses.

TYPE OF BEDDING	PROS	CONS
Wood shavings	Most popular; soft and absorbent	Expensive and often dusty, which isn't good for horse or owner
Wood pellets	A lot less dusty and sometimes more absorbent than shavings	Often dissolve into a sort of sawdust when they become wet or are walked on
Straw	Cheap and a good choice for mares with foals or horses being treated for wounds or after surgery	Not absorbent and tends to attract flies by the thousands
Sawdust	Cheap and absorbent	Messy, collects in a horse's eyes, and not appropriate for horses with breathing problems

Good Hoof Care

NO HOOF, NO HORSE: It's an old saying but a true one. Few things are as important to your horse's health as his feet.

Horses' hooves grow continuously, just like our fingernails. In the wild, horses naturally wear down their hooves as they travel many miles a day in search of food. In domestic life, horses don't move as much and so need help keeping their hooves at a normal length.

Most horses need their hooves trimmed every four to six weeks. The trim your horse receives should mimic his natural hoof shape, and it should not be too short or too long. It's a good idea to educate yourself as much as you can about hoof anatomy and learn what a good trim looks like. This way you can keep an eye on the work your farrier performs to be certain he or she is doing right by your horse.

If your horse acts sore after he gets his feet trimmed, something is wrong with your farrier's work. Consult with your veterinarian to make sure the trim is correct for your horse, and get a referral to a different farrier if necessary.

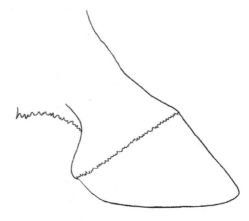

This is a well-trimmed hoof. Note how the heel of the hoof is parallel to the angel of toe.

Round Penning

FOR MOST PEOPLE, riding is the number one priority when it comes to spending time with their horses. But all horses, no matter how old and how well trained, can benefit from work in the round pen.

A round pen is a circular enclosure usually measuring between 40 and 60 feet (12 and 18 m) in diameter. The value of the round pen is that it puts your horse in an environment where she can't help but focus on you. Because the pen has no corners, it encourages forward motion in the horse, leaving no corners where the horse can comfortably stop.

If you have never worked your horse in a round pen, you'll be amazed at how much you can teach her to focus on you using this tool. Here is an exercise to help get your horse to listen to you. What's great about it is that it translates into the saddle.

EXERCISE

Stand in the center of the round pen with a longe whip and ask your horse to go forward. If you regularly longe your horse and she knows how to transition from one gait to another, ask her to go up and down in gaits as she moves around you in the round pen. Change gaits frequently so your horse becomes completely focused on you, waiting for the next command.

If you don't normally longe your horse, start teaching her voice commands for transition while she's in the round pen.

1. Choose words for each gait ("walk," "tee-rot" and "can-ter" for example).

2. Give each command just before you put pressure on your horse to move into that gait.

3. Once she goes into the gait you asked for, tell her she's a good horse to let her know she's doing what you want.

4. Keep her in that gait by putting pressure on her with your body position.

When working in the round pen, always stand so your body is positioned behind the horse's hip to drive her forward. Your longe whip should be in the hand that is opposite the direction the horse is moving. You want to give the horse the impression you are driving her forward with the whip based on where you are holding it.

Spend about fifteen to twenty minutes in the round pen and end your session at a point when your horse is completely focused on you.

The Bashkir Curly

IN 1898, FATHER AND SON ranchers John and Peter Demales were riding a remote Nevada mountain range and they spotted three wild horses. They had seen mustangs before, but not like this. Instead of having a straight hair-coat like other horses, these three had coats made up of tiny ringlets that covered their entire bodies.

Taken with the uniqueness of the horses' appearance, the Demales did not forget them and went back to their homestead with colorful stories of the curly horses.

While the Demales may have been among the first settlers to notice this curly-coated horse, the Sioux and Crow Nations had known about curly horses in other parts of the American West for many years before this. Today, just about everyone in the horse world has heard of the Bashkir Curly.

WHERE DID THEY GET THOSE CURLS?

Of unknown origins, this horse with the curly coat comes in just about every horse color imaginable. The breed's curly coat resembles that of a poodle and is only present during the winter months. The coat sheds out in the spring, along with the majority of their curly manes and tails.

The curly hair of the Bashkir Curly has been shown to be very similar to that of mohair, which is a certain type of coat found on a particular breed of goat. Like mohair, Bashkir Curly coats can be woven and spun into yarn. In fact, a number of Curly aficionados make an assortment of handmade clothing items out of the curly coats their horses shed every year.

Another unique aspect of the curly coat is its propensity to be non-allergenic. Most people who are allergic to horses have no problem being around Curly horses—even those horses that have shed out their ringlet coats for the summer.

Bashkir Curlies are used in a variety of different disciplines, including dressage, Western events, driving, and trail riding.

Bashkir Curly

Historical Reenactments on Horseback

HISTORY BUFFS WHO RIDE HORSES sometimes participate in military reenactments. These reenactments are held all over the world, including Australia, Russia, The Netherlands, France, Germany, Greece, and the United States.

While most reenactments are done strictly on foot, some are still done on horseback. In the United States, replays of battles from the Indian Wars are especially dependent on horses to replicate famous moments in history. An international group called the Vikings also does horseback reenactments, but mostly in the United States.

You don't need a fancy horse to participate in reenactments, but you do need a sense of adventure, along with a budget to buy period clothing and tack for your horse.

You also need to enjoy rough and tumble sports if you want to participate. Reenactors usually use real weapons with blank bullets, and they can get fairly physical. When part of a reenactment, you pretend to be in real battle, and people can get knocked off their horses and "killed"—all part of the fun.

Reenactment groups can be found everywhere, for all periods of history, and a quick search on the Internet will turn up more than you even imagined. Contact a group in your area to find out what it takes to become involved with their group. Plenty of fun lies in store!

Doctorin' Horses

IT TAKES FOUR OR MORE YEARS of intensive study to become an equine veterinarian these days, but 150 years ago, veterinary medicine was a lot simpler. It was also a lot less accurate.

In *The Horse and His Diseases*, a manual on horse doctoring published in 1860, the author, a veterinary surgeon, gives this remedy for constipation, called a diuretic ball:

- Yellow resin, 2 ounces
- Turpentine, 4 ounces
- Soap, 3 ounces
- Salad oil, 1 ounce
- Oil of aniseed, half an ounce
- Powdered ginger, 2 ounces

Rub the last two ingredients together in a mortar, with a little linseed powder. Melt the first three articles over a slow fire, and then mix in the powders. Divide the mass into eight balls, and give one a day.

Friends for Horses

HORSES ARE MOST HAPPY when they can live with members of their own species. Unfortunately, reality dictates that this is not always possible. If you find yourself only able to keep one horse on your property, consider getting him a stablemate to keep him company. Here are a few suggestions:

- *Other equines.* If you can't keep a full-size horse on your property, the next best thing is another type of small equine. Miniature horses make great companions for full-size horses, as do ponies and even burros.

- *Goats.* Horses and goats seem to enjoy each other's companionship. Both are herd animals and have similar habits and attitudes about life. Plus, goats are lots of fun.

- *Dogs.* Not all horses like dogs and vice versa. If you have a dog and horse that get along, let them spend as much time together as you can. Both will enjoy it.

- *Cats.* Some horses adore cats, and some cats even like horses. Cats have been known to cuddle up on horses' backs, probably for the warmth. Depending on the horse, this cuddling may be welcome.

- *Humans.* You can do a lot to help your horse ease his loneliness just by spending time with him. For many horses, human companionship is the next best thing to another equine.

Minerals for Good Health

JUST LIKE HUMANS, horses need minerals to keep their bodies functioning properly.

The major minerals horses need are much the same as what we need: calcium, magnesium, phosphorus, potassium, sodium, chloride, and sulfur.

Horses also need trace minerals: cobalt, copper, iodine, iron, manganese, selenium, and zinc.

All of these minerals come together to help horses metabolize fats, proteins, and carbohydrates. They also work to keep muscles, nerves, and bones functioning properly.

The best way to ensure your horse is getting the minerals she needs is to feed her a good diet consisting of quality hay, pasture, or commercial feed. If the hay in your area is lacking in any of these minerals, your veterinarian will advise you on how to supplement your horse's diet.

Basic Clipping

To CLIP OR NOT TO CLIP: That is the question. Some people believe in clipping their horses; others do not. Your horse's breed, what you do with him, and your own personal preferences determine whether or not you should clip.

Your options for clipping include whisker trimming, fetlock trimming, bridle path creation, body clips, and ear clips.

If you want to neaten your horse's appearance because he's going to be a show, have photos taken, or just needs to look good walking down the trail, consider doing just the minimum amount of clipping. That would include trimming muzzles, fetlocks, and ears. If you have a breed that traditionally wears a bridle path—3 to 5 inches (7 to 13 cm) of clipped-down mane behind the ears—you can add this to the list.

Make sure your horse is used to the clippers and has no problem with you working around his head. If you aren't sure, don't tie your horse. Have someone hold the lead rope as you slowly approach him with the clippers to see his reaction.

Remember to only use horse clippers on your horse. Dog clippers or human clippers won't go far when you try to cut through thick horse hair.

EXERCISE

To trim the muzzle, set your clippers on low and gently run the clippers over your horse's lips.

To trim the fetlocks, run your clips down the horse's fetlock joint and pastern, in the direction that the hair grows. You want to remove the tufts of hair that are sticking out on this part of his leg.

When trimming the ears, be conservative. Nature gave horses hair in their ears to protect them from biting insects.

Unless your horse is going to a show where ears are expected to be shaved, only clip off the tufts of hair that stick way out of his ears. Your horse may not like this type of clipping. Many horses are touchy about their ears, especially when they hear a loudly buzzing clipper coming at them.

If you want to give your horse a bridle path, identify about 3 to 5 inches (7 to 13 cm) of mane just behind his ears and cut this off with a scissors first, as close as you can get to his neck. Neaten up with the clippers. This will give a nice area for your horse's halter or bridle crown piece to rest.

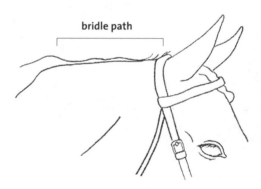

The length of your horse's bridle path should depend on whether you show him or not. Some breeds expect bridle paths to be longer, others shorter.

Mules

ONE OF THE MOST OFTEN ASKED questions by non-horsy people is "What's the difference between a mule and a horse?" The mule is closely related to the horse; it is actually the offspring of a horse and a donkey. Technically, the animal is a mule if the mother is a horse and the father a donkey. If it's the other way around, the animal is a hinny. Both are called mules to keep it simple. Hinnies tend to be smaller than mules because their dams are smaller.

Female mules are called mollies, and male mules are called johns. Mules are sterile, although in extremely rare cases, some mollies have given birth to foals. No johns have ever been shown to reproduce. This sterility is the result of an uneven number of chromosomes, which is what you get when you cross two animals of different but related species.

Mules are famous for their hardiness. They can carry heavier loads than horses and tend to stay sound longer. In the days of the Old West, mules were used to do a lot of the work considered too strenuous for horses to do, such as pull heavy wagons through the desert or carry trappers deep into uncharted wilderness.

Mules come in all horse colors and in different heights, measuring anywhere from 11 hands (miniature mules) to 17 hands. Mules are shown in nearly every discipline, including dressage, Western, jumping, and gymkhana. They make great trail mounts, especially in rugged country.

Mules

Wild Horse Auctions

In 1971, the U.S. Congress passed the Wild Free-Roaming Horses and Burros Act, marking the beginning of the Wild Horse and Burro Adoption Program. Managed by the Bureau of Land Management (BLM), the program is responsible for finding homes for wild horses and burros that have been removed from public lands.

Throughout the year, the BLM holds wild horse and burro auctions around the United States, sometimes in permanent holding stations for these animals, other times in temporary locales. Horse lovers are invited to attend and bid on horses that are kept in pens at the site. You must fill out an adoption application first and be approved before you will be allowed to take home a wild horse or burro.

Bids start relatively low for a single horse or a mare-and-foal combination. If you win your bid, you must have a halter and a trailer with you so you can take your wild horse home.

Wild horse and burro auctions take place on the Internet, too. Photos are posted along with short descriptions of the animals, and potential adopters are invited to bid after filling out an adoption application.

Many wild horse and burro adoption events also feature training sessions by trainers experienced working with wild horses. By watching these experts at work, you can learn a lot about how to train your newly adopted wild equine. Since wild horses and burros are taken off the range and put out for adoption almost immediately, they have had very little handling and have never even worn a halter. They don't know the basics that most horses and burros know, such as how to lead and not to be afraid of humans. They require a lot of basic training, but it's well worth it in the end. Owners of adopted wild horses and burros often report wonderful and deep bonds with their equines, who usually turn out to be incredible companions.

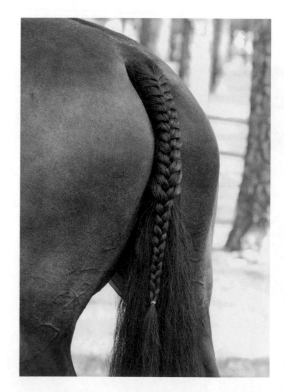

Misty of Chincoteague

IF YOU HAVE A HORSE-LOVING CHILD or were one yourself, you've probably heard of Misty of Chincoteague. This famous pony was the subject of a 1947 book by Marguerite Henry and became a household name among animal-loving children throughout the world.

Based on a true story, *Misty of Chincoteague* is set on Chincoteague Island off the coast of Virginia, and focuses on a pinto filly who is captured in the area's annual wild pony round up. Her trials and tribulations captured the hearts of so many readers that Misty was followed by several sequels and a feature-length film starring Alan Ladd.

As a result of Henry's story, the island of Chincoteague has become a popular tourist destination, especially in the spring when the annual wild pony round up and auction takes place. People come from all over the eastern seaboard to adopt and take home their own version of Misty.

Spooking

SPOOKING IS ONE OF THE MOST oft-reported problems among horse owners, and it's one of the most annoying equine behaviors. It's a rare horse who doesn't do it.

Spooking can be a hard behavior to stop, probably because it is rooted in evolutionary history. Horses are prey animals and are wired to react quickly to perceived danger. Although saber-toothed cats and meat-eating monster bears no longer prowl the Earth, you'll be hard pressed to convince a horse of that.

Here's how to contend with spooking.

- Accept the fact that spooking is a natural behavior for horses. Expecting spooks will happen, especially on the trail, is the first step in learning to cope with them.

- Learn to stay calm and in control. The one-rein stop is an invaluable tool in this regard because you can quickly regain control of your horse in the event of a major spook that sends her bolting in the opposite direction. (For more on the one-rein stop, see Day 202.)

- Desensitize your horse as much as possible. Expose your horse to a lot of different stimuli, always reassuring her that you are nearby and that she's okay. Whether its farmyard animals, floating plastic bags, or roaring garbage trucks, the more time your horse spends around these things, the less spooky she will be.

Aging Your Horse

EVERYONE KNOWS YOU CAN TELL A horse's age by her teeth, but do you know exactly how to do that?

You can always just ask your vet to tell you your horse's age, or you can just look at her registration certificate if she has one. But it's always a good idea to be able to judge for yourself. Not only will it help you become a more knowledgeable horse person, but it may come in handy in the future if you are shopping for another horse.

When examining your horse's choppers, keep in mind that as a horse gets older, her teeth change in length, color, shape, and markings. The surfaces of the teeth also wear down as the horse ages, and teeth also change shape. Dental cups, the dark marks in the surface of the horse's teeth, appear as the horse matures to adulthood, and then disappear as the horse enters her senior years.

Another giveaway that a horse is up there in years is the Galvayne's groove, which is a line in the upper incisors. It starts when a horse hits around ten years of age, and it gets longer as the horse gets older. When a horse reaches around age twenty, the groove reaches from the top of the tooth to the bottom.

The accompanying diagram shows how a horse's teeth change over time.

CHANGE IN INCISORS OVER TWENTY YEARS

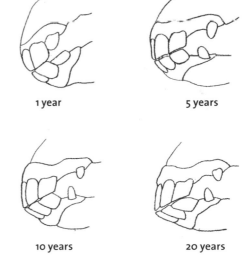

1 year

5 years

10 years

20 years

Over time, a horse's teeth change in shape and markings. This illustration shows the normal changes in a horse's incisors from young foal to twenty years.

The Once-Over

WHETHER YOU SEE YOUR HORSE every day or only on the weekends, you should always give him a thorough inspection as soon as he comes out of his stall, paddock, or pasture.

The once-over will give you a good sense of your horse's general health and attitude. Do it as you groom, but before you ride so you know whether your horse is up to work that day.

EXERCISE

Observe his movement. As you lead your horse out if his enclosure, watch his movement. Check to see if he is favoring any of his legs, or if he is walking stiffly. (If your horse has diagnosed arthritis and lives in a stall, he will probably be stiff but should warm out of it as you walk.)

Examine his legs. Tie your horse to a hitching post or cross ties. Look over his legs from top to bottom, looking for lumps or areas of swelling. Slowly run your hands up each leg, starting from the coronet band to the hock, feeling for heat.

Check out your horse's hooves. You can do this part as you clean them out with your hoof pick. Check for rocks, nails, and other foreign objects. If your horse wears shoes, grasp each shoe and try to move it to see if it's loose. Use your nose to make sure you don't detect any foul odor from the hoof that could indicate thrush. Check the outside of the hoof for quarter cracks.

Examine changes in the skin. As you begin brushing your horse, keep an out of for lumps, bumps, scabs, cuts, or areas of hair loss. When you brush his face, take a good look at his eyes to be certain they are clear and not swollen or excessively teary.

Glance at your horse's nostrils, too. Keep an eye out for discharge. Clear, watery discharge is normal, but thick, white or yellow discharge may indicate an infection.

If you notice areas of concern as you inspect your horse, contact your veterinarian for advice.

Lumps and Bumps

Keep an eye out for the following skin conditions in your horse. Should you find one of these problems, contact your veterinarian.

- Hives: Small or large bumps that appear in clusters

- Ringworm: Starts as a small area of hair loss and worsens with time

- Sacroids: Benign tumors that can be raised or flat

- Seborreha: Crusty skin on the front of the hind legs

- Melanoma: Lump under the skin that are usually black in color

Quarter Horse

THE MOST POPULOUS BREED OF horse in the world is the American Quarter Horse, supported by the largest horse registry and association in the United States, the American Quarter Horse Association.

Developed in the American West in the 1800s as a working cow horse, the breed name comes from the fact that these horses can run a quarter of a mile faster than any other breed.

The Quarter Horse is famous for its easygoing disposition, trainability, and solid good looks. Although seen mostly in the Western disciplines, Quarter Horses are versatile creatures, and they also compete in dressage, jumping, and driving.

Quarter Horses come in a wide variety of equine colors, including sorrel, bay, black, gray, roan, palomino, dun, and buckskin. Pinto-marked Quarter Horses are registered as Paints, and they are considered a different breed. (See Day 43 for more on these colors.)

Because many Quarter Horses also carry Thoroughbred blood, they can range in size from 14.2 to 16 hands. Appendix Quarter Horses, which are half Thoroughbred and half Quarter Horse, are the type of Quarter Horse most often used for racing.

Quarter Horse

Cowboy Mounted Shooting

ONE OF THE MOST FUN equine activities to watch is cowboy mounted shooting, which is a sport that harkens back to the days of the Old West.

In cowboy mounted shooting, skilled riders dressed in authentic 1800s cowboy (or cowgirl) apparel are mounted on well-trained and fast horses. The riders race against one another, two at a time in an arena as they try to pop as many balloons as possible tied to posts, shooting a .45 caliber pistol loaded with blanks.

The event is timed, and whichever rider pops the most balloons in the fastest time is the ultimate winner.

The winner of each race advances to compete with the winners of other match races, until the two fastest and most accurate horse and rider teams battle it out for the top spot.

The Wild Color

TAKE A LOOK AT SOME OF the oldest indigenous wild equids in the world, and you will see one thing in common: a dun coloration. Now look at certain breeds of modern-day horses, and you'll also see this same color. Many experts believe that the dun coloration is the original color of the horse.

The classic dun coloration is characterized by a tan body with dark legs, muzzle, mane, and tail. A black dorsal stripe is always present, and dark stripes can sometimes be seen on the horse's legs.

Different variations of dun exist, including red dun and grulla. The dun gene is a simple dominant gene in the horse, which means only one parent needs to be a dun for the foal to have the coloration.

Duns are plentiful in certain breeds of horses, especially various strains of Spanish Colonial Horses, Quarter Horses, and Norwegian Fjords. This wild color is clearly a throwback to the original wild horse. For more on wild horses, see Day 8.

The Importance of Clean Tack

IT'S NOT THE MOST fun thing to do, but it's a requirement of all equestrians: tack cleaning.

The majority of horse tack—bridles, saddles, and the many accessories that go with them—is made of leather. Because leather is a natural product, made from animal hide, it must be regularly cleaned and conditioned to retain its strength and luster. Nothing is worse than stiff, dry, cracked leather. It's not only unpleasant to work with, but it can break easily, at the most inopportune moments. Few things are as scary as being out on a trail ride in the wilderness and having your bridle break.

Set aside a day to get your tack clean. You can purchase all the supplies you need at your local tack and feed store. You'll need tack sponges, leather cleaner, leather conditioner, a bucket of warm water, and a clean towel.

It's a good idea to take your bridle apart first so you can get into all the nooks and crannies, but remember how it looks before you disassemble it so you will know how to put it back together! Then use the sponges, leather cleaner, and water to scrub all the leather parts on your bridle and saddle, dry with a clean towel, and then follow with conditioner. (See days 293 and 294 for step-by-step details.)

Acupuncture for Horses

ALTERNATIVE THERAPIES SUCH AS acupuncture have been growing in popularity for decades, and not only in the human market. Acupuncture for animal companions is also in greater demand, especially for horses.

Horses can benefit in a number of ways from this ancient form of medicine. Just about every equine malady can be treated with acupuncture, including cardiovascular disorders, chronic respiratory conditions, skin disorders, gastrointestinal problems, allergies, neurological disorders, and even behavioral problems.

Acupuncture is the application of small needles to different points on the horse's body. The idea behind it is to elicit a physiological response that will help treat just about any disease. Acupuncture was originally developed in China, and Eastern practitioners say it works by acting as a

valve in the body to release electrical life energy where it is needed. Western medicine still hasn't determined exactly how it works, but research is ongoing.

Acupuncturists believe there are meridians, or series of points in the body, that correspond to the major organs and other areas that affect overall health. The meridians determine where the needles are placed.

Your regular veterinarian is unlikely to be certified in acupuncture, so if you want to explore this method of treatment, you'll need to find a veterinary acupuncturist. Your veterinarian may be able to recommend one. If not, you can get a referral from the American Academy of Veterinary Acupuncture.

Volunteering at Rescue

YOUR HORSE IS LOVED and well-cared for, but unfortunately that's not the case for many equines. Horses, donkeys, and mules often end up in abusive or neglectful situations, and in need of dire help.

If you love horses and want to help equines in need, volunteer at an equine rescue. All you need to do is contact an equine rescue within driving distance and offer your assistance.

Often, they are small groups with limited funds that are stretched thin trying to help as many horses as they can. Many horses at rescues are in desperate need of a caring person to show them that humans can be trusted.

Most equine rescues need people to groom and exercise the horses, clean stalls, administer medications, and sometimes even feed the horses. They almost always need help with fundraising, public relations, and even legal issues. Without the help of horse-loving volunteers, they wouldn't be able to do the great work they are doing.

The best way to find equine rescues is to use the Internet. A search for equine rescues in your area will undoubtedly reveal at least one group in need. When you contact them, describe your experience with horses, what you are willing to do to help, and any professional expertise you have that they may be able to use. You may even want to offer a foster home for a horse in need.

The Trakehner

ORIGINALLY FROM EASTERN GERMANY, this breed goes back to the sixth century BC. The Scythians first bred the ancestors of today's Trakehners for travel and warfare. In the 1700s, they used their horses for war mounts to fight the Prussian army. By the 1900s, Trakehners were well known throughout Europe as riding horses with great endurance and heart.

The Trakehner is considered one of the warm-blood breeds (a European horse bred for sport), and it is a large, elegant horse with a lot of muscle. Most stand about 16 hands in height, although some can be as small as 15.2 hands. They can come in almost any color, although bay, gray, chestnut, and black are the most common. Some Trakehners have been seen in roan and pinto patterns.

Trakehners are best known for their talents in jumping and dressage, and they are often seen in international competition. They are lighter in build than most other warmbloods.

Trakehner

85

Steer Daubing

IF YOU LIKE CHASING COWS, you'll love steer daubing, the sport of marking a steer on its side with a stick dipped in chalk.

In this exciting sport, horse and rider break from a gate the same time the steer is released next to them. The horse and rider chase the steer and try to daub the animal with chalk (or sometimes flour) on the side. The event is timed. The horse and rider team that daubs the steer in the shortest amount of time is the winner.

Like many cattle events, steer daubing comes from real ranch work. Cattle sometimes needed to be marked to distinguish them from the rest of the herd for "doctoring" or other purposes, and the easiest way to do it was to chase them down on horseback.

Western horse shows and rodeos often offer steer daubing classes. Before you can try this event, your horse has to have experience working cattle You can get this experience by working with a trainer who specializes in training horses to cattle or by buying a horse that has worked cattle on a ranch or already been trained to work with steers. It takes considerable skill to get close enough to the cow and accurately mark the animal in the designated spot. You and your horse will have to practice a lot before you are ready for competition.

Darley Arabian

ONE OF THE MOST FAMOUS Arabian horses in the world is not known for his accomplishments within his breed, but actually for being the foundation of the Thoroughbred horse.

The Darley Arabian was a handsome bay stallion reported to have come from the Nedj, the central tableland of the Arabian peninsula, known as the cradle of Arabian equine nobility. He grew up under very harsh conditions, as all horses in that region, and proved himself to a hardy and proficient sire.

The stallion was bought by a British horse breeder named Thomas Darley and brought to England to stand at stud. He sired a great many foals, and along with the Godolphin Arabian and the Byerley Turk, spawned the Thoroughbred breed in the 1700s.

Why a Helmet?

IT'S A WONDERFUL FEELING to gallop along with the wind blowing through your hair. Despite this truth, you should seriously consider wearing a helmet when you ride.

It's unfortunate but true that head injuries are all too common among equestrians. When you fall from a horse, the chances of hitting your head are great. Although our skulls are hard and do a lot to protect us, the impact is often enough to cause serious damage—and even death.

For this reason, it's best to play it safe and always don protective headgear before you ride. Helmet manufacturers have developed some innovative, streamlined, and fashionable designs that are much more attractive than models of the past, and they are also much more comfortable.

When shopping for a helmet, look for one that is certified by a reputable safety organization. In the United States, helmets are certified by the American Society for Testing (ASTM) and Materials and the Safety Equipment Institute (SEI). Other countries have safety organizations that certify helmets as well. These certifications are necessary to ensure the helmet will protect you in the event of a fall from a horse.

The Right Fit

It's important to make sure a helmet fits you right so you'll get the best protection in the event of a fall.

Before purchasing a helmet, try it on. The helmet should fit snugly on your head. You shouldn't be able to move it on your head from front to back or side to side in any significant way. Remember: You want it to stay in place if you fall and strike your head on the ground.

Although many riders prefer to keep the chin strap loose on a helmet, it's vital that the strap be snug to help the helmet remain stable. A snug chin strap feels annoying at first, but you'll get used to it.

If you have never purchased a helmet before, buy your first helmet at a tack store that provides good customer service. A knowledgeable salesperson can help you find a helmet that gives you the right fit.

Gastric Ulcers

HUMANS AREN'T THE ONLY ONES who get stomach ulcers. Horses are plagued by them, too. Often the result of stress, frequent dosing with non-steroidal anti-inflammatory drugs, and low-fiber diets, gastric ulcers in horses are unfortunately all too common. In fact, one study showed that 90 percent of all performance horses in training have some degree of stomach ulcers.

DIAGNOSING ULCERS

A classic symptom of stomach ulcers is frequent, unexplained colic episodes. Most horses show no symptoms, however. The only way to definitely diagnose them is to have a veterinarian examine the horse using an endoscope. The endoscope is inserted through the horse's nose, down through the esophagus, and into the stomach. The veterinarian can actually see the ulcers using this method rather than simply surmising their presence based on symptoms.

TREATING ULCERS

The treatment for ulcers in horses is medication specifically for ulcer treatment, called omeprozane. Horses receiving non-steroidal anti-inflammatory drugs for another health condition should be fed alfalfa hay to help protect the stomach. Stress should also be reduced to help the horse's stomach heal.

PREVENTING ULCERS

The best way to prevent gastric ulcers is to feed your horse a diet high in roughage—that is, hay. Keep your horse's stress to a minimum if you can, and talk to your veterinarian about preventative medication if he or she prescribes anti-inflammatory drugs for your horse.

♥ Observe Your Horse

HORSES ARE FOR RIDING or driving, but we can learn a lot about them by just watching them be horses.

EXERCISE

Spend an hour just observing your horse. If she's in a stall, turn her out in a paddock and sit nearby, watching her. If she's in a pasture with her buddies, even better.

Take note of your horse's behavior. You'll likely see a lot of grazing and foraging, which will help you come to really appreciate the drive horses have to eat. Watch her ears move as she picks up sounds coming from different directions. Take note of how she raises her head high to get a better look at something that has caught her attention. Observe how much bigger she seems to grow in appearance as she tries to figure out if she is seeing friend or foe.

If your horse is in a pasture or paddock with other horses, study her herd behavior. Watch how she uses body language to send messages to the other horses, and how masterfully she reads theirs. Notice how the movements and behaviors of the other horses affect her movements and behaviors. And take note of what happens if one of the other horses is removed from the enclosure. You'll probably see signs of anxiety as the herd is "broken up."

Take all the information you have gleaned from your horse in this exercise and use it to help understand her behavior when she's with you. The most skilled horse people in the world are the ones who can read horses the best.

Connemara

THE RUGGED, DAMP, AND ROCKY landscape of Ireland is the original home of the Connemara pony, an Irish breed

The ancestors of the Connemara pony first came to Ireland with Celtic warriors from elsewhere in Europe more than 2,500 years ago. These small horses, which pulled war chariots and carts, escaped and became feral, living in the mountains of the Connemara Isles. More than 1,000 years later, a Spanish armada sank off the Irish coast. The horses on board swam to safety and bred with the wild mountain ponies. The result was the early Connemara.

Although Connemaras are called "ponies," many of them are horse sized. Measuring anywhere from 13 to 15 hands, Connemaras have big bones and compact bodies. They are known for having hard feet, and for being sure-footed and athletic.

Connemaras come in gray, bay, brown, and dun, with some roans, and, once in a while, a black, chestnut, or palomino. Sometimes pinto Connemaras occur, but they are not eligible for registration.

Connemaras are well known for their easy-going attitude. They are willing to work, easy to train, and able to perform in many different disciplines, especially any discipline that involves jumping.

One of the Connemara's biggest talents is jumping. Some people believe the breed became good jumpers while living on the rocky slopes of the western coast of Ireland.

Connemara

Dressage

DRESSAGE IS AMONG THE OLDEST riding disciplines in the world, dating back to ancient Greece. Classical dressage is still practiced much in the way it was originally performed in ancient times, while a more modern version of the discipline is also practiced. The sport has long been popular in Europe, and it has gained a lot of fame in the United States over the past two decades.

Dressage consists of a series of movements that emphasizes the horse's natural carriage at various gaits. The horse and rider team performs in a rectangular-shaped arena marked with block letters around the perimeter that serve as targets for particular movements during a dressage test.

Horse and rider teams compete at different levels, depending on their training. They are scored on how close to perfect they perform each movement. Though riders are technically competing with each other in dressage tests, most are primarily concerned with improving their individual score from one test to the nest. (The major exception to this is international competition dressage, such as the Olympics, where winning with the best score is the priority.)

Dressage training is an excellent foundation for any horse, regardless of what you plan to do with him. Riders trained in dressage learn to have an independent seat, and they can become very skilled at communicating with the horse.

Dressage Moves

The following are some of the movements seen in dressage.

- Trot and canter half-pass: The horse travels on a diagonal line keeping his body almost parallel with the arena fence while making both forward and sideways steps in each stride.

- Piaffe: The horse essentially trots in place.

- Passage: The horse moves in a slow-motion, suspended trot.

- Canter pirouette: The horse canters almost in place in a 360-degree circle.

The Chariot

WHEN YOU THINK OF THE CHARIOT, you probably envision ancient wild races, with Roman drivers pushing their horses on as they try to beat several other teams.

Chariots were simple two- or four-wheeled open carts with nothing more than a floor with a waist-high semicircular guard in front. They were used for racing in ancient Rome, but they also had other purposes. They served as simple means of transportation in many ancient cultures, and they were used in the Middle East, the Near East, and Europe from 3,000 BC on.

Originally developed by the Mesopotamians, the first chariot was a fast, light cart pulled by two horses abreast. Later chariots were designed to be pulled by three and four horses as well.

Because chariots were so light, heavy draft horses were not needed to pull them. Light horses were used with chariots, which made them invaluable as fast vehicles in times of war.

Horse Insurance

YOU PROBABLY HAVE medical insurance for yourself, but did you know you can also get it for your horse?

Major medical policies for horses are similar to medical policies for humans. Most policies cover partial medical costs that originate from diagnostic procedures, surgery, medication, and veterinary exams. A deductible for each incident is the norm. Premiums are paid in one lump sum, and the cost depends on the value of the horse and the terms of the policy. You can expect to pay from $500 (£345) or more per year for a major medical insurance policy on a horse.

Along with major medical, mortality is part of the coverage. If your horse dies, you will be reimbursed the stated value of the horse, assuming the death was not caused by your negligence. Most insurance companies will require you to seek all possible medical solutions to save a horse before they will agree to pay out on a mortality claim.

The plus side of insuring your horse is that you'll have a good portion of your veterinary bills paid should your horse develop a serious illness or become injured. The negative side to insurance is that you may never need to use it after paying all those premiums. But that's if you are lucky. If your horse does develop a veterinary problem, you can be assured that the condition will be excluded when your policy is renewed the following year. Also, pre-existing conditions are not covered, nor are horses over the age of fifteen.

That said, major medical insurance is usually a good idea for your horse if you can afford it. The peace of mind it gives is well worth the expense.

Thrush

EVER CLEAN YOUR HORSE'S HOOVES out and smell something really foul? Chances are your horse is suffering from thrush, which is a degeneration of the frog tissue (the frog is the triangular area on the underside of the horse's foot) accompanied by a secondary bacterial infection.

Thrush happens when a horse stands for prolonged periods in wet bedding or manure, or when the hooves are not cleaned out daily. The damp material softens the frog tissue and allows bacteria to take hold. You may notice that the area around your horse's frog is darker in color than normal, and areas of the frog my crumble when pushed with a hoof pick, but this may not be the case. The foul odor of thrush is the best way to detect it.

Fortunately, treating thrush is relatively easy. Over-the-counter remedies sold at tack and feed stores work to kill off the bacteria. Good hoof hygiene is also mandatory to lick thrush.

To prevent thrush, keep your horse's stall dry. Make sure bedding is changed often so your horse isn't standing in urine-soaked shavings. Pick up manure frequently because manure-packed hooves are more prone to thrush. In wet weather, be certain your horse has a dry area in her outdoor stall where she can stand to get out of the mud.

The best way to prevent thrush is to pay close attention to your horse's foot care. Don't neglect her hooves. Clean them out daily, even on days when you can't ride.

Riding on the Lunge Line

MAINTAINING YOUR BALANCE on the horse is probably the single most important aspect of riding. Without balance, you won't stay on your horse for long. Good balance also makes it easier for your horse to carry you.

A great way to improve your balance is to ride on the lunge line. The lunge line is a rope measuring anywhere from 15 to 25 feet (4.5 to 7.6 m) long that attaches to your horse's halter or bridle. The other end is held by someone who stands about 10 feet (3 m) or more away while the horse moves around him or her in a circle. By having an experienced person—whether a trainer, instructor, or another skilled horse handler—lunge your horse while you ride, you can concentrate on improving your balance.

EXERCISE

If your horse knows how to work on a lunge line, get a qualified person to help you. Tack your horse up as you would to ride him, but fit him with a lunge line as well. In a safe arena, mount up your horse and start riding him on the lunge line at the walk. After you and your horse have warmed up, start working on your balance by riding with one arm out to your side as you hold the reins with the other. Start with your inside arm and then switch to your outside arm.

Once you feel comfortable with this, it's time for both arms to come up. Drop your reins and let the person holding the lunge line control your horse. If you feel off-balance, this is the place where you need to stay. Work only at the walk with both arms up for about thirty minutes. Practice this as often as you can until you feel pretty secure at the walk. Be sure to have the horse lunged in both directions.

The next step is try these exercises at the trot, and then eventually the canter. When you can ride on the lunge line with both arms out at the canter, your balance is excellent.

Paso Fino

THE PASO FINO IS A handsome breed developed in South America from horses originally brought to the New World by the Spaniards in the 1500s. The breed is most often seen in Cuba, Puerto Rico, and Columbia, and is becoming more popular in the United States.

Paso Finos are gaited horses, and they are considered one of the smoothest horses in the world to ride. The breed's gaits are the classic fino, paso corto, and the paso largo. The classic fino gait is the slowest gait, and it is about the speed of a fast walk. The paso corto is the same speed as a trot, and the paso largo is the speed of a fast canter. Some Paso Finos can also canter in addition to these other three gaits.

Paso Fino horses usually measure in at around 14 to 15 hands. They have a short back, a gracefully arched neck, and a medium-sized head with a straight profile. They come in bay, black, brown, buckskin, chestnut, dun, gray, grulla, palomino, pinto, and roan. They are known for their brio, which means "controlled spirit." Horses with brio have lots of energy, but they are completely under the rider's control.

Paso Finos make great trail horses because they can go long distances at a gait that is comfortable for the rider. They are also popular at gaited horse shows.

Paso Fino

Equestrian Vaulting

VAULTING IS NOT A TYPICAL equine sport, but it is one that is slowly growing in popularity. Essentially gymnastics on horseback, vaulting requires a well-trained horse and a flexible and energetic equestrian.

In vaulting, the horse canters on a lunge line while a vaulter performs a series of acrobatic maneuvers on the horse's back. Similar to the type of riding often seen in circuses, vaulters are judged alone and in teams, where they perform required maneuvers or freestyle arrangements, just like in horseless gymnastic competitions.

To be successful in vaulting, a competitor must be extremely athletic. In fact, a background in gymnastics is a huge asset. Horses used for vaulting must be specially trained and be quiet, steady animals who will keep their cool regardless of what is going on around them and on them!

Equestrian vaulting consists of many different moves that require considerable skill.

- Flag: The vaulter moves from sitting on the horse to his or her knees and extends the right leg straight out behind, holding it slightly above his or her head so the leg is parallel to the horse's back. The left arm is stretched straight forward, at a height nearly that of the right leg. The right foot is arched and the sole facing upward.

- Mill: The vaulter moves from sitting on the horse to bringing the right leg over the horse's neck. He or she left brings the left leg to a full arc over the horse's hips. The right leg follows it, and the left leg moves over the neck to complete the full turn.

- Scissors: The vaulter moves from sitting on the horse and swings into a handstand. The vaulter then turns to face the inside of the circle that the horse is moving in crosses the outer leg over. The vaulter then comes down and lands so that he or she is facing backward on the horse. The maneuver is then reversed.

- Stand: The vaulter moves from sitting on the horse onto his or her shins and onto both feet. He or she lets go of the grips and straightens up with both knees bent. The vaulter must hold the position for four full strides.

The First Equine Movie Star

THE FIRST EQUINE MOVIE STAR was discovered in northern California in the early 1800s. Photographer Eadweard Muybridge shot a series of photos of a trotting horse named Abe Edgington pulling a sulky. The horse's owner, Leland Stanford, hired Muybridge to photograph his racehorses so he could better understand their movement. Muybridge ended up discovering the art of motion picture in the process.

Muybridge accomplished this feat by placing twelve cameras with special lenses and an electronically controlled mechanism meant to operate special shutters.

Wires were placed under the racetrack at 21-inch (53 cm) intervals and triggered the release of the camera shutters as the sulky wheels rolled over them.

The twelve pictures took about half a second to be recorded. They showed Abe Edgington trotting in motion rather than in a single, still photograph—a first.

After this historic event, Muybridge invented a machine called a "zoopraxiscope," the first film projector, designed to put together the pictures he had shot so he could easily show the fluid motion of the sequence.

Arena Maintenance

IF YOU ARE FORTUNATE ENOUGH to have an arena on your property, you have a place where you can work your horse on a regular basis. You also have the responsibility of keeping that arena in good condition so your horse stays comfortable and safe when he works. Here's how.

1. Make sure your fences and gates are in good repair. Inspect the enclosure carefully, looking for sharp edges that may hurt your horse and loose screws and hinges that could compromise the security of your arena.

2. Examine your footing, the surface that you ride on. Good footing is mandatory if you want your horse to stay sound. The footing layer is of primary concern, and it should be deep enough to reduce concussion to the horse's legs without causing muscle and tendon strains.

3. If your riding surface has become compact or has blown away due to frequent windy weather, you may need to add more. Sand, decomposed granite, or any number of manmade arena materials can work as a riding surface. If you live in a climate that gets a lot of rain, consider adding sand. Even though it can more expensive, you'll get more use out of your arena after bad weather if you use this material.

4. Make sure whatever you add to the arena has been sifted for debris. You don't want rocks, nails, sticks, and other foreign objects inside your arena.

5. Drag your arena frequently to aerate the riding surface and keep it from getting compacted. You don't need a tractor do this; an all-terrain vehicle with an arena drag attached to it will do the trick.

Dental Care

YOUR HORSE'S TEETH SHOULD BE at the top of your preventative care list. Horses with tooth problems can develop serious health issues, such as colic and infections.

Horses in the wild don't need dental care because they wear their teeth down naturally as they graze on a variety of different plants. Domestic horses, on the other hand, tend to eat the same thing every day, which wears their teeth down in an uneven manner.

For this reason, horses living in captivity need to have their teeth filed down—or floated—on a regular basis. Otherwise, sharp points develop on the back molars, causing pain and ulcerations in the mouth.

Horse veterinarians perform routine dental care as part of their normal services. Ask your vet to examine your horse every six months to see if her teeth are in need of special care such as an extraction of a problem tooth, or if issues have arisen from temporal mandibular joint. Your vet can do this as a matter of practice when he or she comes out to give your horse her bi-annual vaccines. Your vet should do a thorough exam of your horse's mouth, keeping an eye out for other dental problems in addition to uneven wear.

Signs of Equine Dental Disease

- Eating slowly
- Having difficulty eating
- Being reluctant to drink cold water
- Excessive salivation
- Bad breath

Also, some horses hold the head to one side while eating, are reluctant to take the bit, or shake their heads while being ridden. Another sign of possible dental disease is the presence of whole, unchewed grain in the stool.

Read a Horse Book

JUST BECAUSE THE WEATHER isn't great and you'd prefer to stay indoors doesn't mean you can't indulge your horse obsession. Instead of riding, read a good horse book instead.

If you like fiction, you'll find no shortage of horse stories to choose from. One great classic suitable for both kids and adults is Anna Sewell's *Black Beauty*, which was first published in 1877. The book brought attention to the inhumane way many horses were handled back then, and it was instrumental in changing people's attitudes about how to treat horses. The book led to laws protecting horses in Victorian England.

If you enjoy reading novels for kids, books such as *The Black Stallion* by Walter Farley, *Misty of Chincoteague* by Marguerite Henry, and *My Friend Flicka* by Mary O'Hara are all classics worth reading. A great adult novel to curl up by the fire with is *Seabiscuit: An American Legend*, by Laura Hillenbrand.

Nonfiction horse books abound, covering just about every equine-related subject imaginable. Read about how to train your horse, how to improve your riding, how to better care for your horse, and how the horse's mind works. You can even explore the spirituality of horses or delve into their history with humankind.

Belgian

THE BELGIAN'S STORY BEGINS in the Middle Ages when the breed's ancestors, heavy war horses were bred for battle. When their war days ended, these large horses went on to work on the farms of Europe, plowing fields and pulling wagons. Centuries later, the Belgian people began to carefully breed their farm horses, creating the Flemish, Brabant, and Ardennes breeds. It is from these breeds that the horse known in the United States as the Belgian was created.

Belgians are plentiful today, but fifty years ago, only a few were left in the world. Motorized equipment had replaced horses on farms, making Belgians and other draft breeds obsolete.

People who still loved Belgians fought to keep the breed alive, and they succeeded. Today, the Belgian outnumbers all other draft horse breeds in the United States and Europe combined.

The Belgian today is the same horse that plowed farm fields before the tractor was invented. Heavily muscled, the Belgian has a large head and a huge neck, with a powerful, round body.

Pulling is a sport that has long been a tradition in the Belgian breed. Pulling competitions began as casual contests between farmers in the early part of the century.

Belgian pulling teams are grouped by how much they weigh, and they are usually divided into lightweight, middleweight, and heavyweight divisions. The team that pulls the heaviest weight the longest distance in one continuous movement is the winner.

Not all Belgians are competition horses. In many places, these horses still do the work they were bred for. In forested regions, Belgians are used in small logging operations, where they are used to haul trees that have been cut down through standing forests. In the Midwest, where the American Belgian had its beginnings, the horse can still be seen working on Amish farms.

Belgian

Ride and Tie

RIDE AND TIE IS AN exciting equine activity that emphasizes teamwork between two humans and a horse. The sport started in the United States, and it is getting interest in other parts of the world, particularly Germany and Australia. It is essentially an endurance race, but unlike regular endurance riding, ride and tie requires some of the race be run on foot by human team members. The humans on the team take turns riding the horse. The team member not riding is running, and vice versa. Since the horse moves faster than the human on foot, riders will get off a horse, leave the horse tied to a bush or tree for the runner to find at a strategic point so he or she can mount up. Meanwhile, the team member who had been riding takes off on foot.

The human team members alternate when they ride the horse and when they run. The team that finishes the race first with a sound horse is the winning team.

Ride and tie races are typically 20 to 100 miles (31 to 161 km) in length, and consist of anywhere from 10 to 50 teams. Mandatory veterinarian checks are part of the course.

Ride and tie events are sanctioned by the Ride and Tie Association, which has established rules for these races and keeps track of winning teams around the country. The majority of races take place in California, although ride and tie events are held all over the United States.

Centaurs

HALF MAN, HALF HORSE: That is the centaur, a bizarre creature from Greek mythology that has remained in the human imagination for thousands of years.

In ancient times, the centaur represented humankind's animal side. Centaurs—and their female equivalent, centaurides—behaved in wild and sometimes violent ways in Greek and Roman mythology.

Centaurs persist in modern culture, and they have appeared in very successful films in recent years. Disney's *Fantasia* featured centaurs cavorting about. In the Harry Potter series, centaurs have superior intelligence and an aversion for humans. And a centaur plays a pivotal role in the film version of C.S. Lewis's *The Chronicles of Narnia: The Lion, the Witch, and the Wardrobe.*

Exceptional riders are sometimes called centaurs because they seem to be at one with their horses. The entire concept of centaurs is believed to have come from humans riding horses and how the two together function as one.

Bucking

ONE OF THE SCARIEST MISBEHAVIORS a horse can throw at you is a buck. Her head goes down, and her back end up goes up, as her hind feet seem to point to the sky. Small bucks are not too hard to sit if you have good balance. But a hard buck can unseat even the best of riders.

Horses usually buck for a few reasons.

• Excess energy that they need to get out

• Pain, usually in the back

• Defiance, hoping to get out of doing what they are being asked to do

If your horse bucks hard and often, you have a problem. To solve it, explore the reasons for her behavior.

• Start with an exam by your veterinarian to make sure the horse is not experiencing pain that is driving the behavior.

• If your horse gets a clean bill of health, try giving her more exercise, especially before you ride. Lunge her or work her in a round pen and let her get her bucks out before you get on.

• If that doesn't do the trick, consider that she may be bucking in the hopes that you'll stop asking her to work. If that's the case, and her bucking is hard enough to unseat you, you may need help from a professional trainer.

Equine Allergies

HORSES CAN DEVELOP ALLERGIES much like people can. They can be allergic to something in the air, something they are eating, or something that is coming into contact with their skin.

Your horse probably has allergies if he is coughing a lot, breathing loudly, has hives on his skin, or gets frequent diarrhea or loose stool. You should have your veterinarian take a look at your horse if he is exhibiting any of these signs.

If allergies are the culprit, your vet can give you suggestions on how to deal with the allergies.

Soaking your horse's hay is one remedy if dust is causing your horse to have breathing problems. If your horse is allergic to something he's eating, your vet will suggest you gradually switch him to a different kind of hay. Hives can be the result of an airborne allergy, as well as diet, and they can be treated with doses of steroids.

But not all itchy skin is caused by allergies. Flies are another cause of hives and itchy skin, and should be kept at bay with a good fly control program. (For more on controlling flies, see Day 18.)

Arena Exercises

Riding in the arena can be fun if you are working toward a goal. It can also be stimulating for your horse if you make it interesting for her.

Before you ride in the arena, have a firm idea of what you want to do with your horse. Arena exercises that you have memorized can come in handy when you sense your horse is becoming bored and needs something to challenge her both physically and mentally.

EXERCISE A

Even though the walk is the slowest gait, you can still do good work here. This exercise will help your horse become more responsive and supple, and it will teach you to use your legs to communicate.

1. Set up three barrels that are 12 feet (3.7 m) apart.

2. Go to the end of arena and face the barrels. Then walk toward them.

3. As you get to the first barrel, turn your horse to the right and make a counter-clockwise circle around the barrel.

4. At the second barrel, turn your horse to the left and make a clockwise circle around it.

5. Go around the third barrel counter-clockwise.

6. Turn around and do the pattern again, going in the opposite direction.

EXERCISE B

The trot is a more challenging gait to ride than the walk, and it requires better balance from you and responsiveness from your horse. This exercise will help improve both. Be sure to use your legs to cue your horse in the direction you want her to go.

1. Start at one end of the arena and begin to trot down the rail.

2. Gradually turn your horse to the inside of the arena and begin making an S-pattern.

3. Continue repeating this S-pattern until you get to the other side of arena.

4. Repeat it again going the other way.

The more often you practice these exercises, the better your horse will bend around your leg when she turns. Your balance will improve, too, as you learn to ride these patterns.

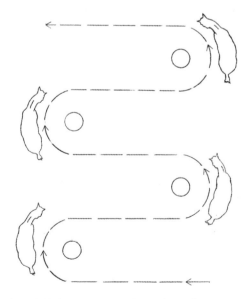

The serpentine pattern can be performed at a trot, and it is a good exercise whether you are an English or Western rider.

Colorado Rangers

EVERYONE INVOLVED IN HORSES has heard of the Quarter Horse and Appaloosa, but not everyone knows about another breed that has been around as long as both of these: the Colorado Ranger.

The roots of the Colorado Ranger (also known as the Colorado Rangerbred) lie in the Middle East, where General Ulysses S. Grant befriended Sultan Abdul Hamid II of Turkey in 1878 and was given a gift of an Arabian stallion named Leopard and a Barb stallion named Linden Tree. The two horses were subsequently used in a program designed to create a new breed of light harness horse to be called the Americo-Arab.

The advent of the automotive engine thwarted plans for the new breed, and the two stallions were sent to Nebraska for a summer to stand stud on the property of a rancher named General George Colby. Here Colby bred the stallions to his mares of mixed breeding (some reportedly spotted), producing excellent working horses.

The reputation of Colby's fine ranch horses soon spread, and not long after, the Ira J. Whipple family of Colorado purchased a double-bred grandson of Leopard from Colby, along with mares sired by Leopard or Linden Tree. In doing so, they brought the legacy of these fine horses to the state of Colorado.

The typical Colorado Ranger stands from 14.2 to 16 hands in height and has stock-horse type conformation. Its build is refined while still being solid enough for hard ranch work. Some horses in the breed retain a concave (dished) profile as a result of the Ranger's Arabian genes, and many possess considerable stamina.

Colorado Rangerbreds come in just about any solid color seen in horses, particularly bay, chestnut, gray, black, and brown. The Appaloosa-type coat patterns most often seen in the breed are leopard, frosted blanket, blanket with spots, and snowflake.

Along with having a compact body and powerful hindquarters, the Colorado Ranger is known for being willing, eager to please, and loaded with good cow sense.

Colorado Ranger

Competitive Trail Riding

TRAIL RIDERS WHO ENJOY competition have found their sport in an event called competitive trail riding. Most widely sponsored by the North American Trail Ride Conference, or NATRC, competitive trail riding takes place in regions all over the United States and Canada. It can be done with any kind of horse or tack, and it doesn't require a large cash outlay for participation.

Competitive trail rides take place over a two- or three-day period. Horses and riders are placed in divisions based on their skill level. Novice horses and riders cover anywhere from 20 to 25 miles (32 to 40 km) per day, while those in the two upper divisions of Competitive Pleasure and Open ride 30 to 50 miles (48 to 80 km) per day, sometimes for two days.

The terrain on the trails vary according to the region and the specific venue. Some rides cover strenuous trails that require steep climbs. Others are mostly flat.

Unlike endurance, competitive trail competitions are not races. Instead, riders are judged on their horsemanship, and horses are evaluated on their manners and conditioning. Horses and riders camp out the night before the ride, which teaches horse camping skills to participants. Judges observe horses and riders throughout the prescribed trail, sometimes stopping participants and asking them to perform certain basic maneuvers such as backing up, mounting and dismounting, and negotiating a trail obstacle. Scores are calculated at the end of the ride, and awards are given that evening in camp.

El Morzillo

ALTHOUGH MYSTERY SURROUNDS the details of horses brought to the New World by the Spanish conquistadors, one horse stands out as an individual. His name was El Morzillo, and he was the favorite mount of General Hernán Cortés.

A black stallion reported to be a great war horse, El Morzillo was Cortés' mount when the Spaniards rode into present-day Honduras. A long splinter became lodged in the horse's hoof, and he became lame, forcing Cortés to leave him behind in the care of the Indians.

Never having seen a horse before, the native peoples considered El Morzillo a god and built him a temple.

They brought him chickens and fruit as offerings, apparently denying him what he really needed to eat out of sheer ignorance. El Morzillo eventually died, but his legacy remained with the Indians who cared for him. When Spanish priests arrived in the area in 1625, they found the Indians worshipping El Morzillo's image.

Catching Runaways

WHEN HORSES BREAK FREE from their confines, whether it be busting out of their stalls or pulling back when tied, all heck breaks loose. If other horses are around, they all react with great excitement. It's as if they are saying "Yeah! Go for it!"

Most horses will quickly give up their newfound freedom for a bite to eat. The hay stack is usually the first and only destination once a horse realizes he's free. But occasionally, a horse decides to make the most of his freedom by galloping around the property like a nut, tail in the air and hooves a-flailing.

Catching a loose horse isn't usually hard. If the horse stops to eat, just quietly approach him with a halter and lead rope and slip the rope over his neck while he's munching. Horses that run from you are more challenging, but eventually a calm approach yields success. Get help if you can, and ask people to form human barriers so the horse is cornered and can't run away. Once most horses realize they are surrounded, they quickly give up.

Whatever you do, don't punish the horse once you catch him. If you do, you'll have a much harder time rounding him up next time because he will remember the punishment and decide it's in his best interests to stay away from you. Never run after a horse either. The horse can easily outrun you and will be happy to prove it if you start trying to chase him down.

All-Important Salt

SODIUM AND CHLORIDE COMBINE together make salt, which is an essential major mineral for many mammals. They are electrolytes necessary for bodily functions. Salt is an essential part of the equine diet, and it should be provided at all times.

Lack of these minerals can cause a horse to experience fatigue, the inability to sweat, and muscle spasms.

Horses lose salt through urination and sweating, and it must be replaced. The best way to provide salt is free-choice loose salt in a bucket. Some horse people prefer natural, loose salt, believing it is healthier than processed salt. Others find that salt blocks are more convenient. Many equine nutritionists recommend a plain salt block rather than one with other minerals added so horses aren't forced to take in minerals they may not need just to get at the salt. This could result in toxicity.

Grazing In-Hand

WE ARE OFTEN SO BUSY RIDING and training our horses, we forget to just spend quality time with them. One way to do this is the let them graze in-hand.

Grazing in-hand simply means that you let your horse eat as she would if she were wild, except that she's wearing a halter and you are on the other end of the lead rope.

Nature designed horses to graze for many hours a day. It's not something most horses get to do in captivity, so when they have moments where they can do it, they really enjoy themselves. As you observe, you'll discover the true nature of your horse, the herbivore.

EXERCISE

Find a good spot for your horse to munch on plants that are growing out of the ground. This can be a lawn, an overgrown field, or a pasture. Make sure you know what kind of plants your horse will be eating, and verify they are not poisonous before you let her eat. Be sure they haven't been sprayed with pesticides either.

Lead your horse out to the designated area and stop. It won't be long before she puts her head down to check out what's beneath her feet. She'll soon start nibbling and will get lost in the act of grazing.

Observe your horse as she's eating. You'll see how her sensitive and dexterous muzzle selects the leaves she wants to eat and directs them into her mouth. She's selective and won't eat everything she comes across. Her sensitive nose helps her discern what seems tasty and what doesn't.

As your horse grazes, you'll notice that she takes small steps. Move with her as she does, taking note of how this slow but steady movement provides lubrication for her joints and muscles and helps keep her circulation going.

Don't let your horse graze for more than an hour a day if she hasn't been doing it before. Overloading her digestive system with foods she's not normally used to can cause colic.

111

Canadian Horse

IN 1665, WHEN CANADA WAS STILL a French colony, Louis the XIV sent the struggling settlers a shipload of sixteen horses. In 1670, he sent another shipment. The French horses that arrived on Canadian soil were of Norman, Breton, Arab, Barb, and Andalusian breeding.

Life was harsh in colonial Canada—known as New France—and the difficult climate and lack of good pasture took its toll on the new horses. Only the strongest horses survived to propagate.

By the time New France had grown from a tiny colony to an area of nearly 20,000 people in Montreal in the 1700s, those first French-imported horses had changed considerably. The rigors of their life and work meant only the toughest survived, and the scarcity of food left them small, never more than 15 hands. This diminutive but powerful horse plowed fields, pulled logs, carried small children, and raced for sport.

Today, the Canadian Horse is known for its easygoing and willing temperament. The breed has a somewhat stocky build, with a short, straight head; a fairly arched neck; a strong, short back; and an abundant mane and tail.

Canadian Horses are most often seen in black, although chestnut, bay, and dark brown are also colors within the breed. Standing 14 to 16 hands in height, the breed has grown a bit since its days in colonial Quebec, which makes it suitable for a variety of sports, such as driving, jumping, dressage, and distance riding.

Canadian

Halter Classes

THE CLOSEST THING TO A beauty contest for horses is the halter class, which is an event that shows off a horse's conformation to a judge well-versed in the breed. The judge compares the horse to the breed standard, which is maintained by the breed club. The judge places the horses in the class according to which ones are closest to the standard.

Halter horses go through a considerable amount of preparation—called fitting—before they are shown in conformation classes. This often involves placing them on a high-grain diet and daily conditioning with exercise.

Some horses even wear a neck sweat, which is a synthetic wrap designed to shrink the size of their necks to make them more attractive for the show ring.

Although considerable preparation goes into getting a halter horse ready for exhibition, halter horses are bred, not made. Certain lines within the Quarter Horse, Paint, and Arabian breeds are known for producing winning halter horses.

The History of Horseshoes

HORSES HAVE BEEN WEARING SHOES for thousands of years. Experts can't seem to agree on exactly when the metal shoe was first used on horses, but they are pretty certain that the Romans used a type of hoof boot to protect their horse's hooves. They also know that by the time of the Crusades, iron horseshoes were the norm.

At some point during the Middle Ages, horseshoes became a good luck charm. In some cultures, the shoe is hung on a door with the ends pointing up to catch and hold good luck. In other cultures, the shoe points down so the luck will pour down into the household. It's important that the shoe used be found by the person whose home it graces.

Today, the horseshoe is a topic of controversy in the horse world. Advocates of the barefoot method of hoof care, which calls for horse hooves to be trimmed according to the way feral horse hooves wear on their own, maintain that horseshoes are not necessary, and that they are in fact harmful to horse's feet because they are unnatural. Those who believe in shoes for horses say they are necessary for protection. (See more about going barefoot on Day 361.)

Water Rules

AT ONE TIME IN THE NOT-SO DISTANT past you could dispose of your horse's manure by spreading it around your pasture or in your arena. You didn't have to worry about carting it away. But because of increased government vigilance over the nation's water supply, more and more horse owners are required to follow strict rules when handling their horse's manure.

The argument for carefully disposing of horse manure is a simple one: Government agencies, such as the Environmental Protection Agency, have found that livestock waste contaminates local waterways.

Although many horse experts argue that manure from cows is actually much more harmful to water quality than manure from horses because of the different kinds of bacteria present in cow manure, all livestock has been painted with the same broad brush.

To help protect the environment and your horse-keeping lifestyle, stay abreast of your community's rules about manure disposal. Failure to do so may result in penalties for you, and it could even threaten the very existence of horsekeeping in your area.

Sarcoids

MANY HORSES DEVELOP benign tumors of the skin, which can show up as raised bumps on various parts of the body. The most common of these tumors are called sarcoids, and they usually appear when a horse reaches the age of seven or older.

Sarcoid tumors usually show up on the head, neck, limbs, and abdomen. They sometimes occur in clusters, or they may be alone. Either raised or flat, they often look like warts or large, firm masses of skin.

In most cases, sarcoids are nothing to worry about. The only time a sarcoid can be life-threatening is if it's located in a place on the body where it interferes with normal function. Examples of this are large sarcoids that develop on the anal area, making it difficult for the horse to defecate. Sarcoids that form around the eyes can also become invasive and destructive to the eye.

Veterinarians don't usually remove sarcoids because they tend to grow back in the same place. Sarcoids that should be removed are treated with cryotherapy, immunotherapy, laser therapy, radiation therapy, and topical chemotherapy.

Going Bareback

RIDERS WHO SPEND A LOT of time riding bareback develop a secure seat and a good sense of balance. For this reason, some trainers insist their students take a few lessons without the security of a saddle.

To help improve your seat and balance, it's a good idea to ride your horse bareback once in a while. Use a bareback pad if you don't want to get your pants dirty, or let your horse go completely *au natural* if he has a comfortable back.

Ride in the arena and practice your transitions from walk to trot to canter. Do 65-feet (20 m) circles and change directions at the trot. If you always ride with a saddle, you may need some time to adjust your balance. After all, you have no deep seat to hold you in and no stirrups to secure your feet. By the end of your session, you should be feeling a lot more comfortable and secure without the help of a saddle.

Practice riding bareback whenever you can to help improve your balance and seat. Don't be surprised if you are pretty sore the next day after a bareback ride since you use a lot more muscles when you don't have a saddle to help keep you in place. It's worth the discomfort. Remember the old adage: No pain, no gain!

Great Bareback Riders

The Plains Indians of the American West were considered the be among the most skilled horsemen the world has ever known. These tribes, which dwelled in the states of Colorado, Kansas, Montana, North and South Dakota, Nebraska, Oklahoma, Texas, and Wyoming, included the Arapaho, Blackfoot, Cheyenne, Comanche, Crow, Kiowa, Lakota, Plains Apache, Shoshone, and Tonkawa peoples.

One of the reasons for their incredible abilities on horseback is that they first learned to ride bareback. They fine tuned their skills to the point where they could shoot arrows and guns at a full gallop while hanging off the side of the horse, a feat that impressed even the well-trained U.S. cavalry.

The Tennessee Walking Horse

THE TENNESSEE WALKING HORSE was developed in the United States in the 1700s. Other breeds that were common at the time—such as the Morgan, Canadian Horse, Thoroughbred, Standardbred, Saddlebred, Narragansett Pacer, and Spanish Mustang—all came together to create the Tennessee Walking Horse.

When the breed was first developed, horsemen in the middle Tennessee region were looking for a mount that was hardy and willing and had smooth gaits. The result of their efforts over a few decades, the Tennessee Walking Horse eventually became well-known throughout the South. Unlike the trot, the Tennessee Walker's rolling gait did not jostle the bones of riders who rode them over long distances. Its special gaits are the flat-footed walk, the running walk, and the canter.

The flat-footed walk is like a regular walk in the sense that each hoof hits the ground separately. However, the flat-footed walk is a lot faster than a standard walk. The strides are longer, so the horse covers a lot of ground.

The running walk is a four-beat gait and is the gait for which the breed is most famous. The running walk is faster than the trot and much smoother.

The canter of the Tennessee Walking Horse is more relaxed than other breeds' and has more spring and rhythm.

The breed comes in a height range of 14.3 to 17 hands and a variety of colors, including black, bay, chestnut, brown, buckskin, gray, palomino, cremello, and perlino. Tennessee Walking Horses also come in different patterns, too, including pinto and roan.

Intelligent and willing to learn, the Tennessee Walking Horse is capable of doing just about any job asked of it. The breed is used for many different types of riding.

Saddleseat

THE ENGLISH DISCIPLINE of saddleseat riding has its roots in the Southern United States where it was first developed in the 1700s for its comfortable seat over long distances. Based on the English park seat, saddleseat was most often used by plantation owners who relied on gaited horses to help them oversee their land.

Saddleseat differs from other types of English riding in several ways. The saddle is very flat, completely lacking in the deep seat seen in dressage saddles or even the shallow seat of hunt seat saddles. The way the rider sits in saddleseat differs from that of dressage and hunt seat as well.

In saddleseat, the rider's legs extend in front of the torso as opposed to in being in line with it, almost as if sitting on chair.

The idea behind saddleseat riding is to allow the horse the greatest freedom of movement in the forehand. High-stepping horses such as Saddlebreds and National Show Horses, as well as gaited breeds like the Tennessee Walking Horse, are often ridden saddleseat, especially in the show ring. Other breeds are shown saddleseat as well, including Arabians and Morgans that have been trained for a high-stepping gait.

Hightower

ONE OF THE MOST-OFTEN-SEEN equine actors was a horse named Hightower. This chestnut gelding appeared in so many films that nearly everyone who has ever gone to the movies has seen this horse on the screen.

Hightower was a stunt horse who appeared in many films in his long career, but he also had some significant roles. He played Ginger in the 1974 remake of *Black Beauty*.

He was also Pilgrim, the horse trained by Robert Redford's character in *The Horse Whisperer*. And he was the horse Julia Roberts took off on in the film *Runaway Bride*.

Owned and trained by Hollywood horse trainer Rex Peterson since the age of two, Hightower was one of the most intelligent, kind, and trainable horses the film industry had ever known. He died at Peterson's ranch in Tehachapi, California, well into his twenties. A Breyer horse model honors his many achievements.

Safety Review

IT'S EASY TO GET COMFORTABLE around horses when you spend so much time with them. But one of the worst mistakes a horse person can make is to become complacent about safety. Horses are big animals, and they can easily hurt or even kill a human without meaning to. Even the quietest, gentlest equines are capable of accidentally causing great bodily harm under the right circumstances.

Staying safe around horses should be your top priority. Remember the following basic rules when working with your horse.

- **Stay alert.** Even if you know your horse very well, be aware of what he is doing at all times when you are working around him. Never leave him tied unattended, and always pay attention to objects and other horses close to him.

- **Take nothing for granted.** When you first started working around horses, you were probably taught never to duck underneath a horse's neck, walk behind a strange horse, or sit on the ground next to a horse. If you have forgotten these very serious safety rules, bring them back into your life. All it takes is a sudden spook or well-placed kick in any of these situations to put you in the hospital.

- **Wear a helmet.** Many people prefer to feel their hair blowing in the wind when they ride, but studies have shown that serious head injuries can—and often do—easily result from a fall from a horse. (See Day 95 for more on helmet safety.)

Cushing's Syndrome

EQUINE CUSHING'S SYNDROME used to be called Cushing's Disease. Cushing's Syndrome is even more accurately labeled pituitary pars intermediary dysfunction (PPID). This condition occurs when a portion of the pituitary gland becomes unable to function properly. The ACTH hormone and blood cortisol levels are chronically too high. Horses with this condition, who are often older, may also be insulin resistant.

You can tell a horse has Cushing's Syndrome if she has a long, wavy haircoat and sweats a lot because of it. These horses are prone to developing laminitis, chronic infections, and loss of muscle mass, giving them a pot-bellied look. They often have increased water intake and urine output, too.

Cushing's Syndrome can't be cured, but it can be managed. Drugs such as pergolide or Cyproheptadine (cyproheptadine hydrochloride) can help, although they are expensive and must be given throughout the horse's life.

The Perfect Bath

EVERYBODY LOVES A CLEAN HORSE. Horses don't seem to care too much about whether their coats are shiny, but humans sure do.

Giving your horse a bath is one of the most enjoyable and satisfying activities you can perform if you like spending quality time with your equine companion. Bath time gives you a chance to pamper your horse while also reinforcing his ground manners.

Follow these steps to the perfect bath. You'll need a garden hose with a shower nozzle, two large sponges, horse shampoo, and horse conditioner.

1. Starting on the left side of your horse, use a garden hose with a shower nozzle. Let the water run on your horse's shoulder and then slowly wet the entire left side of his body except his head.

2. Using a large sponge and horse shampoo, lather up the wet side of your horse. Remember to scrub under his belly where the cinch goes and down his legs.

3. Use the hose to thoroughly rinse off the shampoo. You will probably see brown water come off your horse's coat. Keep rinsing until the water runs clear and free of suds.

4. Move over to the right side of your horse and repeat the entire process. Don't forget to wash your horse's mane, which will either lie on the left or right side of his body.

5. Next, wash the tail. Wet it thoroughly and then lather up with shampoo. Rinse thoroughly. Follow with conditioner for easy detangling.

6. Time to wash your horse's head. Rather than spray your horse in the face with water—something many horses hate—soak a clean sponge and wash his face off with water. Don't use shampoo here; you don't want to get any in his eyes.

7. Wash your horse's forelock the same way. Avoid using shampoo because it may get into his eyes.

Friesian

THE FRIESIAN IS A GLAMOROUS HORSE with a legendary and romantic past. According to some, the Friesian goes back to the Ice Age, when a large primitive horse called *Equus robustus* is believed to have lived in Friesland, the area of Europe now known as The Netherlands.

In the sixteenth and seventeenth centuries, Andalusians were bred to the descendants of *Equus robustus*, bringing refining blood to the early Friesian. Serious horse breeders, the people of Friesland worked hard to develop and preserve this horse, which was unique to their culture.

During the Middle Ages, Friesian horses spread to other parts of Europe, and they served as heavy war horses. Some historians also believe that Friesians were brought to the New World with Dutch settlers in the 1700s, and they might have contributed to the Morgan, Canadian, and the Tennessee Walking Horse breeds.

Crossbreeding resulted in the eventual disappearance of the purebred Friesian from the United States for several centuries. Then, during the mid to late 1970s, the breed was imported into the United States. Over the next few decades, Americans took notice of the breed, whose popularity has soared over the past fifteen years.

Friesians are well known for their jet black coats. A white star on the forehead is also permitted, but no other white markings may be present.

The breed's long, wavy mane and tail are also important characteristics. The tail is low set, and the fetlocks are heavily feathered. The head of the Friesian is relatively small for the breed's large stature, and it features expressive eyes and small ears.

The Friesian's body type is unique among horses, and it features a high-set neck with a high crest; and a broad chest with a slightly accentuated croup. The legs are hardy with solid bone structure. Stallions stand at least 15.3 hands by the age of four, while mares and geldings must be at least 14.3 hands to be registered in the adult studbooks. Most Friesians measure from 15.2 to 16 hands, although some are smaller or larger.

High-stepping action is a part of the breed's movement, and the Friesian's easygoing disposition is one of its most treasured traits.

Friesian

Team Penning

ONE OF THE MOST POPULAR Western sports these days is team penning.

In team penning classes, three horses and riders make up a team and sort three designated cows from a small herd. Once the cows are sorted, the riders must pen them in a corral located at the opposite end of the arena. The event is timed, and the fastest, most accurate team wins.

Team penning classes are officiated by two different judges. The judges watch the action from different positions around the arena. Two timekeepers keep track of each team's time.

Just about any horse can participate in team penning. The horse just needs to be a fast, willing mount with good cow sense.

If you live in an area with a lot of horses, you shouldn't have any trouble finding team penning lessons in your community.

Cow Sense

Some horses are born with a very special talent called cow sense, which is the horse's inborn ability to anticipate a cow's behavior.

Certain breeds are known for their cow sense, particularly the Quarter Horse, Paint Horse, Appaloosa, and Andalusian. Some believe these were inherited from these breeds' Spanish equine ancestors, who were developed to work cattle on the Iberian peninsula hundreds of years ago.

Epona

Epona was the Celtic goddess of horses, and she was responsible for caring for them, along with donkeys and mules. She has become a popular icon for the horse in modern times.

Although Epona is believed to have been born in Celtic mythology, she was integrated into Roman religion. She was worshipped throughout the Roman Empire, mostly by people who depended heavily on the horse for their survival, such as farmers and cavalrymen.

Epona was depicted in several ways on various works of art: as a horse herself; mounted on a horse, sidesaddle; or riding in a cart pulled by horses. She was also shown as a woman standing or sitting, flanked by horses.

Symbols representing fertility, such as cornucopias, were sometimes depicted with her. She was probably a goddess of fertility as well.

Small shrines to Epona were common in the house, as well as in the stables, where she was asked to keep watch over the equines. Temples were erected in her honor, and sacrifices in the form of animals, incense, and wine were offered.

Epona hasn't lost her identity these many centuries later. Today, she represents the grace, beauty, and mysteriousness of the horse, and she can be seen in the names of horses, on jewelry, and on labels for products designed for horses.

Stable Lighting

When the sun is shining and you are spending time with your horse, lighting is the last thing on your mind. But if you have ever found yourself trying to muck stalls or untack your horse in the dark, you know how important stable lighting really is.

Here are some key places that need lighting to keep in mind when you are planning or redesigning your stable.

Work space: The area where you tack and untack your horse should have lighting that allows you to see what you are doing without casting a lot of shadows. If possible, use multiple light sources that are overhead but angled. This will prevent shadows that will keep areas of your tacking area in the dark while you are working.

Stalls and pastures: It's a good idea to have light in your horse's stall or pasture. A sick horse or one in another kind of trouble may need your help in the dark. You may also find the need to do barn chores such as mucking after the sun goes down. Having a nearby light that can brighten up this space should you need it can prove invaluable.

Tack room: You can opt for a sophisticated lighting system in your tack room installed by an electrician if your budget allows, or simply purchase a battery-operated lantern designed for camping and place it near the door so you can turn it on when you first come in.

Encephalomyelitis

A NUMBER OF VIRAL DISEASES affect the horse, including encephalomyelitis, which used to wreak havoc with horse populations. Fortunately, vaccines for this illness are in widespread use and have kept epidemics to a minimum. Encephalomyelitis is spread through the bite of an infected mosquito. The best way to prevent the disease is to vaccinate regularly.

Encephalomyelitis can be found in three strains: Western equine encephalomyelitis, Eastern equine encephalomyelitis, and Venezuelan equine encephalomyelitis. Each strain can cause severe neurological symptoms and death.

Horses infected with the encephalomyelitis virus can be lethargic, have no appetite, and run a high fever. Some get diarrhea. If the horse isn't able to fight off the virus, the next set of symptoms can include circling, seizures, and stumbling. A more progressive symptom is head pressing, blindness, and coma. Death shortly follows.

Diagnosis of encephalomyelitis can be made with a blood test, although some vets begin treating the disease based on symptoms. Because encephalomyelitis is caused by a virus, no cure is known. Supportive care, such as intravenous fluids, anti-inflammatory drugs, and anti-diarrhea medications, can help the animal fight off the disease.

Get Involved with 4-H

IF YOU HAVE A CHILD WHO LOVES horses, or even if you don't, consider getting involved with a 4-H horse project in your area. With activities that focus exclusively on a particular animal, 4-H club projects provide great opportunities for children to learn about livestock, especially horses. You can also offer to be a 4-H leader for a horse project in a local 4-H club. If no horse project exists, offer to start one. (4-H stands for "Head, Heart, Hands, and Health.")

Most 4-H horse projects offer children the following opportunities for learning:

Equine vernacular: Children learn the different parts of the horse, as well as horse-related vocabulary.

Horse breeds: Leaders help children discover the different breeds of horses and their histories.

Horse health: 4-H is a great way for children to learn how to take care of their horses. Everything from daily care to veterinary issues is covered.

Riding: Children in 4-H learn how to better ride their horses through lessons.

Showing: Horse shows are often a part of 4-H projects.

This variety of fun activities help children discover the world of horses through 4-H. Your child will learn with the help of his or her horse. If you participate as a leader, you can be instrumental in helping kids discover the wonderful world of horses.

To get involved with your local 4-H club in the United States, contact your Cooperative Extension Office. You'll find the number in the government pages of your telephone directory, or at www.csrees.usda.gov/Extension/index.html.

127

American Cream Draft

THE ONLY EXISTING DRAFT HORSE developed in the United States, the American Cream Draft Horse has been around since the late 1800s. The breed's most unique characteristic is its light cream color.

Considered an extremely rare breed and listed as critically endangered by the American Livestock Breeds Conservancy, the American Cream Draft can be traced back to a horse named Old Granny. This draft mare had a cream-colored coat, pink skin, and amber eyes, and she passed these traits along to her foals.

Cream-colored draft horses became more numerous as Old Granny's genes were passed down through the generations.

In 1944, the American Cream Horse Association of America was established. The breed began a sharp decline as more draft horses were replaced by mechanized farm vehicles. By the 1960s, the American Cream was almost extinct.

In 1982, several breeders organized to save the breed from extinction. Although the breed is growing, only 400 horses are currently registered in the United States, and it is virtually unheard of elsewhere.

American Cream Draft

Endurance

TRAIL RIDING IS A popular way to spend time with your horse. But if you also like to compete, consider combining the two by getting involved in endurance.

Endurance events are races that take place over 25, 50, or 100-mile (40, 80, or 160 km) trail courses. The first horse and rider team to get to the finish line is the winner, although most endurance riders consider it a victory if they finish the race with a sound horse.

The welfare of the horse is important in endurance rides that are sanctioned by the American Endurance Ride Conference in the United States and Fédération Equestre Internationale (FEI). Horses and riders are stopped periodically along the trail for vet checks to make sure the horses are safely handling the stress of the event.

Awards are given to the horse with the best condition after each race, to help encourage proper conditioning of horses before they compete.

Almost any breed of horse can participate in endurance riding, although Arabians dominate the sport because of their superior stamina over long distances. Half-Arabians are also popular. Other breeds often seen in this sport are mustangs, Morgans, and Quarter Horses. Heavy animals, such as draft horses and stocky horses, are generally discouraged in this sport, since they are not built for traveling long distances

Endurance riding is an international sport, and FEI-level events take place around the world.

Horses of San Marcos

IN THE YEAR 1204, four magnificent bronze horses were found in Constantinople and brought to Venice. Much controversy surrounds these sculptures, which some historians believe may have been created in the fourth century by the Greek sculptor Lysippos. The horses are life-sized and represent a quadrangle of the type that would be used to pull a chariot.

Whoever created the statues, the four prancing steeds are breathtaking. They are massive and detailed, and they glow in a tarnished copper. Wearing collars around their necks, they seem to be frozen in time.

You can almost see their ears flicker and their muscles ripple, the manes roached (cut short and standing straight up) in a style typical for classical antiquity.

The horses of San Marcos once stood atop the Roman Basilica, but they were removed to the Museo Marciano in Venice to protect them from the scourge of air pollution. Today, four replicas stand in their place atop the Basilica. A sculpture inspired by the San Marcos horses and commissioned by Napoleon can still be seen atop the Arc de Triomphe in Paris.

Safe Tying

Horses can get into trouble quickly and easily. One minute they are quietly standing, and the next they are trying to rip the hitching post out of the ground. That's why safe tying is so important. Here are some essential rules for safe tying.

Never tie your horse by the reins. If your horse pulls back, she could break her jaw or do other serious injury to herself. Only tie your horse using a halter and lead rope, a halter, and crossties.

You can't just tie your horse to any object with a regular knot. Horses are strong and can easily pull down an unsecured fence or a small tree by simply throwing their weight around.

When looking for a place to tie your horse, stick to a hitching post or crossties meant just for that purpose. If you are out on the trail or in a place where you can't find a hitching post, tie your horse only to a large, sturdy object that can't be moved—even by 1,000 pounds (455 kg) of muscle (your horse). Tie your horse as high as possible so she can't get her leg over the rope. A good rule of thumb to have the knot at least as high as the horse's withers.

Use a safety knot that easily releases during an emergency. A number of knots fit this description. The accompanying illustration shows a favorite safety knot of horse people.

QUICK-RELEASE KNOT

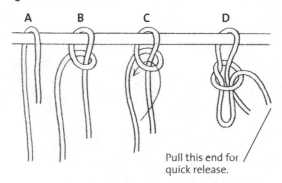

Pull this end for quick release.

A. Drape your lead rope over a post with the other end tied to your horse.

B. Loop the release end of the rope over and around the tie end.

C. Using the release end, pull a loop through as shown. Cinch the knot closed so it resembles the number 4.

D. The knot is untied by pulling the release end. Though the knot itself is secure, it will pull apart.

Equine First Aid

You NEVER KNOW WHEN your horse may injure himself. Horses are large animals that seem to easily hurt themselves, especially when kept in small confines. For this reason, it's a good idea to keep an equine first-aid kit at hand both at the stable and when you are traveling with your horse. This kit can come in very useful while you are waiting for the veterinarian to arrive.

You can buy a first-aid kit for your horse already assembled, or you can make your own. If you assemble your own kit, include the following items.

- Antibiotic ointment to prevent infection
- Antiseptic cleanser for disinfecting wounds
- Equine veterinary bandages for wrapping
- Gauze pads to cover wounds

- Knife with serrated edge for cutting rope
- Rectal thermometer to take your horse's temperature
- Lubricant for inserting thermometer
- Rubbing alcohol to disinfect thermometer
- Scissors to cut bandages
- Tweezers to remove splinters

Keep all these items in a reclosable plastic container near where you keep your horse. Have your veterinarian's phone number on hand, too.

Perfect the "Whoa"

STOPPING MAY BE THE MOST important skill to teach your horse. If your horse doesn't have a reliable stop, she's not a safe horse to ride.

Even if your horse is already adept at stopping, it's a good to practice this skill periodically just to reinforce it. Your horse should be so responsive to your requests to stop that she will stop immediately when you ask her, in any situation.

Practice the following exercises at a walk to perfect your horse's stop.

EXERCISE

If you are riding Western, ask your horse for an extended walk. After a minute, say "whoa" as you put tension on the reins while moving your rein hand backward toward your belly button.

As you do this, sink deep into the saddle and release any leg pressure you were applying to keep your horse at the trot. When the horse comes to a stop, release the reins. If your horse stopped immediately, praise her.

If you are riding English, ask your horse for an extended walk. To ask her to stop, sink your weight into the saddle, and then increase tension on the reins. When she stops, release some of the tension on the reins and praise her.

Perform these stopping exercises first at the walk, then at the trot, and finally at the canter. When your horse stops reliably at each gait, her stop has been perfected. Continue practicing periodically to reinforce this skill.

Icelandic Horse

THE HISTORY OF THE Icelandic Horse starts with the Vikings in 874 AD. The Vikings were invading Europe with the help of their horses, who carried them across miles of terrain and into battle. Some settled in Iceland, along with their hardy, gaited horses.

Because of the remoteness of Iceland, the small horses that arrived in the ninth century via Viking ships remained isolated for nearly 1,000 years. During this time, they learned to survive in the harsh Icelandic countryside, eking out their existence among glaciers, fjords, miles of sand, and rugged mountains.

Only a small horse could subsist on the few grasses that persisted during the cold Icelandic winters, so the breed became diminutive. The farmers who struggled to make a living in the hard Icelandic environment relied on these horses to negotiate the territory, which lacked roads and bridges. Though small, these horses easily carried adult riders over tough trails and through mountain passes.

In 1784, the most severe Icelandic winter on record struck the island, wiping out three-fourths of the horses living there. Only around 8,500 horses successfully endured the harsh conditions that winter and went on to become the foundation stock for today's Icelandic Horse.

In 1969, an international organization dedicated to promoting and preserving the breed, International Federation of Icelandic Horse Associations (FEIF), was formed. The organization had six founding member countries: Austria, Denmark, Germany, Iceland, the Netherlands, and Switzerland. In 1971, France and Norway joined, and in 1975, Belgium and Sweden followed.

FEIF has grown since and now includes Finland, Canada, the United Kingdom, the United States, the Faeroe Islands, Luxembourg, Italy, and Slovenia. The ongoing involvement of FEIF in the breed's management makes the Icelandic Horse the only breed in the world with a single standard and one set of registry and competition rules throughout the world.

The Icelandic Horse stands between 12.3 and 14.3 hands high and is compact with a thick mane and tail. They come in many colors, including buckskin, dun, pinto, cremello, palomino, perlino, smoky black, silver, roan, chestnut, gray, and black, and variations of all these are colors seen in the breed.

The Icelandic Horse possesses two special gaits, the tolt and the flying pace. Icelandic horses can also trot, unlike most gaited breeds. This means they possess five gaits total. The breed is also known for its easygoing, level-headed personality.

Icelandic Horse

Reining

REINING IS A WESTERN EVENT that grew from cattle work. Reining was originally a style of riding that enabled cowboys to quickly maneuver horses around cattle. Today, it's a challenging sport that requires considerable training for the horse, as well as a skilled rider. Reining horses are asked to perform a number of maneuvers in competition, including spins, sliding stops, and figure eights.

Reining classes are popular at Western breed shows, particularly Quarter Horse events. Horses are judged on their ability to execute the required maneuvers with ease and grace.

Horses are judged individually in various classes, including freestyle reining, which requires the horse to perform to music. This popular spectator sport often features horses and riders in costumes, performing creative routines. Similar to freestyle figure skating, freestyle reining allows individual expression while also incorporating required maneuvers.

Vaqueros: The Original "Cowboys"

WATCH ANY WESTERN, and you'll see blond-haired, blue-eyed cowboys rustling cattle and mending fences. But in reality, one of every three cowboys in the West was a vaquero. The work of the vaqueros was well-documented in American painting of the mid- to late-nineteenth century, especially Frederic Remington and Charles Russell.

Vaqueros were Mexican cowboys, and they were the original cowboys of the American West. Revered for their incredible horsemanship and their vast knowledge of working cattle (vaquero literally means "cowman" in Spanish), vaqueros had their own style of horse training that is considered of great value, even today.

Long before North America was settled by Europeans, vaqueros were developing their skills in Mexico. Working vast herds of Spanish cattle on horses descended from the conquistadors' mounts, vaqueros perfected their riding skills and became daring equestrians. As Spanish influence spread northward, vaqueros became an intrinsic part of the culture of the American Southwest. Their skills with a rope became legend, and their saddle style and personal apparel became the inspiration for the American cowboy.

Fire Prevention

ONE OF THE MOST TRAGIC EVENTS that could happen to a horse owner is a barn fire. Barn fires have killed many horses, from famous racehorses to treasured pets.

Barns are particularly susceptible to fire because of the many flammable items kept in their vicinity. Hay, straw, and bedding ignite easily, and horse blankets and other tack go up quickly when fire starts.

You can do a lot to prevent a fire in your barn by following these guidelines.

No smoking. Hang a "no smoking" sign on your barn door and enforce this policy. Cigarettes, cigars, and pipes have no business in a barn, and the same goes for any open flame.

Wire to code. Make sure the electrical wiring in your barn is up to code. Although upgrading the wiring in an old barn can be costly, it is well worth it for safety reasons.

Store manure outdoors. Piles of manure generate their own heat and can burst into flames. Manure kept indoors is a serious hazard for this reason. Many barn fires have started from stored manure.

Avoid heating elements. Using heating elements—such as a portable space heater or a plug-in bucket warmer—in a barn is asking for trouble. Fires often start from sparks from heating elements. If you need a heater in your barn, install a central heating system.

Install smoke detectors. Most barn fires smolder for a long time before they are noticed. A smoke detector will alert you if something is amiss before it's too late.

No flammable liquids. Don't store flammable liquids like gasoline or alcohol anywhere in your barn.

Install a sprinkler system. If you can afford it, install an overhead sprinkler system that will be triggered should a fire break out.

Keep a fire extinguisher handy. In the event of a fire, a fire extinguisher can save lives. Make sure an extinguisher is stored in plain sight.

Provide a water source. Keep a working garden hose near the barn. It may prove invaluable in the event of a fire.

Should a fire break out in your barn, remove the horses as quickly and calmly as you can while someone else calls the fire department. Once the horses are out of the barn, close the door behind you. The old adage is true: Horses will often run back into a burning barn because the barn is their place of security and will be the first place they go to if they are scared.

Nutraceuticals

YOU HAVE PROBABLY HEARD OF nutraceuticals, dietary supplements that provide nutritional effects but aren't considered drugs. Many people take these supplements, especially the more popular nutraceuticals such as Echinacea, St. John's wort, and ginkgo biloba.

Horses can benefit from nutraceuticals, too, just like humans. The most commonly given nutraceuticals for horses are those intended to help joint health. These include glucosamine, chondroitin, and MSM, and many equine vets recommend them for horses with arthritis. Hoof problems and allergies are two other common reasons people give nutraceuticals to their horses.

Your local tack and feed store stocks an array of equine nutraceuticals. But before you run out and spend a fortune on a bunch of these products (they aren't cheap), talk to your veterinarian.

Chances are, your horse doesn't need any of these products in his diet. In fact, you'll be hard pressed to find a vet who will recommend anything other than the three joint supplements already mentioned.

Alternative veterinarians are the exception. They primarily use nutraceuticals to treat ailments in horses. (They may also prescribe acupuncture, massage, and other complementary/alternative modalities.) These vets may prescribe a number of different supplements to help your horse get through whatever health problem she's experiencing. In this case, the veterinarian will tell you exactly what to do and what to give your horse. He or she may even supply the supplements to you. (If your horse is ill, don't add supplements to your horse's diet without first talking to your veterinarian.)

Plan a Riding Vacation

RIDING VACATIONS ARE DESIGNED for everyone from beginners to advanced equestrians. Some destinations provide a horse for you to ride, and others require that you bring your own.

Some riding vacations are hosted by resorts, and they offer other activities besides riding. Others are serious horseback adventures that include hours of trail riding per day, or concentrated periods of intensive riding lessons.

To plan your riding vacation, start researching the different types of opportunities available:

Mixed bag: Vacations offering one-day trail rides use a resort or dude ranch as home base, and they provide guests the options of spending a day riding in the local countryside, taking riding lessons in an arena, or engaging in another nonhorse-related activity. If you are an inexperienced rider looking for an introduction to horses as well as the option to participate in swimming, fishing, or another activity (or have family members who don't want to ride), a resort or dude ranch-based vacation is a good choice.

Riding adventure: If you are serious about taking an extended holiday on horseback and want to see wilderness areas or other remote places where access by car is difficult or impossible, sign up with an equine tour outfitter. Outfitters specializing in horse vacations provide detailed itineraries for horseback treks, which usually include camping or overnight stays in facilities along the way. Make sure you take a few months of riding lessons to get yourself in shape before you embark on one of these vacations. Otherwise, you'll spend much of your holiday feeling stiff and sore.

Learning vacation: Some horseback vacations are devoted solely to study. For riders wanting to spend hours a day perfecting their skills, these vacations are a real treat. The facilities are often luxurious and located in beautiful rural areas. Scenic trail rides are often part of the curriculum.

Bring your horse: Some vacations are for horse owners who want to spend time with their horses. These holidays are usually in rural areas with great trail riding. Accommodations are often rustic, and guides are a part of the package.

Whether you want to roam new terrain, add riding to an eclectic array of activities, or spend time with your own horse, you can find a riding vacation that's right for you. Riding vacation companies have a strong presence on the Internet. A quick search will yield many options.

Some of the best places to visit on horseback in the United States are the Rocky Mountains and Sierra Nevada Mountains and the Pacific Northwest. These areas feature harsh, remote terrain that can only be seen from the back of a horse. Western Europe, such as Ireland and Spain, is also wonderful by horseback because of the profound sense of history and horsemanship in this part of the world. Exotic destinations such as remote Mongolia and Tibet are all the more accessible—and enjoyable—on horseback as well.

Welsh Pony

ONE OF THE MOST POPULAR pony breeds in the world, the Welsh Pony originally comes from Wales. More than 2,000 years ago, Welsh Ponies lived in the valleys of this northern European landscape, braving harsh winters and living off what little plant life grew in the cold environment. These ponies lived almost wild, in herds that were forced to survive on their own with little help from humans.

When a farmer needed a pony for work, he would capture one from the herd and train it to haul a plow, pull a cart, and be ridden. Welsh Ponies were strong, reliable work ponies that helped farm families stay alive in a land that was tough on those who lived and worked there.

In the centuries that followed, different breeds were mixed with the original Welsh Ponies, including the Arabian. Julius Caesar brought Arabian horses to Europe with him after his journey to Africa, and some of these horses found their way to Wales, where they bred with the native ponies. This Arabian blood is noticeable in today's Welsh Ponies, particularly in their small, dished faces.

Welsh Ponies come in four different types: Welsh, Welsh Mountain, Welsh Pony of Cob Type, and Welsh Cob. Each type has a slightly different history, and its own height and build. They measure between 12.2 hands to 15 hands, depending on the type. They can be found in every horse color except pinto and Appaloosa patterns.

Because Welsh Ponies come in different sizes and types, they are popular as show mounts for children. Smaller children prefer the Welsh Mountain Pony, while older children may prefer the Welsh Pony Cob.

Welsh Pony

Heritage Class

ONE OF THE MOST INTERESTING ASPECTS of the many different horse breeds in the world is their varied histories. Whatever a breed's background, the story is often a fascinating one.

Some breed associations have decided to honor their breed's history with a heritage class at horse shows. These classes require exhibitors to show their horses in a costume that reflects the breed's history.

Some popular heritage class breeds include the following.

Appaloosa. The history of these spotted horses is closely tied into the Nez Perce Indians of the Pacific Northwest. Exhibitors often dress their horses in authentic Native American tack and costume, while they don Native American apparel.

Arabian. The Arabian horse developed in the Middle East among the Bedouin nomads. Heritage classes at Arabian shows feature some incredible costumes showing that exotic heritage.

Morgan. A classic American breed, the Morgan is shown in heritage classes under harness. Appointments depict the breed during the 1700s when it was first developed in New England. Antique carriages are one of the highlights of this class.

Other breeds such as the Norwegian Fjord and the Paso Fino also have heritage classes. The American Driving Society has a heritage class that features antique vehicles.

Traveller

BEHIND EVERY GREAT GENERAL, you'll find a great horse... at least that was true when horses were the sole means of transportation during war (until the twentieth century).

One of these great horses was Traveller, an American Saddlebred gelding owned by Confederate General Robert E. Lee. Memorialized in a 1988 book called *Traveller* by Richard Adams (who also wrote *Watership Down*), the gray gelding was a favorite mount of the general.

Traveller was born with the name "Jeff Davis" in the late 1850s, in Greenbriar County, Virginia (now West Virginia). He stood 16 hands, and he had a long, black mane and tail.

General Lee came to own Traveller after buying the horse from a major who had purchased the gelding for use in the war. Lee had seen the horse and took a fancy to him, and it's no wonder. Traveller was described as having bold carriage, a rapid walk, and great muscular strength.

General Lee reportedly loved Traveller because he was relatively fearless, and he had great stamina and a willing disposition. Traveller did spook once while Lee was on the ground holding his bridle, knocking Lee to the ground and breaking both his hands. Lee apparently forgave the gelding, who remained in Lee's stable until his death

Pasture Care

IF YOU ARE ONE OF THOSE lucky horse owners who has pasture for your equine charges, make sure you take good care of it. You can do this by carefully managing the pasture in a way that will provide your horse with the nutrition they need while also preserving the land.

Keep the following pointers in mind.

Rotate grazing. Repeated grazing is tough on a pasture. Divide your pasture into two separate areas and rotate your horses so each side of the pasture gets a break for an entire growing season. This will help the "resting" pasture regenerate.

Take soil samples. In the spring or fall, take a soil sample from your pasture to your local agricultural university. The office will analyze the soil's general health and will let you know if you need to add any particular nutrients.

Control weeds. It's hard to go around a pasture and pull out weeds, but you can do a lot to keep them at bay by mowing aggressively before weeds bud and go to seed. If you do this repeatedly, the good grasses will take over and push out the weeds. (Never use chemical weed killers in your horse's pasture because they can poison your horse.)

Ringbone

WHEN A HORSE DEVELOPS extra bone in or around the joints in the leg, the condition is called ringbone. A potentially crippling ailment, ringbone can be upper ringbone, affecting the pastern joint, or lower ringbone, affecting the coffin joint. Of the two, high ringbone is worse; it causes more pain for the horse.

The trouble with ringbone is that it can be hard to diagnose because it develops gradually. Horses show mild lameness that seems to come and go with activity levels. Only an X-ray can identify the condition for certain.

CONTRIBUTING FACTORS

The following certain factors predispose a horse to ringbone.

Genetics: Horses with a history of ringbone in their families are more likely to develop the disease.

Conformation: Horses with very upright angles on their legs are more likely to get ringbone.

Poor trimming: Poor trimming results in trauma to the joint.

TREATMENT

Ringbone can be treated with therapeutic shoes.

Some proponents of the barefoot method of trimming say this can also help a horse with ringbone.

Anti-inflammatory drugs are often given to horses suffering from this condition.

Surgery is a last resort, and it involves fusing the joint to make it non-functional while still allowing the horse to use the leg.

The only true way to prevent ringbone is to make sure your horse receives proper hoof care.

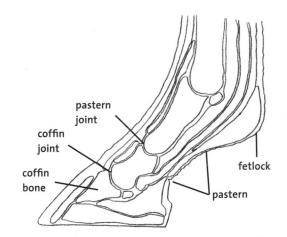

Go Shopping: Tack Store Finds

IT'S HARD TO FIND A HORSE PERSON who doesn't enjoy a visit to the tack store for both pleasure and practicality. Not only is it fun to see all the different horse stuff for sale, but people who own horses are always in need of supplies. In fact, no matter how much horse stuff you have, you and your horse can still benefit from a few hours of tack store shopping. Even if you don't plan to buy anything, it's good to pay the store a visit.

Tack store shopping is good education. Not only does it encourage you to think about what you might need to replace (is your lungeline getting worn and frayed? Are your stirrup leathers ready to break?), it also keeps you up to date on the latest offerings in the horse industry. You'll find out the newest gadgets and tools available, and you may even discover an age-old type of equine equipment you didn't know existed.

Take a few hours and go to a tack store. Make it the largest store you can find. Start in aisle one and walk up and down each aisle, slowly perusing the products on display.

Test your knowledge: Do you know what everything is for? Do you see equipment you can't identify? If so, ask a salesperson. Chances are you don't need it if you don't even know what it is, but you'll become a more educated horseperson if you find out.

If the store is having a sale, keep in mind that items such as supplements and grooming supplies run out at home. Even if you don't need horse shampoo right now, you may want to buy a bottle of your favorite brand if it's on sale, for future use.

Whatever you do, don't walk out of the store empty handed. Even if you don't see anything you want or need, at least buy your horse a bag of horse treats. She'll love you for it.

Lipizzan

THE MARRIAGE OF BERBER and Arab blood with athletic Spanish horses during the Moorish occupation of Spain (711–1492) led to one of the beautiful, athletic: Lipizzan, or Lipizzaner, as it is also known. Originally created as light, fast war horses, the Spanish mounts were prized for their hardiness and intelligence as well as their good looks. With the revival of classical riding in Europe during the Renaissance, they became even more desirable. Hapsburg ruler Maximilian II acquired a number of them in 1562 and brought them to Austria, where he founded the court stud at Kladrub. His brother, Archduke Charles, followed suit in 1580 with a stud at Lipizza (in what is now Slovenia), near the Adriatic Sea. The horses that came to be known for their airs above the ground took their name from Charles's stud. Both studs produced riding horses and carriage horses and occasionally exchanged breeding stock.

In 1735, Austrian Emperor Charles VI opened the Spanish Riding School at the imperial palace in Vienna. Young riders learned the art of haute ecole dressage, the caprioles, courbettes, piaffes, passages, and other movements that enabled military riders to escape dangerous situations or to more easily attack. These sophisticated above-the-ground movements were based on Xenophon's principles of classical riding, which emphasized kindness and rewards during training and formed the basis for modern dressage.

The Spanish Riding School had another equally important purpose: to perpetuate the breeding of the Lipizzan horses. By the nineteenth century, Spanish horses of the type originally used were no longer available, so Arabs were chosen to replenish the strain.

The Lipizzan today has a sturdy body, brilliant action, and proud carriage, but it is best known for its white or gray coat. Foals are born a black-brown, brown, or gray color, and turn white at six to ten years of age, although a rare few retain their birth color. It stands from 14.3 to 15.3 hands, not very tall, but the body is strong with its short, powerful neck, heavy shoulders, well-rounded hindquarters, and short, strong legs. Both mane and tail are long and thick, and the tail is carried high.

While it is still best known for its performances at the Spanish Riding School and throughout the world, the Lipizzan is also a successful dressage and driving horse as well as pleasure mount. It is a rare breed, however, with fewer than 3,000 in the world. Devotees appreciate the Lipizzan for its beauty, intelligence, and athleticism.

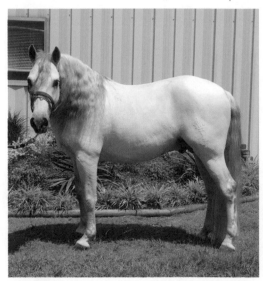

Lipizzan

Horseback Archery

THE PRACTICE OF SHOOTING ARROWS from horseback is older than the saddle, going back thousands of years. The Greeks and Romans practiced this form of warfare, as did the peoples of Mongolia, China, and Japan. The Plains Indians of the American West were also skilled horseback archers.

Recently, this ancient art has been revived, and horseback archery competitions are taking place around the world. The sport was brought back to life in Mongolia in the 1920s, and it is now practiced in Central Europe and the United States.

Horseback archery competitions consist of a course 300 feet (90 m) long. They are divided into three sections separated by posts. Targets are located on the course, and must be shot from a galloping horse. The sport has rules concerning the position the rider must be in when shooting particular targets, and the course is timed. Modern archers use a traditional recurve bow, either genuine or a fiberglass replica.

Any breed of horse can be ridden in horseback archery, although lighter breeds are most often seen. Because the rider needs two hands to shoot the bow, the horse must be well-trained to the leg and seat aids. Horses also have to be calm and not spooky, and they must be able to maintain a consistent speed at the canter or gallop.

Museum of the Horse

HORSES HAVE BEEN A PART OF human history since long before the first written word was penned. Nearly every culture on the planet has been touched—and changed—by the existence of the horse.

It's only fitting, then, that the horse should have its own museum: the International Museum of the Horse, located in Lexington, Kentucky.

Opened in 1978, the International Museum of the Horse encompasses more than 38,000 square feet (3,530 m²) of space at the Kentucky Horse Park. Permanent exhibits celebrate the history of the horse and its relationship to humankind throughout the ages.

Also included in the museum's permanent exhibit are Horse Breeds of the World, describing hundreds of breeds both extinct and living; the Legacy of the Horse, which chronicles the horse in human history; Horses in Sport and Recreation, detailing equine sports and activities; and Sculpture at the Park, showcasing bronze sculptures of horses by various artists located throughout the Kentucky Horse Park.

Temporary exhibits highlight different aspects of the horse–human relationship, such as displays of equine photography, the horse's role in a particular area of history, and the horse in ancient artwork.

Composting Manure

HORSE MANURE MAKES great fertilizer, but you have to know how to compost it first. Composting is the bacterial decomposition of organic matter by placing it in a pile or composting bin to speed along the process. Spread uncomposted horse manure on your vegetable garden, and you'll kill your plants in no time. Use composted manure in your garden and pasture, and you'll see beautiful results.

Composting manure properly is important because you have less odor than you would with an uncomposted pile. Flies are also kept to a minimum if the manure is properly composted. This is because the temperatures reached in a composted manure pile do not permit the development of fly eggs and larvae.

Heed the following guidelines when composting your horses' manure.

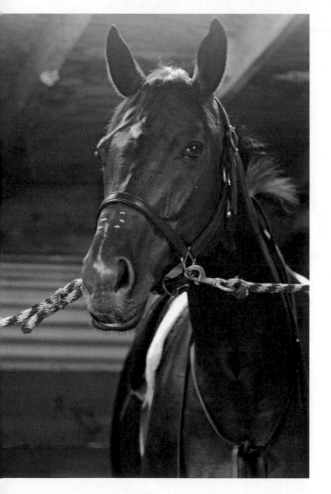

- Make your manure pile at least 3 feet (0.9 m) high to get the high temperature you need to kill flies.

- Turn the pile weekly with a tractor or shovel to speed up decomposition and reduce odor.

- Use a composting thermometer to check the temperature, and keep your manure pile's temperature below 160°F (71°C): to avoid killing beneficial organisms. If the temperature gets too high, reduce the size of the pile.

- Avoid getting the pile wet. Cover it with a tarp during rainy weather.

To learn more about how to best compost manure, contact your local agricultural college or County Extension Agent.

Feeding Senior Horses

SENIOR HORSES ARE truly a joy. They tend to be slow to spook, more cooperative, and just easy to get along with. Older horses do pose some challenges when it comes to feeding, however.

Some senior equines have difficulty keeping weight on. Others tend to get too fat. Most do not have the same energy requirements they did when they were young. Very old horses have difficulty chewing.

When it comes to feeding your senior horse, keep the following in mind.

Regular dental care. Have your senior's teeth checked every six months to make sure he is able to chew his food properly. If you see your older horse dropping food from his mouth as he chews, he may be having dental problems, such as teeth that are unevenly worn or infected.

Watch his weight. If your older horse is getting thinner even though you are feeding him more, have your veterinarian out to exam him. Many older horses have trouble maintaining their weight because their digestive systems don't work as well as they used to. Weight loss can also be a sign of serious disease.

Talk to your vet about putting your older horse on a senior diet. Older horses have different nutritional needs that younger horses, and they can often benefit from commercial feed made for older horses in addition to their regular hay. Senior feed has nutrients that are particularly necessary for older horses to maintain optimal health. Senior horses sometime have trouble chewing and need to be given a complete feed and roughage in pelleted form.

Working on Transitions

EVERYONE WANTS AN OBEDIENT, attentive horse. One way to get this is to practice transitions.

Transitions take place when you ask your horse to go from one gait to another. By asking your horse for transitions, you encourage her to pay attention to you. If you ask for frequent transitions, your horse learns to focus on you as she awaits your next request.

Transitions are best worked on in an arena. You can practice these with other horses and riders present, or by yourself. Don't avoid working on transitions when sharing the area. Asking for transitions while distractions are present is a good way to train your horse to listen to you despite outside activities.

EXERCISE

Here is a pattern for working on transitions with your horse.

1. Enter the arena at the walk. Walk the entire arena once, and then ask your horse for a trot.

2. After one minute of trotting, ask your horse to walk. After a minute of walking, ask for the trot again. Repeat this pattern for five minutes.

3. Once your horse is warmed up, start working on faster transitions. Ask your horse to go from the walk, to the trot, to the canter, and hold each gait for around two minutes. Then do a transition downward from the canter to the trot, and then to the walk.

4. For the next thirty minutes, practice going up and down in your transitions. Go from a canter to a walk, and then to a trot. Then go to the walk, then to the canter. Transition down from the canter to the trot. Continue to mix up your transitions, changing every couple of minutes.

Practicing transitions not only improves your horse's attentiveness, it keeps her from getting bored. It also helps improve your riding skills.

Norwegian Fjord

THE NORWEGIAN FJORD IS considered the oldest breed of horse in Norway, and it is believed to have descended from the ancient Przewalski's Horse, which can only be found in zoos today. (See Day 52.) Experts believe that the ancestors of today's Fjord migrated to Norway and the Scandinavian peninsula around 4,000 years ago. The Norwegians began selectively breeding it 2,000 years ago.

For centuries, the Fjord was used mostly as a draft horse, working the fields and clearing the countryside of timber to make room for farms and villages. The Fjord also doubled as a saddle horse and packhorse.

In the nineteenth century, some Norwegian farmers began keeping records of the owners and colors of various Fjords that were born during this period. In 1910, an official studbook was published by fanciers of the breed to make record keeping more precise. Since that time, the breed has slowly grown and can be found all over the world.

The Norwegian Fjord is an ancient breed that possesses several physical characteristics typical of primitive horses. These include a dun coloration, dorsal stripe, and barred legs. The dorsal stripe extends all the way into the horse's mane, which is trimmed to stand up straight.

Fjords are used for both riding and harness work.

Norwegian Fjord

Polo

IF YOU COULD PLAY HOCKEY on horseback, the game would be a lot like polo. A team sport, polo requires skill and bravery from the rider, and boldness and athletic prowess from the horse.

The objective in polo is to score goals against an opposing team. Each team has four riders. Scoring is achieved when a rider drives a ball into the other team's goal. Riders use a mallet long enough to reach the small ball on the ground. Riders on each team are assigned positions with numbers. Number one plays offense and covers the opposing team's number four. Number two attempts to score, or passes the ball to number one for scoring. Both of these players cover the opposing team's number three player.

Number three is the tactical leader and feeds balls to number two and number one as well as playing defense. Number four is the primary defense player.

Arena polo matches usually consist of four to six six-minute periods, called chukkas. Field polo matches consist of between four and eight seven-minute chukkas, depending on the level being played. Each match lasts around seventeen minutes.

Polo is played on a grass field, which can be as small as the size of a football field or as large as three football fields.

Mounts used in polo are called polo ponies, although they are not true ponies, but horses standing anywhere from 14.2 to 16 hands. Thoroughbreds and Thoroughbred crosses are common in polo, which requires a horse capable of sprinting speed, endurance, and agility. Polo ponies must be calm of temperament since the game can become very exciting, and the horse needs to stay attuned to the rider.

It takes anywhere from six months to two years to train a polo pony for competition. Training includes desensitizing the horse to the mallet, controlling her with the reins held in just one hand (neck reining), and switching directions quickly at a gallop.

Lipizzans of World War II

THE LIPIZZAN, OR LIPIZZANER, breed is world famous for its talents in high-level dressage, made famous by the Spanish Riding School in Vienna. These majestic horses, which are born black, and mature to almost white, are muscular and athletic. They originated in Austria, where they were developed by the Hapsburg monarch in the sixteenth century.

Although most horse people are familiar with the Lipizzans, they don't know the story of how many of these magnificent animals were almost lost.

The story takes place during World War II. The year was 1945, and the place St. Martin in upper Austria. The Soviet army was in the process of invading the region when Colonel Alois Podhajsky, the head of the Spanish Riding School, became concerned for his horses' well-being. He had already evacuated a group of stallions from the Spanish Riding School, and the horses were now refugees in St. Martin.

Word of the horse's plight reached U.S. General George Patton, who was an avid equestrian and had competed with Podhajsky at the Olympic Games. Patton arrived at St. Martin and was treated to a quickly rehearsed performance by the Lipizzans. Patton was so moved, he vowed to help Podhajsky rescue the horses. Upon Patton's prompting, U.S. Undersecretary of War Robert Patterson agreed to place the stallions under the protection of the United States.

Meanwhile, a number of Lipizzan stallions and mares had been taken by the Germans to a Nazi-run stud farm in occupied Czechoslovakia. When the Soviets invaded, the horses fell under their control. Fearing the horses would be slaughtered for food, Patton issued orders for the horses' rescue. On April 28, 1945, the horses were evacuated by U.S. forces and taken to a safe haven elsewhere in Austria.

Rearing

FROM THE HUMAN PERSPECTIVE, one of the scariest maneuvers a horse can execute is rearing. When a horse stands on her hind legs, lifting her forefeet off the ground, the rider fears for his or her life, and with good reason. Rearing horses can easily flip over backward.

Rearing can be caused by the following factors.

- Spooking
- Reaction to a severe bit or mechanical hackamore
- Resistance to the rider
- Excitement
- Play
- To avoid work

In particular, horses that rear to avoid work are dangerous to their riders and need to be retrained by a professional trainer. This is a tough habit to cure and takes considerable work to correct.

You can't do much to stop a horse once she's in the midst of a rear, but you can avoid pulling her over backward by leaning forward and loosening the reins. If you know your horse is going to rear, try to move her forward and use one rein to turn her head to the side to prevent it before her front feet leave the ground.

Deworming

INTESTINAL PARASITES LOVE HORSES, and it's not hard to see why. Horses have 82 feet (25 m) of intestines inside their abdominal cavity—lots of room for worms to play.

Worms can drain your horse of the vital nutrients he needs to stay healthy. They can also cause serious damage to your horse's internal organs. Horses infested with worms are thin, have dull hair, and lack energy. If the parasites are not controlled, they can cause colic and ultimately death.

The worms that commonly plague horses include bots, pinworms, roundworms, and strongyles. These parasites find their way into the horse usually through the mouth, reproduce, and contaminate the environment, where they then infect other horses.

The good news? Controlling worms is easy. Affordable, over-the-counter deworming products are available at tack and feed stores. Your veterinarian can recommend a deworming regimen that will require you to give the horse dewormer two or more times per year. Also consider rotating dewormers so the parasites affecting your horse don't become resistant to a particular ingredient.

Clip Horse Magazines

IF YOU ARE LIKE MOST HORSE PEOPLE, you have a stack of horse magazines piled up waiting for you to read. On a day when the weather is bad and you can't ride, why not spend time reading through those magazines and clipping out stories or images of interest?

Grab a pair of scissors and a binder notebook with clear plastic sleeves inside. Cut out articles you want to keep for reference. Organize them in the binder, using tabs for each subject so you'll have an easier time locating an article when you need it.

Not sure what to save? Articles on equine illnesses are good to have on hand. You never know when your horse, or a friend's horse may come down with something you'll want to learn more about. Behavior and training articles are good for reference as well.

Many horse magazines feature how-to articles for teaching your horse and performing a task around the stable. It's a good idea to clip and save these for future reading.

Once you have finished cutting up the magazines, be sure to dispose of them in a recycling bin.

Consider gathering horse-related articles on the following subjects:

- Health
- Nutrition
- Training
- Behavior
- Foaling
- Grooming

Andalusian

THE ANCESTORS OF THE ANDALUSIAN were painted on Spanish cave walls some 25,000 years ago. Although other prehistoric images of horses appear in European cave paintings, the images in Spain depict a horse that was led by humans, not hunted by them. For this reason, some experts think the ancestor of the Andalusian was the first horse to be domesticated on the European continent.

These early Spanish horses remained on the Iberian Peninsula for centuries, their genetic purity unspoiled. But when foreign invaders and their mounts landed on Spanish shores, the blood of the native horses became mixed with that of other breeds. Eventually, from this melding of bloodlines came a horse known through the continent of Europe as the Iberian. This horse is now known as the Andalusian, named for Andalucia, in the south of Spain.

The Iberian breed eventually became known throughout the continent for its prowess as a warhorse. The Greeks and Romans used these horses, as did the Carthaginians during the Punic Wars.

Over the next 500 years, a series of wars between Spain and other countries seriously affected the breed, and its numbers dwindled. The breed managed to survive in small numbers, and it eventually became popular again because of its use in the Spanish Riding School of Vienna. Here, the Andalusian gained considerable influence, and it was used to create a number of other breeds, including the Lippizzan, the Friesian, the Peruvian Paso, the Paso Fino, and the U.S. Quarter Horse.

The Andalusian is a moderately sized horse, standing anywhere from 15.2 to 16.2 hands. His head has a slightly convex or straight profile. Most Andalusians are gray or white, a few are bay, and even fewer are black.

The breed is used in a number of different disciplines, particularly dressage and carriage driving.

Andalusian

Cattle Drives

IN THE MID-NINETEENTH CENTURY, cattle drives were common ways for a cowboy to spend days or weeks. Moving cattle was an essential part of a cowhand's job. Cattle needed to be herded from winter grazing lands to summer ones and vice versa, as well as to the auction yard when their time was up.

Even with all our modern technology, old-fashioned cattle drives still take place on working cattle ranches. Just like in the old days, cattle need to be moved from winter grazing lands to summer pastures and vice versa. But this time, it's not just the cowboys who move the cattle. Ordinary people come from all over and pay good money to participate.

Many cattle ranches offer cattle drives as part of a horseback vacation package. Guests are put up in nice lodges at night, and they are given a seasoned cowhorse to ride during the day. They move cattle under the guidance of ranch hands, sometimes helping move the cattle to new grazing, or other times just driving them from one area of the ranch to another.

People who choose to spend their vacation time chasing cows often have a nostalgic longing for a bygone era, when equines were the only means of transportation. They gain the experience of being out in the country, communing with nature and working with animals, just like folks did in the old days.

Eclipse

ONE OF THE MOST FAMOUS racehorses of all times was a 16-hand chestnut Thoroughbred stallion named Eclipse, foaled in England on April 1, 1764. Named after the rare solar eclipse that took place on the day of his birth, Eclipse was a direct descendent of both the Godolphin Arabian and Darley Arabian—two of the three Thoroughbred foundation sires, along with the Byerly Turk.

Eclipse won all eighteen of the races he entered, and he finally retired in 1771 due to lack of willing competition. He then went on to sire nearly 400 foals. According to the Royal Veterinary College in London, 80 percent of all Thoroughbreds today show Eclipse in their pedigrees.

Although Eclipse was a British race-horse, a prestigious U.S. racing honor, the Eclipse Award is named after him.

The Right Bit

BITS HAVE BEEN AROUND for centuries. They were first developed when the horse was domesticated to control the horse's movements. The first bits were made of wood, bone, or rope. Metal bits became the norm during the Middle Ages.

Today, most horses are ridden with metal bits, usually made from stainless steel. Bits are designed to apply pressure to the horse's mouth and send a message to stop, slow down, turn, and perform other maneuvers. The shape of the bit affects the way the message is conveyed to the horse. Bits that are severe, or are in the wrong hands, can be painful to the horse.

Bits come in such a variety of styles, it's almost impossible to know which one is best for your horse, and choosing the right bit can be tricky. You should always go for the mildest bit that will get the job done. A mild bit for both English and Western riding has a thick mouth bar that is jointed. Adding shanks to any Western bit increases its strength.

A Bit of Advice

Be sure your horse's teeth are in good shape before you try a bit on her. If your horse hasn't seen a veterinarian in a while, get her mouth checked for sharp points on her teeth and mouth ulcers first.

To see how your horse responds to a particular bit, ride her in the arena first. She should be relaxed and supple while you ride. Flex her head from one side to the other and judge how responsive she is at the walk. Turn her in a circle to see how she reacts. Ask her to stop.

If your horse doesn't respond to you, she is ignoring the bit. This means the bit is too mild for her. Rather than ramp up the pressure by using a harsher bit, consider some training for your horse to make her more responsive.

If your horse starts acting agitated or tossing her head, the bit is too severe for her—or your hands are too heavy. Take a lesson with a professional trainer and get his or her opinion on how you are using your hands, and which bit is best for your horse.

Changing Diets

VARIETY MAY BE THE SPICE OF LIFE, but when it comes to equine diets, variety can wreak havoc with a horse's digestive system and result in a serious bout of colic.

Whenever you need to change your horse's diet, do it gradually. If your horse currently eats three flakes of alfalfa hay per day and you want to switch him to two flakes of grass hay and only one flake of alfalfa, you need to do it slowly. Start by substituting half a flake of the new hay each day for at least three days. Then, substitute an entire flake for another few days. Add another half flake for the next three days, and then finally substitute the second flake of alfalfa for the grass hay until your horse is on two flakes of grass hay and only one of alfalfa.

Use the "half flake, three days" formula whenever switching food on your horse. If you want to introduce a new, pelleted feed to your horse, start with ½ pound (225 g) a day, and then move up to 1 pound (455 g) in three days. Increase the pellets by ½ pound (225 g) every three days.

If you want to switch your horse from hay to a lush green pasture, do so with great care. A sudden introduction to pasture can cause colic or founder. Start by grazing your horse on the pasture for only an hour a day for the first three days, and cutting back slightly on his hay. (Your veterinarian can tell you just how much to cut back, depending on your horse's age and condition.) Increase grazing time to two hours on the fourth day, and maintain this for three days and cut out a little more hay. Follow by adding an hour of grazing every few days, reducing the amount of hay slightly as you go. When your horse is spending at least eight hours grazing at a time with no ill effects, you can let him graze at will without hay supplementation, assuming your pasture can sustain your horse. (If you aren't sure, contact your veterinarian for advice.)

Just a Flake

In the world of horses, a flake is not just an unreliable person. It's also a measurement of hay.

Flakes are sections of hay that can be found in a square-shaped bale. The size and weight of a flake varies, depending on how the bale was divided at the time the hay was bundled. For most stabled horses, one or two flakes of hay constitutes a meal.

Watch a Horse Show

HORSE SHOWS ARE BOTH entertaining and educational, and they are a must for every horse lover. Whether you are an avid competitor or just a casual rider, you can learn a lot by being a spectator at a show.

Get a copy of a local equine publication or find a local equine community calendar on the Internet to get a list of upcoming shows in your area. Pick a show to attend that is completely out of your realm of knowledge. For example, if you are a Western rider, go to a show that features hunt seat, jumping, or dressage. Read up on these competitions beforehand so you have a sense of what is going on as you are watching. You'll be amazed to see these equine athletes in action.

If you are an English rider, go to a Western show. You can watch a gymkhana event where horse and rider teams run barrels and bend poles. Or you can attend a show with rail classes, such as Western pleasure, horsemanship, and trail classes.

Feeling really bold? Go to a breed show. Pick a breed you know nothing about, and do a little advanced reading on the types of classes you'll be seeing. If you select a breed with a strong connection to its natural heritage, you'll likely be treated to a display of costumes and traditions you never knew existed.

While attending these shows, talk to the exhibitors and other spectators. Most of the people in the stands will know someone who is competing, and they can tell you about the sport or breed. You can also learn a lot about the types of horses used in the event and spend time meeting these equines.

After you've spent the day at a horse show learning about a different discipline or breed, you'll be an even more well-rounded horse person.

Hanoverian

A MEMBER OF THE FAMILY of warmbloods, the Hanoverian is a German breed originating in the former kingdom of Hannover. In the 1600s, they were used as warhorses, and they went on to be bred to Spanish, Oriental, and Neapolitan horses. The horses that resulted from these breedings were used as farm horses and riding horses and to pull coaches. These early Hanoverians had a much lighter build than they do now.

As cars began to replace horses as transportation, breeders started working on making the Hanoverian into a competition horse. As a result, Hanoverians are known for being very athletic.

Standing 15.3 to 17 hands high, Hanoverians are strong, sturdy horses. They are most often seen in chestnut, bay, brown, black, and gray. They are most well known for their skills as show jumpers, although many are also used for dressage. Hanoverians have competed successfully in the Olympics.

Hanoverian

Steeplechase

THE SPORT OF STEEPLECHASE is one of the most exciting and dramatic of all equine sports. First conceived in Ireland in the 1800s, the sport got its name from the very first race that took place in a part of the countryside where church steeples were the tallest landmarks.

Today, steeplechasing is most popular in the United States, United Kingdom, France, and Ireland. The horses used in this sport are Thoroughbreds, and nearly all of them come from flat racing.

Steeplechase races are similar to flat races except the horses are expected to go over hurdles as they make their way to the finish line. In the United States, one-day race meets take place mostly in the spring and fall.

The races are 2 to 2 ½ miles (3.2 to 4 km) long on the turf, and include 11 to 12 jumps. Steeplechase jumps in the United States can be either National Fences, which measure 52 inches (1.3 m) in height, or timber jumps made of posts and rails at varying heights. Fence types and heights vary in other parts of the world where steeplechases are conducted, which is primarily England and Australia.

Steeplechase races are exciting to watch, but falls and spills are common. The courage of both horses and riders in these events is peerless.

The Legend of Bayard

FANTASTICAL HORSES HAVE ALWAYS made their presence known throughout the ages, appearing in just about every culture in the world. For the French, a magical horse named Bayard grew from French epic poems and became a legend in his own right. He was known throughout Europe, with the Italians calling him Baiardo and the Dutch referring to him as Beiaard.

Bayard first appeared in a twelfth-century French fictional work as the horse of hero Renaud de Montauban. Because he was a magical horse, Bayard could carry Renaud and his three brothers all at once. He could also understand human language.

Renaud is forced to give Bayard to Charlemagne, who punished the horse by tying a large rock around his neck and forcing him into a river. Instead of drowning, Bayard breaks free by smashing the stone with his hooves. He escapes from the river into the woods, where he goes on to live wild for eternity.

A monument to Bayard can be seen in Belgium, outside the city of Dinant. Called "Bayard rock," it is a huge rock formation with a natural cleft. According to legend, Bayard created the cleft when he struck the rock with his powerful hooves.

Trail Etiquette

TRAIL RIDING SHOULD BE A RELAXING and safe way to spend time with your horse. One way to help make it so is to practice good trail etiquette.

When it comes to behavior on the trail, you should adhere to some basic rules. Follow these tenets and you, your horse, and other riders will have a more pleasant time.

Approach slowly. When approaching another rider, if you are trotting or loping, slow to a walk and maintain your slow place until you are well past the other horse.

Pass quietly. Don't trot or canter up to a rider that is ahead of you on the trail. You are likely to spook the horse and endanger the rider. Instead, drop down to a walk and pass calmly by. Make sure the rider knows you are there before you come right up behind him or her.

Also, avoid yelling or doing anything that might spook the other horse. Some horses are more easily spooked than others, and some riders are less equipped to handle the situation. Your horse might be bombproof, but the one coming toward you might be ready to explode.

Deal properly with spooking horses. If you see another rider in trouble ahead of you on the trail, either offer to help (if you can) or stop and wait until that person has his or her horse under control before you proceed.

Go slowly around blind curves. When riding on winding single track trails, go slowly around blind curves. This is for your safety as well as the safety of others since a hiker, a mountain biker, or another rider might be coming the other way.

Wait for dismounted riders. Don't try to ride past someone who is attempting to mount their horse. Stop and wait until the rider is safely in the saddle before you proceed.

Keep your dog under control. If you ride with your dog in tow, keep him on a leash or have him under strict voice control at all times. Don't allow your dog to approach other horses on the trail. This is for the safety of both the horse and your dog.

Chiropractic Treatment for Horses

HORSES ARE GREAT CANDIDATES for chiropractic treatments, too. And why not, since they carry us around on their backs?

Equine chiropractic is based on the theory that spinal and joint dysfunction can affect the overall physical well-being of horses. Chiropractors believe that the spine and all its associated structures (including nerves, blood vessels, muscles, and ligaments) can be helped by chiropractic treatments.

Chiropractic is used to help horses heal from injuries, especially those that result from compensatory issues. In other words, if one part of a horse's body hurts or is weak, she will put more pressure on another part to compensate. The part that is used to compensate will then develop its own problems.

Veterinary chiropractors adjust a horse's spine, just like regular chiropractors do for humans. This helps to restore proper alignment and return the horse's normal range of motion, which relieves pain and enhances the horse's health.

Some chiropractors who work on horses have veterinary degrees, while others do not. Many veterinarians recommend only using chiropractors with veterinary degrees because these individuals have a very thorough, working knowledge of the entire horse's body, although many horse owners use non-degreed equine chiropractors and report excellent results.

Organize Your Horse's Records

HORSE OWNERS ARE AMONG the busiest people around. Not only do they have the same obligations as most other people, but they also have the added responsibility of riding and caring for their horses, too, which can take up hours a day depending on whether the horse is kept at home or at a boarding stable.

This is why it is so essential to be organized when it comes to your horse's records. Keep shot records, farrier receipts, and training details in one central location. That way, you can find them easily when you need to and keep better track of what your horse needs and when.

Take a few hours to organize your horse records. Here are some options on how to do it.

File drawer: Gather all of the receipts you have from your veterinarian, trainer, farrier, and anyone else who has performed a service related to your horse. Create a series of folders labeled for each subject and file the receipts in these folders. Place them in alphabetical order in a file drawer, along with your horse's registration certificate (if she has one), show records, and other paperwork.

Notebook: Get a loose-leaf notebook and create a page for each of the different areas of your horse's care. Set aside several pages for vaccines, another for veterinary procedures, another for teeth floating, another for deworming, another for farrier care, and so on. Using your receipts, write down the dates and details of each procedure in chronological order.

Record book or software: You can buy a record book specifically designed to keep track of a horse's health and training, or purchase a software program created for this. If you have several horses, a software program might be a good investment since these are usually designed for owners of multiple horses.

It's also a good idea to have a tickler file or another kind of reminder system to let you know when your horse is due for vaccinations, deworming, farrier work, and other procedures. Free reminder services are available on the Internet. Once you sign on, they will send you emails reminding you when it's time to tend to your horse's regular needs.

Saddlebred

THE SADDLEBRED'S ORIGINS WERE IN a horse breed called the Narragansett Pacer, which was created in the Narragansett area of Rhode Island. British colonists in the New World used Galloway and Hobbie horses from the British Isles to develop the Narragansett horse, which possessed a wonderfully smooth riding gait.

In the early 1700s, breeders had begun crossing Thoroughbreds with the Pacers to get a bigger, more versatile horse. This resulting breed came to be known simply as the American Horse. This breed inherited an ambling gait from the Narragansett Pacer, and colonists used it during the American Revolution and into the early part of the next century.

Eventually, Morgan, Canadian Pacer, and Hackney horses were bred to the American Horse, resulting in a new breed called the Kentucky Saddler, and eventually the Saddlebred. By the mid-1800s, this breed had become very popular throughout the Eastern United States.

When the Civil War began in 1861, the Saddlebred carried men into battle, including the war's most prominent generals. General Ulysses S. Grant owned two Saddlebreds, named Charger and Cincinnati, while General Robert E. Lee rode a gray Saddlebred gelding named Traveller. (See Day 164.) The Saddlebred not only helped fight the war, it also aided the South during Reconstruction.

In 1891, the National Saddlebred Horse Breeders Association was formed, later to be called the American Saddlebred Horse Association.

The American Saddlebred has an elegant and refined appearance. Standing anywhere from 15 to 17 hands, they come in palomino, chestnut, bay, black, gray, brown, and pinto.

Saddlebreds are born with three gaits and some are trained to have five. In addition to the walk, trot and canter, five-gaited Saddlebreds also know how to slow gait and to rack.

The Saddlebred is used widely for show, in gaited classes, jumping, and dressage. The breed also makes a great trail horse.

Saddlebred

Horse Expos

FOR HORSE LOVERS, one of the closest things to heaven on Earth is an equine expo. These celebratory fairs, which are centered on the horse, feature everything from equine-related vendors to breed exhibitions to educational clinics. Expos are a great way to spend a day with your horsy friends, learn how to better handle your horse, and learn more about horses in general.

Horse expos are becoming more popular, and they take place in various parts of the country. They tend to be big events that go on for several days and draw some of the most famous clinicians in the horse world. They provide great opportunities to learn about how to train and care for your horse.

If you are looking for horse stuff to buy, horse expos are the place to go. Many vendors give special show discounts, and you can purchase everything from fly spray to horse trailers at a lower-than-normal price.

Breed demonstrations are often a big part of horse expos. In large venues, horse stalls are set up to temporarily house horses that represent each participating breed. Live exhibitions featuring breeds showing their stuff are usually part of the expo as well.

The Spanish Jennet

Long before the Age of Exploration of the fifteenth and sixteenth centuries, a distinct type of horse could be found all throughout Europe. Called the Spanish Jennet, this popular mount was a small saddle horse of Iberian origins with a naturally smooth ambling gait. The horse had a compact build and an overall dramatic look.

Spanish Jennets can be seen in paintings dating from the Middle Ages. Their low-set tails, round croups, high-set necks, and convex profiles are trademarks of the breed.

The Spanish Jennet was among the horses brought to the Americas by the Spanish conquistadors in the sixteenth century. These popular gaited horses went on to contribute to a number of breeds native to the New World, including the Spanish Mustang, Peruvian Horse, and Paso Fino.

Some researchers believe that the Tennessee Walking Horse, Saddlebred, and Missouri Fox Trotter, among others, owe their smooth gaits to the Spanish Jennet.

Although the original Spanish Jennet is now extinct, a group of horsemen are striving to promote a modern version of the breed. The Spanish Jennet carried genes for pinto and spotted, Appaloosa-type patterns, passing these on to horses in the Americas. The Spanish Jennet Horse Society recognizes pinto and altigrado (spotted) horses of Paso Fino and Peruvian Horse breeding.

Should You Breed Your Horse?

MANY HORSE OWNERS BELIEVE that if they have a mare, they should breed her at some point in her life. After all, wouldn't it be fun to have a foal around?

Before you breed your mare, you must make some considerations.

Just like with cats and dogs, more horses exist than homes. Thousands of horses go to slaughter each year because they are unwanted, and most of them are not old or lame. They simply have nowhere else to go. You must have a good reason to breed your mare if you plan to contribute to the horse population. Here are some contributions to consider.

Your contribution to the breed. Does your mare contribute something important or unique to her breed, and will there be a lifelong market for your foal? If your mare is not registered with a breed registry, you shouldn't even consider breeding her unless you plan to keep the resulting foal the rest of its life. The market for grade horses (the term for horses of unknown breeding) is small, and many of these horses end up in the slaughterhouse.

Also, unless your mare has great conformation and terrific skills that should be preserved and passed down to another generation, it's better to leave her a maiden, especially if you can't find a suitable stallion to complement whatever faults your mare possesses.

Cost in time and money. There are several costs involved in having a foal. Your first will be the stud fee. Next, you'll be spending money on prenatal care. Once the foal is born, you'll have to have a vet check the baby over. All this expense is to be expected, but what happens if something goes wrong with mom or baby? You could spend a fortune in vet bills, and worst case scenario, you could lose both the foal and your beloved mare in a medical emergency.

Before you go out looking for a stallion to breed your mare, please be responsible and refrain from breeding your mare just for the fun of it.

Stocking Up

HAVE YOU EVER NOTICED the lower part of your horse's legs looking puffy when you go to get him out of his stall? And after a bit of exercise, the puffiness goes away? If so, your horse is experiencing a condition called "stocking up."

Stocking up is caused when blood and lymph fluid pools in the lower part of the horse's legs. This is usually the result of stall confinement, lack of exercise, and sometimes overfeeding. The fluids dissipate when the horse is exercised, and it returns after he has been standing in his stall for several hours.

The condition of stocking up is not painful to a horse, and it isn't associated with lameness. But it can be distressing to see because it temporarily distorts the appearance of your horse's legs.

To help prevent stocking up, give your horse plenty of exercise every day. Provide him with the largest stall or paddock you can to encourage him to move around more when he's not being worked. If you are feeding your horse alfalfa, consider switching all or some of his diet to grass hay as this may help. Talk to your veterinarian about changing your horse's diet.

To help reduce the likelihood of your horse stocking up after a ride, hose down his legs with cold water. This may keep fluids from settling there.

Teach the One-Rein Stop

THINK ABOUT IT: You trust your horse with your life every time you mount up. If your horse is sensible and well trained, it's a risk worth taking. But even the most reliable horse can be frightened or excited, and you can lose control. This is where the one-rein stop comes in.

The one-rein stop is your emergency brake when you are riding. With this technique, you can bring your horse to a stop in just about any situation.

TEACHING THE ONE-REIN STOP

Your horse must know what you are asking for when you use it in an emergency so she will be programmed to respond.

1. Teach your horse to give to lateral pressure with her head. While you are on the ground and your horse is wearing just a halter, stand behind her shoulder and pull her nose toward her side with the lead rope. Don't let up on the pressure until she moves her nose on her own toward her side. If she gives even just a little bit, release the pressure and praise her.

Practice this on the other side of her body, too, and do it repeatedly over a few days until she quickly and willingly gives to the pressure of the rope. Your goal is to have her touch her side with her muzzle without resisting. Once she is doing this with the halter and lead rope, switch to practicing with a bridle and reins until she gives in to the pressure without hesitation.

2. Your next step is to teach this from the saddle. (Do not use a leverage bit or mechanical hackamore.) At the stop, ask your horse to bend her head first to one side, then the other, touching her muzzle to her side.

If you have taught your horse well on the ground, she should catch on quickly that you are asking her for the same thing. If not, you'll need to teach her in increments like you did from the ground until she catches on.

3. Once your horse has mastered steps 1 and 2, teach her to yield her hindquarters. As you pull the rein to the side to ask for her head, move your inside leg back behind the girth and ask the horse to shift her hindquarters away from you. Your horse should yield her hind end as her head turns. Practice this repeatedly, on both sides, over a period of weeks. Continue to reinforce it from time to time. This is the move you want your horse to make when you are trying to stop her from running away, bucking, or rearing. You are taking control of her head and disengaging her hindquarters. Your horse can't use her hindquarters for power when she is yielding them.

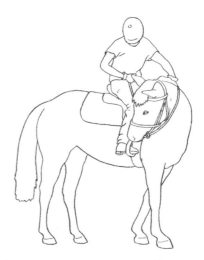

The key to the one-rein stop is pulling the horse's head around and disengaging the hindquarters.

The Sorraia Horse

ONE OF THE MOST ANCIENT and rare breeds of horse is the Sorraia. Of Iberian origin, these horses appear in prehistoric cave drawings throughout the Mediterranean, and were first identified by a zoologist in 1920 as living in the wild in Portugal.

Believed to be the ancestors of today's Andalusians, Lusitanos, and Spanish Mustangs, the Sorraia is now found primarily in Portugal and Germany, where a few small herds are maintained.

The Sorraia is distinct in both its conformation and color. Most Sorraias stand between 14.1 and 14.3 hands, although horses as small as 12.3 hands

are sometimes seen. The Sorraia's head is one of its most distinguishing features, and is large with a convex profile. The ears are long, and the neck slender. The withers are high and the croup slightly sloping. These horses also have long pasterns and are known for their soundness.

The Sorraia's color is unusual in that it is always dun or grulla. All have a dark dorsal stripe, and some have barring and "cobwebs" on the legs. The ear tips are dark, and the mane and tail frosted with white.

Sorraias are known for their great endurance and ability to collect, making them good dressage horses. Although they often have an independent nature, they are very trainable.

Only two hundred Sorraia are alive today, and a movement is afoot to save the breed from extinction. In 2006, the Sorraia Mustang Preserve was established in Ontario, Canada. A few years earlier, two Sorraia stallions were imported to the United States. The American Heritage Horse Association (AHHA), a consortium of breeders in the U.S., has established a separate studbook for the Sorraia. The AHHA is using Spanish Mustangs with the same mitochondrial DNA as the Sorraia to help resurrect an American version of the breed.

Sorraia

Pole Bending

ONE OF THE SEVERAL EXCITING gymkhana events offered at rodeos and Western breed shows, pole bending is a timed class that features one horse and rider team at a time.

Pole bending works like this: A series of six poles set 21 feet (6.4 m) apart, attached to heavy bases, are set up in a line. A horse and rider start at a gallop and race past the poles to the end of the set. They then return back, weaving in and out of the poles in a serpentine pattern. When the horse reaches the last pole, he turns around it and weaves back down through the poles the way he came.

The horse then runs back across the timer line. If the horse knocks any of the poles down, the team is given a five-second penalty. The horse and rider team that completes the poles in the shortest amount of time is the winner.

Horses must be agile to be successful in pole bending. They must also be able to switch leads in between poles to perform the serpentine pattern at a gallop.

Xenophon

THE TITLE OF "HORSE WHISPERER" has been used to refer to a number of modern-day natural horsemanship trainers, but the original holder of this title was a Greek soldier and historian named Xenophon. A contemporary of Socrates, Xenophon was a gifted writer as well as a magnificent horseman.

In 350 BC, Xenophon wrote a treatise called *On Horsemanship,* in which he explained the selection, care, and training of horses for use in war and peace. Many of Xenophon's recommendations are still common practice among horsemen today. His advice to always treat the horse with kindness and patience is surprising to some who may think that ancient horsemen used brute force to train their mounts, based on the harsh bits and other equipment they used during those times.

On Horsemanship includes advice from Xenophon on the selection of a war horse. He noted that a good war mount should be sound, gentle, fast, and obedient, and pointed out that a nervous, skittish, or vicious horse is not acceptable for use in war. A suitable horse should also be willing to leave other horses behind when asked, and should be amenable to having a bit placed in her mouth.

Xenophon also explained how to teach a horse "collection," which is a way of moving that requires the horse to use her muscles differently than she normally would when being ridden. Collection is a big part of the discipline of dressage, making Xenophon the author of the oldest surviving work on this discipline.

Biting

HORSE BITES ARE ONE OF THE most painful types of bites you can get from a barnyard creature. When jaws strong enough to masticate tough, fibrous plant material come down on human skin, the results are excruciating.

Horses usually bite people for one of two reasons: They are trying to play, or they are being aggressive. Some horses who are hand-fed bite out of impatience, or in an attempt to coerce you into giving up the food.

Although a painful bite can hardly be seen by a person as invitation to frolic, biting is a common play signal between horses. Horses who bite out of playfulness are not doing it to be mean, but the bite hurts just as badly. You can tell if a horse is biting out of playfulness by the expression on his face. If his ears are up and his bite was more of a nip than a gaping-mouth attack, chances are he is trying to play.

On the other hand, aggressive horses deliver bites with their ears pinned back and teeth bared: very clear signs.

ADDRESSING THE ROOT CAUSES

If you have a horse who bites, you need to teach him that this is completely unacceptable behavior. You also need to consider the root cause of the behavior. A horse who delivers play bites may need more exercise or stimulation to get rid of his excess energy. A horse who bites out of aggressiveness may be in pain or experiencing another kind of problem. This is especially likely if the horse has never been a biter before but suddenly begins attacking people.

First try to deal with whatever underlying issue may be triggering your horse's biting. Have a veterinarian examine your horse to see if he's in pain if he has suddenly started biting. If your horse is a play biter, give him more exercise and stop feeding treats to him by hand.

If the biting continues, start teaching your horse that his behavior cannot continue while also protecting yourself from his powerful teeth.

Begin by learning to anticipate your horse's behavior. Pay close attention to him and notice the cues he gives you just before he opens his mouth to bite. Head him off at the pass by yelling "Quit!" at the top of your lungs and jerking on the lead rope if he makes a move to bite you. You can also raise your elbow and let him bang into it with his head as he moves toward you to bite. If he tries to bite you when you are leading him, hold your fist up near his mouth so he smacks into your knuckles when he swings his head around to bite.

If all your attempts to stop the biting fail, contact a professional trainer for help. Biting is a serious problem that shouldn't be ignored.

Newborn Foal Care

BABY HORSES ARE ADORABLE, but they are fragile creatures that require close watching and good care.

Assuming your mare has a normal delivery, the foal will be born front feet and head first. The mare will lick the fetal membrane off the foal, and the baby will try to stand about half an hour after birth. If the foal is not standing within two hours, call a vet.

Once the baby is standing, she should make her way over to the mare's udders to nurse. If the foal cannot find the udders after ten minutes of searching, help her by gently guiding her in the right direction.

You can do this by putting your arms around the foal's neck at chest level and around the buttocks as you help her walk. If the baby finds the udder but can't seem to nurse, call a veterinarian immediately.

Within the first twelve hours of birth, the foal should pass sticky, dark stool called meconium. If she doesn't, you'll need a vet to help you. Without passage of the meconium, the foal can die.

182

A veterinarian should give your foal a full examination within twenty-four hours of birth just to make sure everything is all right. Call for an appointment as soon as you can.

Basic Brushing

WE ALL KNOW HOW TO brush a horse. . . or do we? Do you have a system that really gets the dirt out and brings out your horse's natural shine? If not, give this one a whirl.

First assemble all your tools.

- Ruby currycomb

- Stiff body brush

- Soft dandy brush

- Small, stiff detail brush for hard-to-reach places

- Clean towel

First, curry your horse with the rubber curry-comb. Begin just behind the throatlatch and work in a circular motion as you cover every part of his body. Don't forget to go down his legs all the way to the coronet band, underneath his belly, and on his back legs beneath his tail.

This will raise a lot of dust and dirt to the surface of your horse's coat. Brush it all out with the stiff body brush. Remember to brush with the lay of the hair. Don't stop until all the dirt and dust are gone from your horse's coat. Clean your brush periodically by rubbing it vigorously back and forth across the currycomb.

Use the stiff body brush to groom your horse's forelock, mane, and tail. Don't use a comb or bristle brush for this as these will pull and break the hairs.

Next, take your small detail brush and groom behind your horse's ears (sweat accumulates there from the headstall), on his elbows, and beneath his fetlocks.

Using the soft dandy brush, go over your horse's face. Start between his eyes and work your way down to his muzzle.

Next, go over your horse's entire body with the dandy brush. This will remove the fine layer of dust that remains on the surface of your horse's coat.

Finish off with the clean towel. Wipe your horse's entire body to add sheen and sparkle to that newly cleaned coat.

Missouri Fox Trotter

THE MISSOURI FOX TROTTER developed in the Missouri Ozark mountains of the United States, where pioneers from Kentucky, Illinois, Tennessee, Virginia, and Arkansas settled after the Show Me State was given statehood in 1821. The horses they brought along crossed with each other over the decades, and the result was a surefooted horse with the ability to negotiate the rugged mountain terrain. These horses were used to plow, work cattle, haul logs, and transport people. In time, the breed was given the name Missouri Fox Trotter because of its smooth, four-beat gait.

In 1948, an association formed to maintain the breed's studbook. The association took the name of Missouri Fox Trotting Horse Breed Association in 1958, and it was reincorporated as a stock company. In 1973, the organization changed to a membership association. The studbook remained open until 1983.

Today, Missouri Fox Trotters can be found in all fifty states, in Europe, and in Canada.

The Missouri Fox Trotting Horse stands between 14 and 16 hands and comes in palomino, cremello, perlino, chestnut, black, brown, bay, buckskin, gray, roan, and pinto.

Horses of this breed are born with the ability to perform the fox trot and the flat foot walk, in addition to the canter. The fox trot is a collected gait that features a walking step in the front and a trotting step behind. The flat foot walk is a four-beat gait that differs from the fox trot in that it features a steady, equal, four-beat cadence produced by the hooves.

Missouri Fox Trotters are shown in jumping, Western classes, parades, gymkhana, and competitive trail riding. They are also common as family and pleasure horses, and they are known as being gentle and good for beginners.

Missouri Fox Trotter

184

Horsemanship

MANY WESTERN SHOWS these days feature a horsemanship class, where horse and rider are expected to execute a specific pattern in the arena. The pattern is done at the lope, and illustrates the rider's skills at controlling the horse.

Horsemanship patterns vary according to the particular show, but most require the horse to back up, pivot, and circle. The horse is expected to always be on the correct lead. Cones are used to designate areas of the pattern where horses execute maneuvers.

Horsemanship classes are popular because you don't need a fancy horse to do well. As long as your horse is well groomed and well trained, you can succeed.

Just about every western breed association offers horsemanship classes in shows. Open western shows often feature horsemanship, as do smaller schooling shows and even 4-H events.

Comanche

THE BATTLE OF LITTLE BIGHORN, which took place in 1876, is famous for the fact that General George Custer and all his men were wiped out by the Sioux and Cheyenne. One of few equine survivors of this historic battle was a remount horse named Comanche.

Comanche, a 15-hand bay gelding, was the personal mount of Captain Myles Keogh, who led two of the companies defeated in the battle. Keogh chose Comanche in 1868 after the horse was reportedly captured on the range and trained by the U.S. army as a remount. Comanche was reportedly a Morgan–mustang cross.

Keogh and Comanche fought in many battles, and Comanche was badly wounded in one. According to legend, Comanche continued to obey his rider despite his injury, endearing him even more in Keogh's heart.

Two days after the Battle of Little Bighorn, Comanche was found seriously wounded among the many dead men and horses on the battlefield. He was taken to North Dakota by steamboat and nursed back to health by army veterinarians. He was later shipped to Fort Riley in Kansas and became a pet to the soldiers at the fort. He was never ridden, only served as a mascot in parades.

When Comanche died in 1890, he was granted full military honors. His remains were sent to the University of Kansas, where he was taxidermied and put on display in the university's National History Museum. He can still be viewed there, and he is the museum's most popular exhibit.

Cleaning Brushes

IT'S ONE OF THOSE TASKS you never get around to doing: cleaning your grooming brushes. But it's important to do this at least once a month. After all, if you don't clean your brushes, all you are doing is putting dirt back on your horse when you groom him.

The best way to clean brushes is to soak them in warm water. If your brushes are made from synthetic bristle, add mild dishwashing soap to the water, stir them around, let them soak for about twenty minutes, and then remove them. Rinse them thoroughly and let them dry in the sun.

For brushes with natural hair bristles, use warm water and a dab of horse shampoo. Wet the bristles and rub the shampoo on them to build up a lather. Work the shampoo in between the hairs. Rinse the bristles thoroughly with warm water until the water runs clear with no more shampoo foam. Shake the brushes out and let them dry in the sun.

Poisonous Plants

IT'S A MYTH THAT HORSES won't eat plants that aren't good for them. In most cases, horses can't tell the difference between a toxic plant and a safe one. And a horse that is very hungry will eat any plant she comes across, regardless of its smell or taste.

It's your job as a horse owner to protect your horse from toxic plants by keeping these weeds out of your horse's pasture. Or, if you are trail riding, keep your horse from snacking on this potentially deadly flora.

Here are just a few common plants that can be toxic to horses.

- Azalea (*Rhodedendrum*)
- Black walnut (*Juglans nigra*)
- Boxwood (*Buxus*)
- Buckwheat (*Fagopyrum esculentum*)
- Buttercup (*Ranunculus*)
- Castor bean (*Ricinus communis*)
- Cotton (*Gossypium*)

- Fern palm (*Cycas circinalis*)
- Round ivy (*Glechoma hederacea*)
- Hemlock (*Conium maculatum*)
- Hydrangea (*Hydrangea*)
- Indian paintbrush (*Castilleja*)
- Lantana (*Lantana*)
- Mesquite (*Prosopis*)
- Milkweed (*Asclepias*)
- Oleander (*Nerium oleander*)
- Red maple (*Acer rubrum*)
- Tobacco (*Nicotiana*)
- Wild cherry (*Prunus avium*)

Some of these plants cause digestive disturbances when eating in small quantities, while others can result in death if ingested. Make certain your horse stays clear of these plants. If you suspect she has eaten a toxic plant, contact your veterinarian immediately.

Watch a Horse Movie

FEELING SICK OR THE WEATHER got you down? Curl up with a blanket, a cup of tea, and good horse movie.

Horse movies have been around since the beginning of the film industry. In fact, as mentioned on Day 108, the first moving picture ever made was of a horse. Shot by film pioneer Eadweard Muybridge in Stanford, California, it featured a trotting horse named Abe Edgington.

Horse films comprise a sprawling library of films. Old Westerns going back to the silent film era feature plenty of horses. One, called *The King of the Wild Horses*, features a black Morgan stallion named Rex who was considered a renegade of his time.

Just about any movie starring cowboy William S. Hart will include his famous pinto sidekick, Fritz. And silent movies star Tom Mix was never far from his faithful mount, a sorrel gelding named Tony.

Films from the golden age of Westerns also feature some equine stars. Champion, Gene Autry's sorrel wonder, shows his stuff in a number of films, including *Tumbling Tumbleweeds*, *Red River Valley* and *The Singing Cowboy*. And don't forget about Roy Rogers and Trigger. Trigger's best work can be seen in *Son of Paleface*, also starring Bob Hope.

National Show Horse

ORIGINALLY A CROSS between the Arabian and the Saddlebred, the National Show Horse is now its own registered breed in the United States. With the grace of the Arabian and the showiness of the Saddlebred, the National Show Horse is the quintessential exhibition horse.

The breed was considered a crossbred until the early 1980s, when a group of fanciers established a registry. Today, horses that are at least 25 to 95 percent Arabian, with remainder being Saddlebred, are eligible for registration.

The National Show Horse is a flashy animal with a long neck, high-stepping action, and considerable spirit. The head is relatively small, and the eyes are large. The tail is high set and carried up when the horse is working. National Show Horses come in all colors seen in the Arabian and Saddlebred.

The breed is shown in halter, country pleasure, English pleasure, Pleasure Driving, Fine Harness, Western pleasure, hunter pleasure, show hack, and equitation. Three-gaited classes are also popular, as well as five-gaited events.

National Show Horse

Therapeutic Riding

THERAPEUTIC RIDING IS THE USE of horses to aid people dealing with mental or physical challenges. Riding centers established to provide horseback therapy help people of all ages deal with a variety of issues.

Specially trained instructors work with students using riding as a means of physical and emotional therapy. Students are taught how to ride, and in the process they develop skills that help them overcome their particular disabilities.

For example, children with autism are helped by the facilitation of communication and social skills. Because the horse's stride is similar to that of a human's, kids with physical disabilities experience the rhythm and feel of walking.

Hippotherapy, another equine-assisted therapy, involves hands-on work by a physical therapist during riding. This helps improve neurological functioning in both children and adults.

(For information on becoming a certified instructor in therapeutic riding and hippotherapy, see Resources for the North American Riding for the Handicapped Association [United States and Canada] on page 316.)

Idaho Gem

THE VERY FIRST MEMBER of the equine family to ever be cloned was a mule named Idaho Gem. Produced as part of a joint effort between the University of Idaho and Utah State University, the mule was born to a horse mother and was the clone of the full brother to a successful racing mule named Taz. It took many attempts before a successful cloned mule foal was delivered to term. Since then, several other mule clones have been born.

Don Jacklin, an Idaho businessman and former president of the American Mule Racing Association, funded the project. In 2006, Idaho Gem ran his first race and won. Since then, he set the record for a 350-yard (320 m) course by running the fastest time by a three-year-old mule. In his racing career thus far, Idaho Gem won two firsts, two seconds, a third, and a fourth out of six total races.

Saddle Pads

THERE WAS A TIME WHEN NOTHING came between a horse's back and his saddle. Things have changed, however, and nowadays horses wear saddle pads when being ridden.

Saddle pads come in a vast assortment of sizes, shapes, colors, and materials. Western saddle pads tend to be thick to help evenly distribute the rider's weight across the horse's back. They are often in Southwest designs in keeping with the Western theme, although some are solid colors. Western pads often have a leather pad at the front, or else a cut-out area to provide more room for the withers. Some therapeutic Western pads feature shock absorbent material inside the pad to help keep the horse's back from getting sore.

English saddles also use pads, although these pads are much thinner and lighter than their Western counterparts. Styles vary along with the saddle type. Riders using close-contact saddles typically use pads that are a few inches (centimeters) thick and are cut to follow the design of the saddle. Dressage riders often use thin, quilted square pads that are designed primarily to protect the saddle.

When choosing a saddle pad for your horse, your budget will be your primary factor. Pads range considerably in quality and price, with simple pads being the most affordable. Therapeutic pads featuring special materials meant to provide additional benefits above and beyond what ordinary pads provide will be considerably more expensive.

Arthritis

ARTHRITIS IS A COMMON PROBLEM in horses, and not just old ones. Even youngsters can develop this issue if they are genetically predisposed to it.

Arthritis is often the culprit in lameness in horses. This inflammation of the joints results in pain and stiffness. The knees, hocks, and fetlocks are the most often affected joints, and the condition worsens over time.

Arthritis can be seen in four different types: degenerative joint disease, septic joint disease, immune-mediated arthritis, and traumatic arthritis.

Degenerative joint disease is by far the most common type of arthritis seen in horses. The hocks are the joints most often affected, with the fetlocks a close second, and the stifles third.

Symptoms include chronic stiffness, swelling around the joint, and difficulty performing. Treatments for this type of arthritis are aimed at reducing swelling at the joint. Non-steroidal anti-inflammatory drugs, corticosteroids, and nutraceuticals are often prescribed.

Horses with arthritis do best when given daily exercise. Nothing is worse for an arthritic horse than standing around in a stall all day. A hand-walk for thirty minutes a day can do wonders to get an arthritic horse's joints loose and help him feel better. Pastures are even better for these horses since they can exercise at will and keep themselves limber.

Lunging Transitions

IMAGINE HAVING TO TRAVEL AROUND and around in a circle, over and over again. It would get pretty boring, right? Your horse feels the same way when you make her work repeatedly on the lunge line. You can make lunge-line work more interesting for your horse while fine tuning her training at the same time. One good way to do this is with transitions.

By using frequent transitions on the lunge line, you make things more interesting for your horse, and you teach her to listen closely for your commands. Her focus will stay on you more completely once she catches on that you are going to ask for something different on a frequent basis. (Evidence of this is how her inside ear is always cocked toward you.)

Frequent transitions also teach your horse to collect herself, which is something all horses should know. When you work on transitions in the saddle, they will come more easily because you have practiced on the lunge line.

EXERCISE

Start your horse on the lunge line at the walk. Have her do two complete circles, and then ask her to trot. After she has trotted half way around the circle, ask her to walk. Half way around the circle, ask her to trot again.

Repeat this for the first ten minutes of your session. Once your horse is warmed up, you can add cantering to the transitions. Ask your horse to go from the walk to the canter, and then back down to the walk. Let her canter at least one time around the circle before you ask for the downward transition. Change it up by asking her to go from the canter to the trot, from the trot to the walk, from the walk to the canter, and from the canter to the walk.

Half way through your session, change directions and repeat the entire process again. Don't work your horse more than forty-five minutes total. Less is better when you first start working on these transitions. Be sure to cool her down the last five to ten minutes at the walk.

Miniature Horse

THE MINIATURE HORSE IS A diminutive copy of a regular-sized horse. It originated in Europe when, in the 1600s, small horses were bred as pets for the rich. Some of these mini equines found their way to Dutch and English coal mines in the 1700s, and they were enlisted to pull carts under ground. These "pit ponies," as they were called, rarely saw the light of day, and they were even stabled underground.

Valued as mining horses, pit ponies were brought to the United States in the 1900s and put to work pulling coal wagons in the Appalachian Mountains. Eventually, Shetland Ponies were bred to them, which resulted in the modern Miniature Horse.

Another type of Miniature Horse, the Falabella, was created in Argentina, in the rugged Argentine Pampas. Measuring no more than 40 inches (1 m) at the withers, the Falabella looked just like a regular-sized horse, in miniature. In 1970, twenty-five Falabellas were imported to the United States, and a breeding program started in Pennsylvania. The breed is considered rare, with only 900 horses alive today.

In the United States, the Miniature Horse became a recognized breed in 1971 by the American Miniature Horse Registry. In 1978, another breed registry, the American Miniature Horse Association, was also founded The Falabella Miniature Horse Association was created in 1973.

All horse colors are eligible for registration with these organizations, including pinto and Appaloosa patterns.

Driving is a popular activity for owners of Miniature Horses, who are too small to be ridden by anyone but very young children. They can be trained for different kinds of driving, including trail driving, parade driving, and single or multiple hitch. They are shown in open or country pleasure, obstacles, and roadster classes, too.

The most common function for Miniature Horses is as pets. Many people who don't have room or finances for a full-size horse keep Minis as companions.

Miniature Horse

Treasure Hunts

JUST ABOUT EVERYONE EMBARKED on a treasure hunt or scavenger hunt as a child: Establish a list of items you must find, then traipse around knocking on neighbors' doors in a race to collect all the items on the list. The team that finds the most items wins.

Scavenger hunting can also be done on horseback. A popular horse camp activity, horseback treasure hunts involve teams of riders that go out on the trail and try to collect all items found on a list written by the camp counselors.

These items can include everything from a particular type of flower, a certain color pebble, or the bark of a uncommon tree. Similarly, the team that retrieves the most items from the list is the winner.

Riding instructors say that horseback treasure hunts are fun for kids learning to ride, and treasure hunts also help boost their skills. Riders practice turning, stopping, starting, dismounting, and mounting, all while participating in a scavenger hunt.

Balius and Xanthas

THE GREEK HERO ACHILLES did not conquer Troy by himself. He had the help of two divine horses, named Balius and Xanthas, who pulled his chariot.

Balius and Xanthas were brothers who were sired by none other than Zeus himself. Their mother was a harpie (a death-spirit with a bird's body and a woman's head). They were given to Achilles by his father, King Peleus, after the horses were gifted to Peleus by the god Poseidon.

Patroclus was Achilles's comrade in arms, and he cared for Balius and Xanthas in the stable. When Patroclus died on the battlefield, the two divine horses stood by him and wept. When Achilles found his friend dead, he reprimanded Xanthas for not protecting Patroclus. Hera, Zeus's wife, broke divine law and gave Xanthas the gift of speech so he could tell Achilles that a god had killed his friend—and that the same god would soon kill him. Xanthas's ability to speak was then taken away from him by one of the Furies, a goddess of revenge. Xanthas never spoke again.

Arena Etiquette

IF YOU TAKE GROUP LESSONS or ride in an arena, you need to be aware of arena etiquette. You and your horse are sharing space with others, so courtesy is essential.

Here are some basic rules of arena etiquette.

- If you need to mount or dismount your horse in the arena, go to the center to do it. Stay off the rail.

- When passing a horse that is going in the opposite direction you are riding, pass left shoulder to left shoulder. This means you will either stay close to the rail so the rider going the opposite way can pass you on your left, or you will stay closer to the middle of the arena. (If you are going clockwise, you will be on the inside of the arena. If going counter-clockwise, you'll be on the rail.)

- If you see a rider lose control of a horse or fall off a horse, stop your mount immediately. If the other horse starts panicking and running around the arena, get off for your own safety since this behavior can be contagious among horses.

- Always close the arena gate behind you when you enter or exit an arena.

Hoof Cracks

HORSES GET MINOR CRACKS and chips along the edge of the hoof all the time. This is normal as the hoof grows out and begins to break off. But what is not normal is a vertical crack that starts from the coronet band down toward the toe. These are called hoof cracks, and can be dangerous.

Hoof cracks are often caused by inappropriate hoof care, such as a trim that is wrong for that horse's hoof and leg. It causes an imbalance of the horse's weight on that hoof, resulting in a stress crack. If the crack develops toward the back of the hoof, near the heel, it is called a quarter crack and must be addressed by a farrier. Some farriers put egg-bar shoes on horses with quarter cracks to help protect the hoof from further cracking until it grows out.

Pre-Ride Stretch

Horses aren't the only athletes in the human–horse team. Riding takes athletic skill in humans, too. Just ask any first-time rider how they feel the day after they ride. Muscles they didn't even know they had hurt.

The demands of riding on the muscles and ligaments are why it's always a good idea to warm up with stretches before you ride. Do each one of the following stretches before you get up on your horse. It only takes five minutes total, and it is well worth it:

- **Stretch your neck.** Tilt your head slowly first to the right, with your ear toward your shoulder, and then to the left. Tuck your chin forward into your chest, and then back up toward the sky. Then, turn your head as far to the right as you can while keeping your shoulders straight. Do the same to the left. Follow this routine four times, holding each stretch for at least five seconds.

- **Stretch your quads.** Stand up straight and bend one leg up behind you. Hold your ankle so your knee is bent. Slowly pull your ankle so your knee points out behind you. Hold for ten seconds and switch to the other leg. Repeat this twice for each leg.

- **Stretch your hamstrings.** Stand up in front of a fence and brace yourself with one hand. Reach one leg high up onto the fence and bend forward. Hold for ten seconds. Repeat on the other leg.

- **Stretch your inner thigh.** Sit the ground with your knees bent out to the sides and the soles of your feet touching each other. Push down gently on both knees. Do this twice for ten seconds each.

- **Stretch your lower back.** Lie on your back with your knees to your chest. Wrap your arms around your legs just below your knees and pull your knees toward you. Hold for five seconds and repeat three times.

Hamstring stretch

200

Back stretch

Quad stretch

Dutch Warmblood

FIRST CREATED TO BE A multi-use farm and riding horse, the Dutch Warmblood is the result of breeding a native Dutch horse with English, German, and French horses. The Dutch maintained strict standards for breeding these horses because they were so important to the livelihood of Dutch farmers. Horses that were lacking in soundness, intelligence, or disposition were culled from breeding programs.

Today, the Dutch Warmblood is now considered a world-class equine athlete. They are famous for their jumping abilities, as well as their talents in dressage, three-day eventing, and driving.

Dutch Warmbloods stand between 16.2 and 17 hands and come in black, brown, bay, chestnut, and gray. Pinto and roans may turn up as well. They have a distinctive appearance, with an arched, muscled neck, and powerful hindquarters.

Dutch Warmblood

Reined Cow Horse

A SPECIAL EVENT SHOWCASING the talents of Western stock breeds has emerged in recent years. Called reined cow horse, or working cow horse, this sport elicits precise reining skills on the part of horse and rider, along with solid cow sense in the horse.

Reined cow horse works like this: Horse and rider enter the arena alone and perform a prescribed series of reining patterns. This involves cantering circles, doing spins, and completing sliding stops. When the pattern is complete, a single cow is let into the arena. The horse and rider must control the cow in the arena, directing it where the rider wants it to go. This is known as fence work. Of course the cow has her own ideas about where to go, and that's when it gets interesting.

The National Reined Cow Horse Association (NRCHA), a U.S. organization, governs all-breed events in the sport of reined cow horse, and it has affiliate clubs in Europe and Canada. Classic Western breeds such as the Quarter Horse, Appaloosa, and Paint have working cow horse classes at their breed shows, which are the equivalent to reined cow horse events.

Perfecting this activity takes a lot of training and practice, especially with cows. Those involved with the sport become hooked on it because of the great adrenaline rush it provides.

Marengo

BEHIND EVERY GREAT WAR HERO is a good horse. Napoleon was no exception. The horse that carried him through many battles was a gray Arabian stallion named Marengo.

According to legend, Napoleon rode Marengo in all of his major battles, from Moscow to Waterloo. The horse was supposedly captured by Napoleon's army in Egypt after a battle, and he soon became Napoleon's mount.

Because no official record exists of Marengo in Napoleon's stable registers, some historians believe the name Marengo may have been a nickname for a horse named Ali, who was ridden extensively by Napoleon.

The great general reportedly liked giving nicknames to both horses and people, and just about every horse he rode had one.

After the battle of Waterloo, Marengo was captured by British forces and taken to England where he was put on exhibition. When Marengo died in 1831, his remains were sent to London Hospital to be prepared for display. The hide was lost, but the skeleton was kept at the Royal United Services Institute Museum in London for public viewing.

Herd Behavior

IF YOU CAN COUNT ON HORSES for one thing, it's to be highly tuned in to other horses. This is an expression of herd behavior, which is an instinct that has been programmed into horses for millions of years. Try to take a horse away from his buddies, and you will see this instinct in action.

Herd behavior developed in horses as a means of protection from predators. Horses live by the motto "There's safety in numbers," and in the wild, a horse alone is often a worried horse.

When humans ride horses and ask them to be in situations that fly in the face of that herd instinct, things can get tense. In essence, horses with a strong herd instinct don't want to leave the safety of the barn where their buddies live, or the safety of the close proximity of a horse they are attached to. Terms like "barn sour" and "buddy sour" get bandied around.

Horses can be taught to override their strong herd instinct, but it takes hard work. By learning to trust the rider and responsively obey his or her commands, a horse can overcome his strong urges to stay close to home or close to another horse, and do what is asked of him.

The herd instinct is stronger in some horses than others, but every horse has some of this, left over from developing in the open plains with hungry predators lurking. Our challenge as riders is to help horses understand that they can look to us for safety and companionship, instead of their equine buddies.

203

Chronic Obstructive Pulmonary Disease

IF HORSES COULD GET ASTHMA, it would be called chronic obstructive pulmonary disease (COPD), which causes difficulty breathing in, and more difficulty breathing out. Horses with this condition can often be heard wheezing loudly, coughing, or experiencing shortness of breath.

Horses have long suffered from this condition, which is also called "heaves" by laymen. An old cowboy term, "broken wind," is also still used on occasion to refer to horses with COPD.

CAUSE

In the old days, people thought horses developed COPD by being run too hard. We now know that COPD is caused by a genetic predisposition to this condition, which involves an inflammatory response that causes restriction of the airways.

Poor ventilation and dusty hay and bedding are some culprits in the development of COPD. Sometimes airborne or food allergies can trigger bouts of this condition.

TREATMENT

The best treatment for horses suffering from COPD is fresh air free of dust and allergens. Soaking a horse's hay before each feeding can also help because it cuts down on dust. In severe cases, veterinarians recommend bronchodilators to open up the horse's airways or corticosteroids to help reduce inflammation of the lungs.

Volunteer for Therapeutic Riding

HORSES PROVIDE A WONDERFUL GIFT in the form of horseback therapy, where children and adults who suffer from both physical and emotional challenges learn to ride. This equine-assisted therapy helps boost confidence, along with helping participants develop both mental and physical skills needed for everyday life.

Programs for therapeutic riding exist all over the world, and many do not charge participants a fee. These programs rely heavily on volunteers, and they can't continue their services without people willing to help.

Most therapeutic riding programs are in dire need of volunteers, and they don't require that you have any experience around horses. People who volunteer at therapeutic riding centers receive on-the-job training. They are taught how to handle horses and work around them. This includes barn chores such as feeding the horses and mucking their stalls.

Spend one day a week or just one day a month volunteering at a local therapeutic riding center. You can easily find one these programs by visiting the website for the North American Riding for the Handicapped Association. (See Resources on page 316.)

Pony of the Americas

An APPALOOSA IN MINIATURE, the Pony of the Americas—or POA—is a popular mount for children.

The breed began quite by accident in Iowa when a Shetland pony stallion was accidentally allowed to mate with an Appaloosa mare. The resulting foal, an attractive black and white colt, named Black Hand because of a handprint-like marking on his flank, became the foundation sire of the breed.

When the Pony of the Americas Club was first created in 1954, Black Hand was the only pony registered with the group. Today, almost 50,000 POAs are listed with the club. The breed is mostly found in the United States, but an affiliate club has been established in Germany.

Fans of the breed attribute this growing success to the fact that the POA is the ultimate child's pony because of its outstanding disposition. The breed's versatility is also a big selling point. POAs have been shown in hunter/jumpers, Western, three-day eventing, dressage, driving, and other disciplines.

POAs come in a variety of pony sizes, usually standing from 11 to 14 hands. They come in a variety of Appaloosa colors and patterns, and they feature Western stock-horse conformation.

Pony of the Americas

Three-Day Eventing

An EXCITING EQUINE SPORT known as three-day eventing, or combined training, is an Olympic discipline that commands tremendous athleticism and courage from both horse and rider.

Essentially a triathlon on horseback, three-day eventing consists of three days of competition in three different disciplines: cross-country jumping, show jumping, and dressage. Each discipline is performed on a different day, consecutively.

Horses have to be talented in all three of these activities, and they must also have great stamina. The same goes for the riders.

This sport requires considerable, specialized training that can take months or years to complete, depending on the horse. It also calls for conditioning and spirit. Thoroughbreds are most often seen in this sport, with warmbloods following second.

Wind Horse

HORSES HAVE OFTEN INSPIRED spirituality through the ages. A symbol called the Wind Horse has found its way into both Buddhism and Native American religions.

In the Buddhist faith, the Wind Horse represents one of the cardinal directions. This symbol originated with the Asian shamanistic faith of Bon. In Tibetan Buddhism, its appearance bespeaks peace, harmony, and wealth. The Wind Horse is invoked in the mornings and during the harvest.

The Wind Horse appears on the coat of arms of Mongolia, and it has wings that help it sail over a green mountain range.

In Choctaw legend, the Wind Horse was a noble creature filled with love and kindness who spent his time helping people who were sick or injured. One day, he met a young boy who was born with only one foot. The child had been abandoned in the forest and no one loved him. Wind Horse grew to love the boy and carried him away to the Hunting Grounds, giving up his own freedom to spend eternity with his young friend.

Safe Turn Out

EVERY STABLED HORSE NEEDS regular turn outs to just run around and be a horse. But turn outs can be dangerous if you aren't careful. Horses can easily injure themselves when running at full tilt. Bowed tendons and fractures can happen when a horse who has been cooped up for days on end suddenly finds herself in the great wide open.

Before you turn out your horse, always prepare her for her time out to make sure she stays safe. Follow these safety rules.

- Hand-walk your horse for at least ten minutes before turning her loose in the turn out. If you can, consider riding or lunging your horse first to warm her up. This will limber up her muscles, tendons, and ligaments, making her less prone to injury.

- If your horse wears shoes, put protective leg boots on her so she doesn't knick herself with a shoe and cause bleeding.

- Try to use a small arena for turn out. This will cut down on the amount of speed your horse can muster up when running, reducing her likelihood of injury.

- Do not turn your horse out with another horse. Horses like to play in the turn out and can inadvertently injure each other, especially if they are wearing shoes.

- Make sure the turn out has a fence at least 5 feet (1.5 m) high so your horse is not inclined to jump out of it.

- Supervise your horse at all times during the turn out. That way if she does hurt herself, you will be there to call for help right away.

- Cool your horse down after a rigorous turn-out. Don't offer her food or water until she's no longer hot, as it will be difficult for her to digest and may cause colic.

Equine Physical Therapy

LIKE PEOPLE, HORSES CAN ALSO benefit significantly from physical therapy and many other types of body work.

The traditional form of physical therapy for horses focuses primarily on veterinary sports medicine and post-surgery rehabilitation.

Equine physical therapists are becoming easier to find these days because some veterinary schools are offering postdoctoral courses in the subject. The need for this type of treatment has increased as more horses are used in intensive equine sports such as show jumping and dressage.

In most cases, a veterinarian will refer you to an equine physical therapist if your horse is in need of rehabilitation. You can also call on an equine physical therapist yourself if your horse is experiencing back problems, unexplained lameness, or even behavioral problems. A good physical therapist might be able to find a problem in your horse's body that is contributing to the issue at hand. With repeated sessions and even at-home therapy, your horse might be able to make a full recovery.

Take a Lesson

WHETHER YOU HAVE BEEN RIDING your entire life or are new to the hobby, everyone can benefit from taking a riding lesson.

If you think you have all the skills you need to ride well and the idea of taking a lesson seems silly to you, consider this: Even Olympic equestrians who compete at the highest levels in the world still take riding lessons. In other words, no matter how much you know, someone else knows more than you. At least when it comes to riding.

If you haven't had a lesson in a long time, find a good instructor in your area and make an appointment for a single ride in your discipline of choice.

Tell the instructor you just want a single lesson right now to gauge your riding level and get a sense of where you need to improve. If possible, ride the instructor's horse instead of your own. You learn more with every new horse you ride because each horse is an individual, and feels and responds differently to each rider.

Do not be surprised if you find that after your lesson, you are yearning for more. The better you ride, the better you feel in the saddle, and the more you enjoy your time with your horse.

Kiger Mustang

MANY OF THE WILD HORSES that roam the western United States trace back to the original horses brought to the New World by the Spanish conquistadors. In 1977, a band was discovered in the high deserts of southeastern Oregon that had Spanish blood as well as mixed genes. These horses had a distinct Spanish appearance and similar color and markings. They also seemed to be able to produce other horses of like conformation.

To help preserve this small band of horses, the Bureau of Land Management (BLM), the agency responsible for managing wild horse herds, moved them to the Steens Mountain wild horse range, near Kiger Gorge. They are now protected in two Herd Management Areas (HMA): Kiger HMA and Riddle HMA.

The BLM rounds up Kiger Mustangs every few years to help keep the breed's wild population in check. These horses are in high demand at auction, and they go quickly.

Private breeders have also started producing Kigers for sale. These horses are registered with the Steens Mountain Kiger Registry and the Kiger Mesteno Association.

Kiger Mustangs come mostly in a dun coloration, with striped legs and a dorsal stripe. A color called "claybank" describes a very pale dun seen in the breed. Bay, grulla, gray, and black are other colors that show in the breed. Excessive white markings are discouraged.

Kigers stand from 13.2 to 15 hands. They are used in a variety of disciplines, including trail riding and Western showing. They can run gymkhana, work cattle, do reining, and even jump and do dressage.

Rodeos

ONE OF THE MOST LOVED spectator sports in the horse world is the rodeo. The event started in the 1800s in the Western United States, where cowboys (and cowgirls) worked day in and day out handling cattle. Rodeos were a way for these folks to show off their skills and their horses. By the 1900s, this casual event grew into a professional sport.

Today, rodeos feature a variety of classes. Gymkhana classes are a tradition at rodeos, and they feature pole bending and barrel racing. (See Day 44.) Calf roping is another favorite, but the biggest spectator draws come from the bull and bronco riding events, where cowboys try to stay on "wild" bulls and horses who are, in reality, trained bucking animals.

Some rodeo events are so popular with spectators that they take place over several days and draw tens of thousands of onlookers.

Rodeos are considered an "all-American" tradition, although some animal rights groups have protested parts of rodeo that involve the rough treatment of animals. Specifically, they object to calf roping because it is hard on the young cattle. They also object to the bucking events because of the way the animals are induced to buck. Although Professional Rodeo Cowboy Association limits use of electric prods, these devices are often used on animals before they are turned loose from the bucking chute.

Trigger

ONE OF THE MOST FAMOUS HORSES to ever emerge from the United States was a part-Thoroughbred palomino stallion named Trigger, who starred in eighty-two movies. The trusty mount of singing cowboy star Roy Rogers, Trigger was named Golden Cloud before he became Rogers's horse. Trigger made his first appearance with Rogers in a film called *Under Western Stars*, in 1938.

Trigger was trained by well-known movie horse trainer Glenn Randall, who taught the stallion to rear on command, as well as many other tricks. Like most famous actors, Trigger had doubles for the most daring stunts, but he did a lot of less-risky-but-no-less-spectacular stunts himself.

Rogers and Trigger also made many personal appearances together in the 1940s and '50s all over the United States.

When Trigger died at the age of thirty-three, Rogers had his remains mounted and put on display in the Roy Rogers and Dale Evans Museum in Victorville, California. The museum moved to Branson, Missouri, in 2003, and it still features Trigger on display.

Whether to Blanket

THE WEATHER OUTSIDE IS FRIGHTFUL. Should you blanket your horse?

This age-old question stumps horse owners the world over whenever winter blows into town. The answer depends on your horse and just how cold he really is.

Although the air may be quite chilly outdoors, if your horse is healthy and has a good winter coat, he will be able to withstand it without being blanketed. Nature equipped horses with winter coats that do a terrific job of insulating the horse against cold and wind.

That said, there are times when you should blanket your horse. Here are some examples.

- If your horse is sick, recovering from an illness, or very thin, blanket him in cold weather.

- If your horse does not have shelter from the rain or snow, cover him with a water-resistant turnout sheet to help him stay dry.

- If your horse is old, it's a good idea to give him at least a light blanket in cold weather. Older horses are less able to generate heat than their younger counterparts.

- If your horse is a very young foal and you are experiencing a cold snap, get him a foal blanket to help him stay warm.

- If your horse has been body-clipped (his winter coat removed with clippers), keep him in a blanket during the winter.

Remember to remove your horse's blanket during the day if the air warms up, and put it back on when the sun goes down and the temperature drops.

Botulism

MOST PEOPLE KNOW BOTULISM as something you can get from eating contaminated canned food. Horses can get botulism, too, although not in the same way most humans get it.

Botulism is a deadly toxin produced by a bacterium called *clostridium botulinum*. The metabolic process of this bacterium produces neurotoxins, which affect the horse's nervous system.

Horses can get botulism in the following different ways.

- They can get the bacterium in their systems via a deep puncture wound or when a wound results in a lot of dead tissue.

- They can get it from accidentally ingesting hay that has been contaminated by a dead bird or rodent during the harvesting process.

- They can accidentally swallow pasture soil that is contaminated with this bacterium.

SIGNS OF BOTULISM

When a horse has botulism, she will show weakness and paralysis. She may have trouble swallowing, or she may drool. She may have trouble standing, and her muscles may quiver. The symptoms get progressively worse until the diaphragm muscle becomes paralyzed, and the horse is unable to breathe. Death soon follows.

TREATMENT

Because botulism is difficult to diagnose other than through analysis of symptoms, vets often treat it without having a definitive diagnosis. The horse is given horse hyper immune plasma, which is very high in antitoxin titers. This treatment is expensive and doesn't always work. Supportive care in the form of fluids, tube feeding, and antibiotics can be the best way to combat the illness. This gives the horse's body time to repair itself on its own.

PREVENTION

The best way to prevent botulism is to inspect your horse's hay for animal carcasses. If you find a dead animal, or parts of one, in a flake of hay, don't feed the rest of the bale. Prevent infection via puncture wounds by calling your vet immediately if your horse becomes seriously injured.

Finding a Trainer

IN AN IDEAL WORLD, horse owners would be able to train their own horses. After all, most people manage to train their own dogs. But horse training is different in several ways, two the most important being—quite simply—that horses are a lot bigger than dogs, and you ride them.

If you have a young horse who needs to learn the ways of the saddle horse world or you are having issues with your horse and don't know how to deal with them, you may need to get professional help.

Horse trainers spend every day working with horses and know how to deal with just about every equine personality out there. A trainer can do a lot to teach your horse the right way to behave and make him safe for you to ride.

So how do you find the right trainer for your horse? What criteria do you use to decide? These are important questions because a poor trainer can make your horse's problem worse instead of better. And if you live in the United States, you don't have any kind of licensing or certification process to guide you when determining whether a trainer is really qualified to handle your horse or not.

You can increase the odds of choosing the right person to work with your horse if you follow these guidelines.

Ask for referrals. The best way to find a good trainer is to get details on how the person works and trains from clients. Ask horse people you know who trained their horse and how they liked the trainer. Check with your veterinarian, too. If you find a trainer who gets repeated good reviews, you are off to a good start.

Find out if the trainer is certified. In many countries, horse trainers are certified or licensed. If you live in a country where this is law, find out if the trainer you are interested in using is certified or licensed.

Watch the trainer work. Spend some time watching the trainer work with horses and students to get a sense of whether or not you like the person's style and way of handling mounts. If you like what you see, take a lesson or two on your horse with the trainer. A good trainer will give you lessons on your horse in addition to riding him.

Once you settle on a trainer, constantly evaluate the situation to make sure you see results. Ask the trainer up front how much time he or she needs to achieve your goals with the horse and hold the trainer to them.

Hackney

A HORSE CALLED THE NORFOLK TROTTER was the predecessor of the modern day Hackney, which is a high-stepped show horse considered rare by the American Livestock Breed Conservancy.

The Norfolk Trotter was bred for style and speed, pulling fancy carriages in England during Georgian times. In the mid-1700s, breeders put Norfolk mares to Thoroughbreds, and the foundation of the Hackney horse was laid. Over the next fifty years, the breed was fine tuned to a swift trotting horse. In 1883, the Hackney Stud Book Society was founded in England.

In the late 1800s, the Hackney horse was popular for pulling fine carriages in both England and the United States. In 1891, the American Hackney Horse Society was founded to preserve the breed in the United States. The Hackney Horse Stud Book Society in England is now called the Hackney Horse Society and maintains a breed registry in the United Kingdom.

The Hackney comes in two types: horse and pony. Both are the consummate show animal, and both feature an elegant conformation and high-stepping gait. In the show ring, Hackney horses compete in driving, riding, and showmanship, and have also been shown in dressage. Hackney horses are over 14.2 hands.

Hackneys ponies, which are 14.2 hands or smaller, are shown in four divisions depending on their height and type. The Cob Tail pony is 14.2 hands and under at the withers. Long Tail ponies measure 12.2 hands or under at the withers, and Roadster ponies measure below 13 hands. Pleasure Ponies are 14.2 hands or under.

Both Hackney horses and ponies come in black, brown, bay, and chestnut. They have a small head, a delicate muzzle and ears, and a long neck.

Hackney

Horse Rescues

EVER SINCE ANNA SEWELL'S best-selling novel *Black Beauty* became a hit in the late 1800s, people have been trying to help horses in need. (See Day 290 for more on *Black Beauty*.) And it's a good thing. As much as we love horses, they are among the most ill-used and neglected animals in the world.

Over the past several decades, horse rescues have sprung up in nations around the globe. Places of refuge for horses that are suffering from abuse and neglect, horse rescues take in horses that are sick, malnourished, injured, or traumatized. Some rescues rehabilitate the animals and try to find new homes for them. Others give the horses a home for life.

Horse rescue groups are private organizations that survive mostly on individual donations. In addition to charitable donations, they often use volunteer help.

Rescues vary in the work they do.

- Rescue and rehabilitate retired Thoroughbred or Standardbred racehorses
- Rescue wild horses that need to be placed by government agencies because they have been rounded up off the range
- Take horses that have been seized by local animal control agencies
- Take owner-surrendered horses or a combination of seized and surrendered
- Place horses in new homes after they have been rehabilitated
- Provide a sanctuary so the horses never have to live anywhere else again

Just about every group takes donkeys and mules, as well as horses.

The Spanish Riding School

ASK ANY PERSON WELL VERSED IN the history of horses, and he or she will be able to tell you all about the Spanish Riding School.

The Spanish Riding School is an old, prestigious training center for Lipizzan horses and riders in Vienna. Called the Spanish Riding School because the first horses trained at the school in 1572 were of Spanish breeding, the academy was an important training center for military horsemanship during post-medieval times.

Now an important tourist attraction in Vienna, the school features a beautiful hall that was built in the 1700s. The Lipizzan stallions who are trained there are exhibited in regular performances for the public. Training sessions with the famous stallions, which are bred elsewhere in Austria, can also be viewed by the public.

The Lipizzan stallions of the Spanish Riding School are taught classical dressage, and they begin their training at age four. It takes four to six years to train a horse all the way to the highest level, which includes airs above the ground, which are very difficult and dramatic maneuvers. The Lipizzans of the Spanish Riding School are most famous for being able to perform these gravity-defying maneuvers, which include the levade, corbet, and capriole.

The Lipizzans occasionally go on tour, taking their performances internationally. Horse lovers line up in droves to see these magnificent horses at work.

Feeding Grain

EVERY HORSE LOVES OATS, but should every horse have grain? This is a question that equine nutritionists have asked for years.

The question you should ask yourself is whether or not your horse should have grain. While grain is a necessity for horses performing regularly at very demanding activities, such as racing and three-day eventing, it may not be necessary if your horse is just used for trail riding or enters a show a few times a year.

It's easier to make a decision about whether to feed grain if you understand what grain really is. The grains most commonly fed to horses are oats, corn, and barley. They contain a lot of carbohydrates, which the horse's body converts into energy. The result is that the horse who eats grain has a lot more vim and vigor than the horse who doesn't. This is useful if your horse is an equine athlete with a demanding training and showing schedule. If you just want to poke around on the trail on the weekends, however, grain can be your worst enemy because your horse will be full of excess energy and may become hard to control. He may also put on too much weight.

Grain also provides nutritional value in addition to energy, which is why some horse experts believe all horses should be fed oats in particular. Oats are a good source of fiber, and they keep better than other grains. Corn, on the other hand, is fed most commonly because it is cheap. It gives horses a good energy boost, although if overfed it can cause colic, laminitis, and diarrhea. Barley is high in protein and harder to digest than the other grains. Too much of it can cause laminitis.

When it comes to whether you should give your horse any of these three, the basic rule is don't feed grain unless you absolutely have to. If your veterinarian or professional trainer tells you your horse needs grain, then by all means, provide whatever the pros recommend. But if you are planning your horse's diet on your own, avoid including grain in the mix. Avoiding grain will save you money, and your horse is more likely to behave if his energy level isn't through the roof.

Equine Influenza

HUMAN BEINGS AREN'T THE only ones who get the flu. Horses come down with it, too. Called equine influenza, it has many of the same symptoms as the human version. Horses develop lethargy, a high fever, and a thick nasal discharge. Some horses come down with a cough. Secondary infections can develop, including pneumonia.

Just as with the human flu, equine influenza is spread between individuals via airborne contact. It is diagnosed based on the symptoms. In most cases, the virus runs its course, and the horse is fine after a week or so. Problems arise when complications occur, such as bacterial infections.

PREVENTION

Just as with human flu, the horse version can often be prevented with a vaccination. Some veterinarians recommend the vaccine twice or more a year, while others only once. The frequency of the vaccine depends in part on how much contact your horse has with other equines. Horses kept in boarding stables are usually vaccinated at least twice a year.

Practice Trailer Loading

FEW THINGS ARE AS STRESSFUL as trying to load an uncooperative horse into a trailer, especially when you are in a hurry to get somewhere. Rather than waiting until the morning of a show or an emergency situation to work on getting your horse to load, you should practice loading when you have nowhere to go.

SETTING UP

Set up your trailer (or a borrowed one) in an area where you have a lot of room to work with your horse. If the trailer has a manger, put hay in it. If not, hang a full hay bag where your horse will tie.

LOADING YOUR HORSE

Ask your horse to load into the trailer. If she goes in the first time, tell her how wonderful she is and tie her. Let her eat for a while and have her stand in the trailer for at least fifteen minutes. Then back her out. She should back calmly and slowly, and not until you ask her to. Don't let her charge backward out of the trailer. If she does this, reload her and work on this problem by having someone stand at the trailer door with a long whip. Be sure he or she stands off to the side so he or she doesn't get kicked, and be sure you aren't directly in front of the horse so she doesn't jump forward on top of you. Have your assistant tap the horse lightly on the rump if she starts to charge backward. Repeat this over and over until your horse learns to walk backward out of the trailer in a calm manner.

WHAT IF SHE DOESN'T BUDGE?

If your horse won't go in at all, you'll need to teach her to load. Different trainers have various methods on how to do this. One common way is to start by leading your horse up to the trailer so she can take a good look at it. Let her put her head down and sniff the floor. Next, step into the trailer and ask your horse to follow. If she refuses, keep asking. Don't look at your horse and start pulling on her head. She will plant her feet. Instead, turn your back on her and cluck to her, walking forward with purpose.

If she still refuses, have someone stand behind her with a whip and cluck to her. Don't touch her with the whip just yet. Just having someone behind her might send her forward. If she still refuses, have your helper gently tap her on the rump with the whip as you ask her to come forward. If she starts moving off to the side or backs up wildly, you may need professional help teaching her to load.

The goal is to get your horse in the trailer and have her find food at the end. She can stand in it for a while, eat, and then come out. Then reload her again. Do this a few times until it is no big deal to go in and out of the trailer.

223

Akhal-Teke

THE NATIONAL HORSE OF TURKMENISTAN, the Akhal-Teke, is an ancient breed that developed from the horses used for raiding. The breed hasn't changed much since the eighth century, and it is the purest living descendent of the ancient Scythian horse. Some experts believe the breed is even older than the Arabian, which is usually considered the oldest living pure breed. Some also believe the Akhal-Teke contributed to the development of the Thoroughbred.

Akhal-Tekes were notably kept by the Terkemenes, a nomadic people who still live in the deserts of Turkmenistan. Because of the Terkemenes' lifestyle, the horses they kept needed to have considerable stamina and sturdiness. The breed became valued as both a rugged warhorse and a fiery mount. Bloodlines were maintained through oral tradition for thousands of years. The Akhal-Teke lived mostly in Central Asia, but they also found their way to Russia, where they were kept by royalty.

In 1935, the Turkmene people made a great effort to call attention to their very special breed. They sent a group of riders on Akhal-Teke stallions over 2,500 miles (4,000 km) from the capital of Turkmenistan, Ashkabahad, to Moscow in eighty-four days. The trip included a segment with a 225-mile (362 km) desert crossing. The trip across the desert took only three days, and the horses managed with little water. The same ride was repeated in 1988.

The Akhal-Teke's conformation is long and lean, making it a natural for this kind of endurance. The average Akhal-Teke stands 15.2 hands, although the horse has a taller appearance because of its upright neck and greyhound-like appearance. Horses of this breed can be found in buckskin, bay, black, chestnut, palomino, cremello, perlino, and gray. They are known for having a distinct metallic sheen to their coat.

Akhal-Tekes are considered a rare breed, and they are listed as "critical" in the American Livestock Breed Conservancy annuals.

Akhal-Teke

The American Livestock Breed Conservancy

The American Livestock Breed Conservancy (ALBC) is a United States–based organization that is a clearinghouse for information on livestock breeds that are in danger of becoming extinct. The organization works to conserve these breeds by encouraging small farmers to become involved with these animals and by calling attention to their plight.

Horse breeds as well as other livestock are listed by the ALBC in one of the following categories, depending on population numbers.

Critical: Fewer than 200 annual registrations in the United States and estimated global population less than 2,000.

Threatened: Fewer than 1,000 annual registrations in the United States and estimated global population less than 5,000.

Watch: Fewer than 2,500 annual registrations in the United States and estimated global population less than 10,000. Also included are breeds that present genetic or numerical concerns or have a limited geographic distribution.

Recovering: Breeds that were once listed in another category and have exceeded Watch category numbers but are still in need of monitoring.

Study: Breeds that are of genetic interest but either lack definition or lack genetic or historical documentation.

Model Horse Shows

THOSE PLASTIC HORSE STATUES that seem to infatuate children are more than just toys to a lot of people. They are actually the subject of model horse shows, which mimic real horse shows—but with model horses being the participants instead of live ones.

The model horse show hobby started in the United States in the 1960s, when little girls who loved horses but couldn't have their own started holding shows. Since the children lived all around the United States, the shows took place through the mail, with photos of the horses entered in various classes. At first, the horses entered were mostly Breyer models, made by Breyer Animal Creations in New Jersey. As the hobby grew more popular, adults started getting involved and learned how to manipulate the models to make them appear original (rather than mass produced).

Using heat, they changed the posture of the models. They painted them, created elaborate tack and customs, and even added real horsehair to the manes and tails.

Model horse show participants started clubs and began holding shows in person instead of through the mail. The model horse manufacturers, with Breyer in the lead, became involved in the hobby and started sponsoring shows. These days, model horse shows feature a wide variety of classes where models are put on display for judges to evaluate. The public is invited to these shows, where vendors sell an assortment of customized and factory models.

Although model horse shows are not as common as real horse shows, they take place often enough to keep the hobby alive.

The Unicorn

THE UNICORN IS ONE OF the most common fantastical equine images. Little girls seem to love unicorns, and the animals have made their way into popular culture in the form of dolls, fantasy paintings, and even movies.

The image of the unicorn as a horse with a single horn in the middle of its forehead is a modern one. The unicorn of ancient Chinese mythology not only had a horn on its head, it also had the body of a deer, the tail of an ox, and the hooves of a horse. This creature was careful never to tread on any living thing. It only ate plants that had died. Seeing it was considered a good omen.

Unicorns also appeared in Greek writings in the third century BC, but they were referred to as "horned ass," rather than horses. The legend of the unicorn, whose horn was considered magical, persisted throughout Roman history and the Middle Ages.

Unicorns are even mentioned in the Bible. In some translations, the first animal Adam named in the Garden of Eden was the unicorn. Noah banished the unicorn from the ark because of the beasts' demanding nature, which is why these animals are no longer seen.

During medieval times, the unicorn became a symbol of Christ, with the horn being a symbol of the Christ and God's oneness. Throughout history, the unicorn has almost universally appeared as a symbol of good.

Mares and Foals

HORSES MAKE SOME OF the best mothers in the world. Watch a mare with her foal, and you can learn lessons about love and parenting that you could never get from reading a book.

From the moment a foal is born, the mare begins cleaning it. This is the beginning of the bonding ritual, securing baby to mother in a tight bond that only death can break. Once the baby stands and nurses, mother stands patiently, letting her little one get as much milk as he needs.

As the baby begins to get stronger over the days, he starts to wander. The mare keeps a close watch on him, and he is never out of her sight. If an unfamiliar horse comes anywhere near the baby, the mare meets him with bared teeth and pinned-back ears. And if the intruder doesn't get the message, flailing hooves are sure to follow.

The mare is the foal's protector, and she is also his teacher. She lets him know which behaviors are acceptable and which are not. Although patient, she is strict. The foal can play with his mom, but he can't be disrespectful. The lessons he learns from her will come in handy in his future dealings with other horses.

If the mare is a saddle horse, the baby can also learn the ways of humans through her. By tagging along on the trail when Mom is being ridden, the foal gets to see the world from a young age. By following along when Mom is being led, the baby gets used to walking with people. And when it's time for the foal to learn to lead, Mom can serve as a motivator as she walks up ahead.

Unfortunately, mares rarely have the opportunity to wean their foals on their own. Humans usually make this happen sooner than the mare would want. (Mares usually prefer to wean at about six months, but humans usually take babies away at three to four months. And trauma results for both mother and baby.) Compassionate weaning takes place at the same age as other weaning; it's just gentler. Considerate horse handlers make the process gradual, moving the baby to the stall next door and keeping him there for a few days before moving him a bit farther and farther away until the two have learned to lead separate lives in a gentle and gradual manner. Given the power of the bond between mare and foal, compassionate weaning should be the norm everywhere.

229

Applying Eye Drops

IT'S NOT UNUSUAL FOR HORSES to suffer injuries to the eye. They can have run-ins with stable doors and fence posts or receive a kick from another horse. Grass seeds or thorns can scrape or puncture its surface. Infection or disease can also affect the eye. For all situations, eye drops may be required for treatment.

Types of eye drops that horses might need include those containing antibiotics for inflammations of the tear sac, artificial tear solutions for horses with keratoconjunctivitis sicca (dry eye), drugs that draw fluid out of the eye or reduce production of fluid for horses with glaucoma, iodine solution for flushing the eyes of horses with eye worms, or even eye drops made from the horse's own blood serum to help cure infection.

You might need to apply eye drops several times daily for weeks, and many horses grow wary of being approached with that now-familiar bottle. Often, applying eye drops to a horse's eye requires patience, skill, and cunning.

If your horse is used to having her forelock combed, her muzzle wiped, or her face brushed, try those acts first, then apply the drops while she is relaxed and not expecting them. An assistant can hold the horse's head still while the drops are administered. Try distracting the horse with peppermints or other treats.

ADMINISTERING THE EYE DROPS

1. Gently lift the horse's upper eyelid while pulling down on the lower eyelid.

2. Place a small amount of the solution in the lower corner of the eye. Avoid putting any pressure on the eye as you do so.

3. Let the liquid flow across the eye. Close the eye and gently rub it to ensure the eye drops are distributed across the entire surface of the eye.

Follow a similar technique for eyewashes or eye ointment.

Use the same precautions you would in giving any medication. Never share eye drops between horses as that is a good way to spread infection. Never give eye drops prescribed for another horse unless your veterinarian gives the okay. Eye drops containing steroids can cause blindness if they are used improperly. The nozzle should be free of dirt or discharge before using. Don't save partially used eye medication. If your horse doesn't need all of it, throw it away. Ask your vet if the drops require refrigeration or special handling.

If your budget permits, your veterinarian may place an indwelling catheter, a tube that allows the eye drops to be administered directly into the eye without handling the horse. A soft rubber tube is inserted beneath the eyelid and then braided into the mane so the drops can be applied from a distance. Another option is a tiny battery-driven pump that allows for a constant infusion of drops into the eye.

Natural Living

THE TREND TOWARD LIVING NATURALLY is well-established in humans, and it's starting to take hold in the horse world, too. With horses, this trend is not just about natural supplements and organic food. It's all about daily lifestyle.

Researchers have studied wild horses to learn how nature designed horses to live. They discovered that wild equines don't need their feet trimmed or shod, they don't need their teeth floated, and they rarely suffer from lameness or colic. The conclusion many horse people have come to as a result of these observations is that horses that live a more natural lifestyle are going to be healthier.

Here are a few suggestions for providing your horse with a way of life that is closer to what he might experience in the wild:

• Feed lots of roughage, and often. Horses have evolved to eat low-quality forage nearly 18 hours a day. If your vet gives you the okay, provide your horse with plenty of grass hay to nibble on throughout the day.

• Consider going barefoot. Many horses do fine without shoes, and some experts believe this is the best way for them to live. Research barefoot trimming, and talk to an experienced barefoot trimmer about the possibility of skipping shoes.

• Provide plenty of exercise. Wild horses travel about 20 miles (32 km) a day in their search for food. Give your horse as much as you can in his living space, and provide him with daily exercise. It is unnatural for a horse to stand in a stall all day, so do whatever you can to get his feet moving.

• Offer companionship. Horses are herd animals and need the company of other horses for their mental health. If your horse lives alone, consider getting him another horse or pony for a companion, or keep him at a boarding stable.

By introducing your horse to as many elements of a natural lifestyle as you can, you'll do a lot to keep him healthy and happy.

New Forest Pony

SOME 3,000 WILD NEW FOREST PONIES still roam England's New Forest, a 90,000-acre (7,078 m²) preserve in Hampshire on England's southern coast from which they take their name, but these days the quiet, willing ponies are also known as versatile equine athletes. Their speed over rough terrain and natural jumping ability ensure their reputation as all-around ponies. They can be found participating in dressage, driving, jumping, Pony Club, polo, and gymkhana, and they have been trained to carry riders who have physical disabilities. The breed is popular throughout Europe, North America, and Australia.

New Forest Ponies are among the eleven native breeds, known as mountain and moorland ponies, that have inhabited England for centuries. They are known to have grazed in the New Forest since at least 1016, when their presence was first recorded. Various other breeds, including Arabs, Hackneys, and other pony breeds such as the Fell, Dartmoor, and Exmoor, were introduced into their habitat over the years, in an effort to improve their type.

Sturdy and tough, New Forest Ponies reflect the environment in which they evolved. That hardiness and a calm, gentle disposition, combined with strength and intelligence, makes them favorites as riding horses for children.

The sporty ponies are elegant yet easy to maintain. They display good movement in all three gaits and have strong, muscular hindquarters with good depth of body.

New Forest Ponies stand from 12 hands to 14.2 hands. Horses of this breed are found in bay, brown, gray, chestnut, roan, and black. Some white markings are permitted on the head and legs, but they must not be the result of scars. Colors and patterns that are not permitted are blue-eyed creams, palomino, piebald, and skewbald.

New Forest Pony

Show Jumping

AN EXCITING SPECTATOR SPORT that is popular worldwide is show jumping, in which powerful equine athletes team up with talented riders to negotiate challenging obstacles in the show ring.

Most people are familiar with show jumping on the Olympic level, when horses and riders compete as teams and individuals for medals. Throughout the world, show jumpers compete for cash prizes at large events. But besides being a high-level sport, show jumping also takes place on a more minor level. At local horse shows around the world, show jumpers participate in events with lower jumps that are still exciting nonetheless.

The rules of show jumping are fairly simple. Horses are expected to negotiate a course of jumps in a prescribed amount of time, garnering as few faults as possible. Faults are accumulated when horses knock down all or part of a jump, or if the horse refuses to take a jump. The horse and rider team with the best time and the least amount of faults wins the competition.

At the highest levels, warmbloods are most often seen in show jumping competition. When the sport is held as part of a three-day event competition, Thoroughbreds predominate. In smaller shows, just about any breed can be seen participating, from Appaloosas to Saddlebreds.

Man O' War

PROBABLY THE MOST FAMOUS RACEHORSE of all time, the legend of Man O' War—nicknamed Big Red—still lives on almost 100 years after his birth. The chestnut colt, foaled in 1917 to a mare named Mahubah out of stallion named Fair Play, won twenty out of twenty-one races by the time he was three years old. He went on to sire sixty-four stakes winners and 200 champions. He also set three world records during his racing career.

Surprisingly Man O' War did not win the Triple Crown. In fact, he didn't race in the Kentucky Derby. In the early 1900s, the Derby, Preakness, and Belmont were not considered the pinnacle of horse racing, and Man O' War's owner, Samuel D. Riddle, felt it was too early in the horse's third year to go the mile and a quarter distance.

Consequently, Man O' War was never even entered in the Kentucky Derby. He did win the Preakness and Belmont one year.

The 16.2-hand colt got better the more he raced, and he won the Lawrence Realization Stakes by more than 100 lengths. After winning a match race in Canada, Man O' War was retired to stud in Kentucky, at Fairway Farms. He lived the remainder of his life there until he died of a heart attack at the age of thirty. He was buried on the farm after a funeral attended by more than 2,000 people, but his body has since been moved to the Kentucky Horse Park in Lexington. Above Man O' War's grave stands a bronze statue of the famous stallion.

Arena Footing

IT'S NOT SOMETHING many horse people think about, but it's an important part of your horse's environment: the footing—that is, the dirt under your horse's feet—in your arena.

Whether you have your own riding ring or are using a boarding stable facility or community arena, it's important to take note of the footing. If the arena where you ride has good footing, your horse's legs will be healthier for it. The good footing will also encourage your horse to move forward with energy—something you want her to do when you ride.

When planning an arena, always consider the footing. High ground that drains well is imperative if you don't want to be sloshing around in puddles for days after a rainstorm. The arena should also be level so you aren't going uphill and downhill when you ride. A 2 degree grade is all you should have, and that's just to encourage drainage.

The base material should be something that provides cushion to the horses and keeps rocks from coming to the surface. A lot of stables use decomposed granite. The top layer can be a mixture of surfaces. Sand is a great choice because it doesn't turn into mud when it gets wet.

If the footing is too hard, it is tough on the horse's joints. Footing that is too deep, on the other hand, puts horses at risk for strains and other injuries. Footings that become muddy or slippery are also a hazard to the horse's well-being. Dusty footing can cause respiratory irritation for both horse and rider. Footing should also be consistent throughout the arena. Arenas that have deep dirt in some areas and hard dirt in others are tough on a horse's legs.

If you have control over the footing in the arena where you ride, do some research and find out how to get the best footing possible for your horse. The expense will pay off in the long run in the form of fewer veterinary bills.

Treating Diarrhea in Horses

LIKE PEOPLE, HORSES CAN SUFFER the discomforts of diarrhea. The gut-wrenching pain and loose, liquid stools can have many causes, including the following.

- Bacterial diseases such as Potomac Horse Fever
- Bacterial agents such as salmonella or clostridium
- Certain antibiotics or non-steroidal anti-inflammatory drugs
- Intestinal parasites
- Eating too much grain
- Ingestion of toxic plants or blister beetles
- Bowel strangulation or obstruction
- Liver disease
- Peritonitis (inflammation of the membrane of the abdominal cavity)

Diarrhea in adult horses can be acute or chronic. Acute diarrhea comes on suddenly and is usually caused by bacterial agents or ingestion of a toxic substance. Chronic diarrhea persists for more than a month and can be a challenge to diagnose. Possible causes include bowel inflammation, noninflammatory colon conditions caused by changes in diet or altered intestinal "bugs" as a result of antibiotic treatment, chronic liver disease or intestinal cancer.

Diarrhea is uncomfortable, and it also leads to dehydration and electrolyte imbalance. In horses, massive fluid loss can occur rapidly because of the large volume of the colon and cecum. Those concerns must be dealt with before a veterinarian can start to find out why a horse has diarrhea.

Supportive care with fluids is necessary to prevent the horse from going into shock or developing laminitis. Horses with severe diarrhea may require hospitalization and intensive care.

TREATMENT

Once the horse is stabilized, a medical history and diagnostic laboratory tests such as fecal exams can help to isolate the cause. Because diarrhea can have so many causes, it can often be difficult to determine the reason for it. A definite diagnosis is reached in fewer than 50 percent of cases seen.

Fortunately, whatever the cause, treatment is similar. It usually involves replacing fluids and electrolytes, deworming the horse if it has a load of parasites, or treating with antibiotics for bacterial diseases.

Health Note

When diarrhea is accompanied by pain, fever, weakness, or depression, it's an emergency situation. Call your veterinarian immediately. Diarrhea in horses is more likely to cause death than diarrhea in other animals or in people.

Work on Your Equitation

EQUITATION, QUITE SIMPLY, is how you sit on a horse. Part of it is about looking good, but the other part is about having balance and security on the horse.

The type of equitation you should strive for depends on the type of riding you are doing. If you are competing in jumping events, you want equitation with a forward seat. If riding Western, you want to sit farther back and deeper in the saddle. Dressage riders ride with longer stirrups than do hunter and jumper riders, which changes their position in the saddle.

When you ride today, spend some time focusing on your equitation. Study the way you should be riding for your discipline. If you take lessons, or have taken them in the past, think about what your instructor told you about lining up your body in the saddle.

Consider your seat and pelvic bones and whether they are making contact with the saddle. Think about where your leg is positioned. It should be directly under you. No matter what your discipline, these basic truths apply.

A good book to study for English equitation is *Centered Riding*, by Sally Swift. Here you will learn all about how to properly sit in the saddle, whatever English discipline you choose, so that you are well balanced. This will give you a more balanced and independent seat, and it will also make carrying you easier for your horse. (If you ride Western or saddleseat, you may find some of Swift's advice helpful, too.)

Thoroughbred

THE THRILLING THOROUGHBRED descends from a small group of stallions imported to England from the Middle East in the late seventeenth and early eighteenth centuries: the Byerley Turk, the Godolphin Arabian, and the Darley Arabian. Those stallions, bred with native English horses as well as some mares imported from the Middle East, put their stamp on a new breed that became known as the Thoroughbred.

Probably an Arab, the Byerley Turk was captured at the siege of Buda, in Hungary, by Captain Robert Byerley. The Byerley Turk was a distinguished sire, and among his descendants was Herod, a fine racehorse who also contributed greatly to the Thoroughbred lineage.

The Darley Arabian was foaled in 1700 and sold in 1704 to Thomas Darley, who purchased him in Syria and shipped him home to Yorkshire, where he was bred to numerous mares, most notably Betty Leeds, who produced the colts Flying Childers and Bartlet's Childers. It was through the Childers line that the Darley Arabian became the great-great-grandsire of the famed Eclipse, from whom more than 90 percent of the world's Thoroughbreds today trace their lineage. The Darley Arabian's influence on the development of the Thoroughbred cannot be overstated.

The Godolphin Arabian was imported to England in 1730 by Edward Coke and acquired by Lord Godolphin, who bred him to several well-known mares, including Roxana, with whom he sired the great racehorse Lath and Cade, the sire of Matchem, another great who gave both speed and a gentle disposition to his descendants. It was said in 1850 that "the blood of the Godolphin Arabian is in every stable in England."

The Thoroughbred is handsome with a well-chiseled head, widely spaced eyes, long neck, evenly curved back, lean, muscular body, and clean, long legs. It stands 15 to more than 17 hands and comes in a range of solid colors, primarily bay, brown, or dark bay, chestnut, black, and gray, and less commonly in roan, palomino, and white. Markings include stars, blazes, stockings, and socks.

Thoroughbreds' Arabian heritage gives them a spirited, bold temperament. Their reputation is as "hot-blooded" racehorses who can reach speeds of up to 40 miles per hour (17.9 m/s), but their versatility and intelligence also make them well suited to such varied disciplines as eventing, show jumping, dressage, barrel racing, and polo. For experienced equestrians, whether they be recreational riders or mounted police, Thoroughbreds are the ultimate mount.

Thoroughbred

Hayrides

It's hard to pin down exactly when the fall custom of hayrides first began in the United States, although some historians believe it started in Kansas in the 1800s. Regardless of how or where it was born, the hayride has become a classic seasonal tradition

The most traditional type of hayride takes place in a horse-drawn wagon. Usually pulled by two draft horses, the horse-powered hayride features a flatbed wagon littered with loose straw and decorated with straw bales. The ride travels through scenic areas and might last a couple of hours. Travelers may be taken to a location where they are served hot chocolate, apple cider, or another treat, after which they make the return trip in the wagon.

A modernized version of the hayride is in a flat-bed truck. This is much less traditional and not as fun, since the grinding of the truck engine and spewing exhaust puts a distinct damper on the experience.

Hayrides usually take place in autumn, but they can be held at any time of the year. Christmas hayrides often take place at night, feature Christmas lights on the wagon, and include caroling by the occupants.

Flicka

A little sorrel filly named Flicka first came to life on the pages of Mary O'Hara's 1941 best-selling book, *My Friend Flicka*. It's hard to find a young horse lover who hasn't read this book or seen one or both of the movies based on this novel.

In *My Friend Flicka*, a Wyoming rancher's son befriends a renegade mustang filly, proving to his disapproving father and himself that he has skills as a horse trainer. The book won the hearts of so many horse lovers that it was made into a movie starring child actor Roddy McDowell.

O'Hara followed up *My Friend Flicka* with two sequels: *Thunderhead, Son of Flicka* in 1943 and *Green Grass of Wyoming* in 1946. These two books were made into movies as well, although neither were as successful as the original.

In 2006, *My Friend Flicka* was remade into a film called simply *Flicka*, starring country music star Tim McGraw. During the making of the film, two horses died, creating a public relations nightmare for the film studio, 20th Century Fox. The American Humane Association, which monitors animal actors used in film productions, investigated and cleared the production company of any wrongdoing, labeling the horses' deaths as unpreventable accidents.

Horse Stretches

MOST ATHLETES STRETCH BEFORE they work out, so why should horses be any different? Since you can't tell this to your horse and expect him to do his own stretches, you have to help him.

Here are some stretches to try on your horse before you ride. He will like these because most of them involve carrots. Walk your horse for about five minutes before you stretch, to help loosen up his muscles. Don't do it if he has worked hard and is tired. If he has an injury, talk to your vet before you do stretches.

EXERCISE

1. Get a carrot and hold your horse on a lead rope with one hand while you put the carrot at the center of his chest with the other hand. He will stretch down to get the carrot.

2. Next, hold a carrot between his forelegs to get him to stretch his neck down even farther.

3. Hold the carrot at his side near the middle of his barrel so he has to stretch to get it. Do the same thing on the other side.

4. Tie your horse or have someone hold the lead rope. Lift his left front leg and pull it gently forward in a straight line using steady motion. Be careful not to twist it to the side. Hold the leg out for a few seconds to give it a stretch. Do the same with the other foreleg.

5. Go to your horse's left hind leg and stand to the side, facing his rump. Reach down and lift the leg as if you were going to clean out the hoof. Gently pull the leg forward toward the belly, being careful not to twist or jerk it. Hold it here for a few seconds, and then walk the leg back toward the back of the horse. Let the horse set the leg down on his own. Do the same thing with the other hind leg.

Navicular Disease

THE NAVICULAR IS A SMALL BONE in the horse's foot that can cause big problems in horses. Horses with navicular, as the disease is known, become unsound in the front feet, suffering pain in the hooves.

Navicular is a common cause of lameness in horses. It appears to develop as the result of several factors, including inflammation of the bursa—located between the navicular bone and the tendon of the deep digital flexor—and decreased blood supply to the navicular bone, which causes it to degenerate.

It's unclear why this happens, but veterinary researchers believe the condition might to some extent be hereditary. Horses that are most prone to navicular are mature riding horses and racing, cutting, and roping horses, in particular those with abnormal conformation of the front feet or legs. Usually both front feet are affected, although one may be worse than the other.

DIAGNOSIS

Navicular is diagnosed through observation of the horse's physical signs, such as lameness. Horses with navicular tend to place their weight on the toe so as to avoid the pain caused by putting pressure on the heel. They also frequently shift their weight. These habits can indicate the presence of navicular. The veterinarian can confirm the disease through the use of hoof testers and nerve blocks.

TREATMENT

There is no cure for navicular, but certain treatments are available to manage the disease for a period of months or years. Medications that reduce pain and inflammation and increase blood flow to the navicular bone can help keep a horse comfortable. Corrective shoeing helps as well.

Some horses suffer severe pain from navicular. In these cases, the veterinarian can perform surgery to cut the nerves in the heels that supply the navicular area, preventing the horse from feeling any pain. This technique can have complications, however, and it should be used only as a last resort.

Your Horse's Personality

HORSES ARE A LOT LIKE PEOPLE; they all have their own personalities. One horse can be shy and retiring, while another can be outgoing and bossy. Age and breed may not even be a factor, although younger horses tend to be more fractious than their older counterparts.

If you haven't already figured out your horse's personality, it's high time you did. You need to have a sense of who your horse is so you can truly understand her behavior. If you are having problems with your horse, the key to solving these issues no doubt lay in her personality.

A number of famous clinicians have published details on the different types of horse personalities out there and how they differ from one another. Linda Tellington-Jones's book *Getting in Touch: Understand and Influence Your Horse's Personality* shows how the shape of a horse's head, ears, eyes, chin, and nostrils can belie her personality. Clinician Pat Parelli breaks down the different equine dispositions in his DVD *Horsenalities*. Trainer Charles Wilhelm details different types of horses in his tome *Build Your Dream Horse*.

All of the different equine personality types described by these experts are right on the mark. Study them, and you'll discover your horse among these distinct descriptions.

Once you have a handle on your horse's personality, it's a good idea to evaluate your own disposition to see how the two of your compare. For instance, if you are a nervous rider and you have a horse that is timid, you may be mismatched. Does this mean you need to get rid of your horse? No, but it gives you insight into why the two of you are having problems. Your next step will be to find ways to boost your own confidence and that of your horse as well.

On the other hand, if you are a fearful rider and your horse is as brave as they get, rarely spooking at anything, and frequently being labeled as "bombproof," you now have a sense of why the two of you get along so well.

You can only learn more about your connection to your horse by discovering her innate personality. A deep understanding of your equine companion will enhance your relationship.

243

Cleveland Bay

SAID TO BE ENGLAND'S OLDEST established horse breed, the Cleveland Bay takes its name from the Cleveland area of northeast England where it was developed. In the Middle Ages, the Cleveland Bay was bred at monasteries for use as pack animals. Its ancestors probably include pack horses from the Yorkshire Dales known as Chapman horses for their association with the itinerant peddlers known as chapmen. Sometime before the end of the seventeenth century, the Chapman horses were bred with Arab Barbs to create a larger, more powerful pack and harness animal.

The breed's popularity spread beyond its original home, and it was frequently used to pull carts and wagons for farmers. Some Clevelands were crossed with Thoroughbreds to produce tall, elegant carriage horses. In 1884, however, the Cleveland Bay Horse Society of Great Britain published a stud book containing stallions and mares whose pedigrees went back more than a century and had not been crossed with other breeds. From then on, the breed was maintained with no outcrosses, and it is known for its uniform characteristics, including size, stamina, disposition, and color. The breed almost became lost after the advent of motorized vehicles, but a few dedicated breeders saved it from extinction.

Today's Cleveland Bay is intelligent and sensible but with a strong character. As its name suggests, this bold and honest horse is always bay in color with black legs, mane, and tail. It stands 16 to 16.2 hands, and its action is true, straight, and free.

Because of Cleveland Bays' stamina, hardy nature, and versatility, they have been used in dressage and show jumping, and true to their heritage they remain excellent carriage and driving horses. Teams of Clevelands compete in driving trials or are driven as singles or in pairs for recreational purposes. They make ideal heavy-weight hunters for the field, and they can be exhibited in the show ring either as in-hand, ridden, or working hunters. Mounted police appreciate them for their soundness and good temperament. Nonetheless, the Cleveland Bay is considered to be a rare breed, with fewer than 125 in North America.

Cleveland Bay

Flat Racing

IT'S WHAT THOROUGHBREDS DO BEST: flat racing. Flat racing is a form of horseracing that takes place on a flat track. The track can be a dirt track or turf (grass track). The horses break from a starting gate. In Thoroughbred racing, they usually run anywhere from three furlongs (³/₈ mile [603 m]) to more than 2 miles (3.2 km), depending on the country's standards.

Other breeds also participate in flat racing in the United States. Quarter Horses, which are sprinters, run at ³/₄ mile (1.2 km) or less. So do Paint Horses and Appaloosas. Arabians flat race from three furlongs (³/₈ mile [603 m]) to 1³/₄ miles (2.8 km).

Wagering is popular with flat racing, particularly Thoroughbred racing. People who bet on flat racing practice handicapping, which is the art of predicting which horses will win based on a variety of factors. The term "handicapped" is used in another context as well. Horses are literally "handicapped" in certain races, which means they are saddled with extra weight to level the field, which may vary based on performance and age.

Thoroughbred racehorses begin their careers at the tender age of two, and they rarely race beyond the age of five. Controversy rages over whether these horses are started too young, before their bones have a chance to fully develop. The death of the champion Thoroughbred Barbaro in 2008 led to an outcry to reconsider the starting age of racing Thoroughbreds.

Mares of Diomedes

MOST HORSES IN MYTHOLOGY are benevolent creatures, mystifying humankind with their beauty and magical powers. But in the case of the Mares of Diomedes, horses take the form of monsters.

In Greek mythology, the Mares of Diomedes were wild and spectacular, but they were also man-eaters. The four fire-breathing horses belong to Diomedes, a giant who lived on the shores of the Black Sea. One of the Twelve Labors, dangerous tasks carried out by Heracles as penance for killing his wife and children, was to steal the Mares. Two different version of this myth exist. In one, Heracles' favorite companion, Abderus, was eaten by the Mares, garnering Heracles' wrath and causing him to kill Diomedes and feed him to the Mares. In the other version, Heracles used the Mares to lure Diomedes to him and then fed the body of Diomedes to the Mares.

The Mares of Diomedes are pictured in both Greek and Roman art as wild, untamable beasts thirsting for blood. Alexander the Great's horse, Bucephalus, was believed to be descended from the Mares. (See Day 3.)

Leather Care

ONE OF THE MOST INTOXICATING SMELLS to a horseperson is the smell of leather. Walk into a tack room, and the scent overwhelms you with warm feelings about time you've spent with horses.

Your leather tack is valuable because you love the way it looks, smells, and feels, and it's valuable also for the work it does for you. You depend on the straps on your leather bridle to stay strong and the leather on your saddle to stay pliable and supple. You need all those leather straps and pieces to be at their best so they can serve you while you ride.

To keep your leather in good shape, you need to clean it on a regular basis, at least once a month. Use products made just for leather when you do. Dry it thoroughly after cleaning.

Store your tack in a dry cool place, out of the rain and sunlight. If you get caught in the rain while riding, dry your tack off with a clean towel when you get back to the barn.

Protect leather saddles with a saddle cover when not in use and dust them in between cleaning with a towel. Treat your leather tack well, and it will last for decades.

Strangles

THIS BACTERIAL DISEASE IS CALLED strangles because affected horses may develop a harsh cough or noisy breathing. Caused by the *streptococcus equi* bacteria, it is a nasty customer that attacks the lymph nodes, which are important to the healthy functioning of the immune system.

Strangles is an infectious disease that can be transmitted between horses directly or indirectly. Shared drinking water is one source of transmission. Another is contact with stalls that have been contaminated.

Seven to twelve days after horses have been exposed to the bacteria, they start showing signs of the disease: fever, depression, and a runny nasal discharge that eventually thickens and usually becomes yellow.

Strangles is most common in younger horses between the ages of four months and five years, whose immune systems are not as developed. Older horses, who have been exposed to more "bugs" over their lives, are less likely to be affected. Horses that have had strangles infections develop some immunity, but their resistance decreases with time.

DIAGNOSIS

As strangles progresses, the area of the throat where the lymph nodes are situated begins to swell, filling with pus. Sometimes an abscess, known as a guttural pouch infection, forms and then breaks open, the thick pus oozing out. If the abscess doesn't rupture on its own, it may need to be lanced and drained by a veterinarian.

When a guttural pouch infection is suspected, the veterinarian will use an endoscope to take a look, obtain a culture via a swab, and flush the pouches with antibiotics. Systemic antibiotics will also be administered to fight the infection.

TREATMENT

The primary treatment for horses with strangles is rest in an isolated stall. In a mild infection, the disease will simply run its course. Some veterinarians prescribe antibiotics to prevent an abscess from forming, but this is controversial because it can reduce the horse's ability to build immunity against the disease, resulting in reinfection. Other veterinarians prefer to give antibiotics only after an abscess has formed and ruptured. Antibiotics, and sometimes a tracheostomy (an incision on the neck to create an airway so the horse can breathe), may be necessary in severe cases, in which the horse has a high fever and severe respiratory difficulty because of the abscess.

Most horses recover, but 15 to 20 percent develop secondary infections or complications. These include laryngeal inflammation, paralysis, and chronic infection of the guttural pouches. These horses become carriers. Some carriers shed the strep bacteria and may have recurrent episodes of coughing and nasal discharge. Others don't show signs of the disease but spread the bacteria to other horses.

COMPLICATIONS

Some horses may experience more serious complications of strangles. Purpura hemorrhagica is an immune-mediated problem that causes severe inflammation of the blood vessels, leading to swollen legs and hemorrhaging of the gums and mucous membranes. It generally sets in three to four weeks after the initial infection. Purpura hemorrhagica is treated aggressively with antibiotics, steroids to dampen any immune over-response, diuretics, leg wraps if necessary, and hydrotherapy, usually in a hospital.

In "bastard" strangles, the strep bacteria make their way to the lungs, liver, or kidneys, causing abscesses in those organs. The abscesses may enlarge and rupture. If this occurs, the resulting inflammation and infection can threaten the horse's life.

Vaccines may not prevent the disease, but they can lessen its severity. A horse who is already showing signs of the disease cannot be vaccinated, and vaccination should also be avoided in horses that have had strangles within the past year. Giving a vaccine to these horses, who already have high numbers of antibodies to the disease, could cause them to develop purpura hemorrhagica. Ask your veterinarian to take a blood sample to check the titer, or level of antibodies, before giving a vaccine.

PREVENTION

Strep bacteria can survive in freezing temperatures, in water, and on various surfaces, including wood and glass. Even the cleanest, best-run facilities can have strangles outbreaks. Nonetheless, practicing good hygiene around the barn and isolating all new horses that come to your property can help to prevent strangles.

Horse Toys

SOME OLDER HORSES DON'T SEEM to mind just standing around, but if you have a young horse—or one who is young at heart—consider providing him with some toys to keep him amused when he's not working.

Horse toys come in all forms, from edible treats to things he can push with his nose or pull with his teeth. Both types attach to the side of the stall or hang from the ceiling, and the edible toys require the horse to work to get at the food attached to the toy.

Mouthy horses particularly like toys that are designed to be picked up. Balls with handles on them are a favorite. (Some horses have been seen tossing these toys and chasing them.) Large toy balls are meant to be bitten at or pushed, and they double as a great despooking item. They help your horse feel confident around a large, unfamiliar object.

Go to a tack store or shop online and peruse the horse toys available in your price range. Think about your horse's personality to figure out which ones are most suited to him. If money is tight, consider making your own toy. A lot of horses love construction cones and can play for hours picking them up and tossing them around. Or, you can devise a contraption that you can attach to your horse's stall to keep him amused, as long as it's safe. Items such as balloons are good, as well as flags and plastic bags. Your horse may act afraid of them at first, but if he's a playful sort, he'll be going at it in no time.

Swedish Warmblood

UNLIKE MANY SPORT HORSES that were originally developed as driving or working horses, the elegant and intelligent Swedish Warmblood has been bred in Sweden as a riding horse for more than 400 years. It was created as a military horse in the seventeenth century. Breeds that contributed to its development included Swedish work horses, Friesians, Hanoverians, Trakehners, and Thoroughbreds. The first official studbook for the Swedish Warmblood horse was developed in the late 1800s. In 1928, breeders founded the Swedish Warmblood Association.

The breed is known for its exceptional athleticism, and as the need for horses in the military went by the wayside in the 1970s, the Swedish Warmbloods were repurposed as sport horses. They make excellent dressage horses, having both the mind and the movement to excel in the sport. They also excel at jumping, three-day eventing, and carriage driving. Some members of the breed compete successfully in multiple disciplines. It's not unusual for Olympic riders on Swedish horses to medal in dressage and combined training.

Swedish Warmbloods stand from 16 to more than 17 hands and are distinguished by a long, muscular neck, rhythmic gaits, willing temperament, and versatility. The ideal Swedish Warmblood is noble in appearance, correct and sound, and has superb competitive temperament, rideability, and movement or jumping ability.

Swedish Warmbloods mature slowly, and they may not reach their full growth until they are seven years old. Young horses are not started until age three, and they don't begin serious schooling until they are four years old. Approximately 3,500 foals are born each year in Sweden, and approximately 150 Swedish Warmbloods are registered annually in the United States.

This is a friendly and sensitive horse with a positive attitude and a competitive nature. Treat it with "horse sense," and it will always give you its best.

251

Swedish Warmblood

Horses for the Blind

GUIDE DOGS FOR THE BLIND are a common sight in cities around the world. These dogs dutifully provide assistance to their sight-impaired handlers. But have you ever seen a guide horse for the blind? If the Guide Horse Foundation has its way, guide horses may become as common as guide dogs.

The Guide Horse Foundation, located in North Carolina, is currently experimenting with the concept of using Miniature Horses as guides for people who are legally blind. Guide horses serve the same purposes as their canine counterparts; they help the sight-impaired find their way out in public. They also receive the same privileges as guide dogs, and they are allowed in all places where guide dogs are allowed, including on airplanes.

The Guide Horse Foundation program uses Miniature Horses that are donated by breeders around the country. It takes years to train a guide horse, and it must be done by a professional trainer. Training even includes housebreaking, which allow the handler to take the horse indoors. All candidate horses are given an intelligence test prior to be accepted into the program. The horse must also demonstrate stamina since guide dog work can be physically demanding. Potential guide horse owners must also receive training so they know how to handle their guide horses.

Guide horses are taught the following jobs:

• Basic leading

• Voice command recognition

• Stationary obstacle avoidance

• Moving obstacle avoidance

• Surface elevation change recognition

• Housebreaking

• Intelligent disobedience, which involves the horse making its own judgments about safety and disregarding the commands of the handler if they would put either the horse or handler in danger

The Guide Horse Foundation is a volunteer-run organization, and it provides guide horses for free to qualified handlers. To have a guide horse, a sight-impaired handler must live in a suburban or rural environment since guide horses need an outdoor living area. All guide horses are placed with another Miniature Horse for companionship.

Black Beauty

IN 1877, WHEN WRITER ANNA SEWELL died soon after completing her first and only novel, *Black Beauty*, she had no idea of what her book would ultimately accomplish. Because of *Black Beauty*, horses would never be thought of the same way again.

Black Beauty is set in late Victorian England. It is the fictional autobiography of a horse, who tells of his trials and tribulations as he is passed from one owner to another. Forced to work under a painful device called the bearing rein, Black Beauty describes with graphic candor the suffering he endures pulling a carriage around London.

After publication, a grassroots movement developed to banish the cruel bearing rein. Attempts to ban the device were successful, and soon other anti-cruelty laws were established in England as well. It was no longer acceptable for horse owners to beat their animals and starve them, which had been regular occurrences at that time.

Black Beauty remains a top-selling book that has been read by just about every horse lover in the world. It has been translated into many languages, and it was the inspiration for four feature-length films.

Before Sewell's death, she said the aim of *Black Beauty* was "to induce kindness, sympathy, and an understanding treatment of horses." She certainly achieved her goal.

Cavalettis

ONE OF THE MOST OFT-USED training devices, a set of cavalettis should be a part of every serious horseman's equipment.

Cavalettis are small jumps measuring anywhere from 6 to 12 inches (15 to 30 cm) in height. They are used to help horses learn where to place their feet when moving. Going over cavalettis helps the horse become aware of her foot placement, and teaches her to collect her gait. It also helps her from getting bored when you are working the arena.

Even just one cavaletti can be used for training, although it's good to have at least three. You can buy ready-made cavalettis, or you can build your own. It's best to use heavy wood for the poles so if the horse hits them with her foot, she will be aware of it and will learn to avoid doing this. Paint the poles a light color so the horse can easily see them on the ground.

When teaching your horse to work with cavalettis, you can start in-hand. Place the pole from the cavaletti directly on the ground and ask your horse to walk over it as you lead her. You can add other poles as well, making sure all are equally distant from each other and at least 6 feet (1.8 m) apart. Once your horse is comfortable walking over them and doesn't step on them or trip over them, graduate to a jog.

Next, work on cavalettis under saddle. Start with poles directly on the ground and gradually raise them. If you are working with a Western horse or one you don't plan to jump, keep the poles low—8 inches (20 cm) or below. Your horse may hop over them. Anything higher may elicit a bigger jump. If you are planning to jump your horse over larger obstacles, working first over cavalettis is a great way to build her confidence.

Travel Care

MOST OF THE TIME, horses themselves are transportation, but on some occasions they must be transported on wheels rather than on their own four legs. Whether you and your horse are heading to the veterinarian, a show, or a trail to meet friends for a ride, getting there safely is an essential element of the trip.

For a horse, walking into a small, dark trailer and then moving along the road without being able to see what's happening is an unnerving experience. As a prey animal, all of a horse's instincts tell him to have a means of escape. When escape doesn't seem possible, the horse will feel stressed. Fortunately, you can make travel more comfortable and less stressful for both of you.

First, teach your horse to load politely. This will save time getting on the road and can be essential in an emergency. Clinics or DVDs can teach you how to accomplish this successfully in one hour or less.

Consider the size of the trailer. It should be large enough for the horse to move its head around, move forward and backward a step, and shift his weight slightly from side to side. All of these factors will help the horse maintain his balance.

Drive thoughtfully. When the trailer moves smoothly at a constant speed, the horse will be less anxious. Avoid sudden starts or stops, going too fast around corners, and changing lanes. Factor in the weight of the horse in the trailer when braking or changing lanes.

You will need to start braking at a greater distance because of the additional weight. The extra weight will also increase the "whip" effect if the trailer swerves, so look ahead as you drive and be aware of any potential obstacles.

Maintain your vehicle and the trailer appropriately. Inflate the tires properly and ensure they have good tread. Check the brakes and lights to ensure that they work. The loaded trailer should pull level. If it doesn't, check the hitch and rebalance your load if necessary. See a mechanic if necessary.

Make your horse comfortable. Ensure that your horse has plenty of fresh air coming into the trailer, especially during hot weather. Try to travel at times when roads aren't congested so your horse won't be subject to the fumes of stop-and-go traffic.

Leave the trailer's interior lights on at night. This helps ensure that your horse won't be startled by the lights of vehicles behind the trailer.

Don't rely on medication to keep your horse calm unless there is no other option. Some horses react poorly to them, and most competitions do not permit the use of depressants and will test for them.

Common sense and taking a little extra care will help avoid major problems in hauling horses.

How to Clean Your Tack

IT'S A DIRTY, BORING JOB, but it must be done. At least once a month, preferably twice a month, you need to clean your tack.

If you are like most horsepeople, much of your tack is made of leather. You probably have a few synthetic pieces as well (such as a girth or halter), as well as metal parts.

1. Gather together whatever pieces of tack you use regularly. This will include your saddle (with the girth or cinch, and stirrups), bridle (with reins, martingales, and other devices you might use), halter and lead rope, breast collar, saddle pad, and other accessories.

2. Put together all the items you will need to clean your tack. Here is a list:

- Two buckets, both containing lukewarm water

- Leather soap

- Leather oil

- Leather conditioner

- Two tack sponges

- Clean rags or towels

- Toothbrush

- Small paintbrush

3. Start with one piece of your leather tack, such as your saddle. Wipe the dust off it with a rag or towel. Put some soap on the damp tack sponge and work it into a lather, using a circular motion. When trying to clean tight spots, use the toothbrush to get into the nooks and crannies. (This is especially necessary if you have a Western saddle with tooling.) If your tack is very dirty, the sponge will need frequently dipping into one of the buckets of water to clean it out.

4. After washing the entire piece of tack with the sponge and soap, use a clean sponge to wipe away all the soap residue. You want to make sure you get the soap off, but you don't want to saturate the leather with water.

5. If your tack is very new, dry, or old, you may want to oil it. Use a paintbrush to apply a light coat of leather oil over it, being careful not to get it on your clothes. Let the oil sit on the tack for at least an hour, then wipe off the residue with a rag or towel.

6. Next, use leather conditioner on the tack. After conditioning, rub it down with a dry cloth to bring out the sheen.

7. For synthetic tack, use a damp sponge and wipe it down. Do this several times until the water runs clean when you squeeze out the sponge. The good part about synthetic tack is that it's easy to care for, so this is all you really need to do to keep these pieces clean.

257

Falabella

THE FALABELLA IS A miniature horse that hails from Argentina. It might descend from Andalusians brought to South America and later abandoned by Spanish conquistadors. Natural selection, for whatever reason, led to horses of a smaller size. They were eventually developed as a breed some 150 years ago by the Falabella family, who still maintain it today. Some of the earliest photos of miniature horses depict the Falabella and date to 1905. Most Falabellas live at the family's farms in Argentina, but they are also found in North America, Great Britain, and other countries.

These little horses are gentle and docile. Outgoing and amiable in nature, they enjoy being petted, and they learn routines quickly, making them good companions for children. Falabellas have a long life span, with some living to be forty-five years old.

A Falabella can resemble any breed, depending on the breeder's preferences. It has fine, silky hair and thin, supple skin. The mane may be short and straight or long, falling on both sides of the neck. Narrow hooves have an oval shape. In color, it is usually black or brown but may also be found in Appaloosa, pinto, bay, or chestnut. All colors are permitted. The Falabella moves with an energetic gait. Most Falabellas stand between 28 and 34 inches, (71 and 86 cm) but there is no height restriction and some are as tall as 38 inches (96 cm).

This is a rare breed, with fewer than 900 registered with the Falabella Miniature Horse Association. Other associations that register the breed are the Falabella Horse Breeders Association and the International Falabella Miniature Horse Society. Only a few thousand are believed to exist throughout the world. That rarity makes them prized by people who appreciate the unusual.

Falabella

Equicaching

ONE OF THE NEWEST SPORTS to hit the world of U.S. trail riding is equicaching, which is essentially a treasure hunt on horseback. With the help of a global positioning system (GPS), riders search for caches hidden by other riders. The caches can contain anything from money to coupons to books to horse shampoo. You only discover what's in the cache when you find it. You then put something in the cache to replace what you took so the next equicacher has something of value waiting for her.

Caches are listed on equicaching websites, along with their GPS coordinates and descriptions of the cache containers. Rules dictate that all caches be placed within 10 feet (3 m) of an established horse trail in an area that allows equestrian use. A log book is included with each cache, and finders must sign the log to indicate they found the cache.

The sport is catching on among trail riders, and caches are being hidden in parks and national forests all around the United States.

Clever Hans

IN THE EARLY 1900s, Germany was all abuzz about a chestnut gelding named Clever Hans who could answer complicated math questions correctly by tapping his hoof. Owned by math teacher William von Olsten, Hans performed to large crowds throughout Germany, rarely getting answers wrong. Hans could respond to answers asked orally, and he could also answer those presented in written form. He could add, subtract, multiply, divide, work with fractions, tell time, keep track of the calendar, differentiate musical tones, and read, spell, and understand German. His notoriety spread beyond Europe, and he was even profiled in the *New York Times*.

Scientists were intrigued and became determined to find out what was going on. Their first suspicion was that the whole display was a trick, put on by von Olsten. After considerable study, they acknowledged that trickery was not involved.

Finally, a psychologist named Oskar Pfungst conducted an investigation and determined that Hans did not really know the answers to the questions, but was performing based on subconscious and subtle physical cues he was getting from von Olsten. Pfungst's findings were widely accepted in the scientific community, although von Olsten never accepted them, maintaining to the end that Hans knew the answers on his own.

Choosing a Farrier

THE EXPRESSION "NO HOOF, NO HORSE" is about as true as they come. If your horse's feet aren't in good shape, she won't be happy or healthy. For this reason, finding a good farrier is essential.

A good farrier is someone who will care for your horse's feet on a regular schedule, in a skilled and caring way. A farrier who doesn't show up when he or she is supposed to, who leaves your horse sore after a visit, or who won't answer your questions is not a good farrier.

The best way to find a good farrier is by referral. Ask other horse owners who they use. If you can find a few people who say glowing things about a particular farrier, consider giving that person a try. You can also ask your veterinarian for a referral. Many horse vets work with farriers on difficult cases, and therefore know who the best professional are in this field.

Keep in mind that having a good farrier doesn't excuse you from knowing a thing or two about your horse's feet. You should be able to tell when your horse's hooves don't look right, and if your horse is sore or lame. Make it your business to study different types of farrier work, including barefoot and therapeutic shoeing. Being an educated horse owner is the best way to ensure your horse gets good hoof care. (For more on hoof care, see Day 68.)

Equine Infectious Anemia

THIS SERIOUS VIRAL DISEASE can be fatal to horses, so it is essential to guard against it. The virus that causes equine infectious anemia (EIA) is transmitted between horses through the bite of a horsefly. It can also be spread through shared use of dental floats, needles, and other equipment that has been contaminated by the virus. Pregnant mares who are infected may lose their foals or pass the disease on to them at birth.

The signs of EIA develop seven to thirty days after exposure to the virus. Horses that have acute EIA are obviously unwell, with signs that include high fever, lethargy, depression, and anemia. It's not unusual for horses with the disease to develop thrombocytopenia, which is a decrease in platelets that causes hemorrhaging from the gums and elsewhere in the body. Their lower legs and the underside of the abdomen may swell, which is a condition called "stocking up."

DIAGNOSIS

To diagnose EIA, veterinarians must draw blood for what is called a Coggins test. Because EIA has the potential to become a widespread threat to other horses, veterinarians in the United States must report its diagnosis to state authorities and submit the blood sample for testing to a laboratory approved by the state. Each state has different requirements regarding frequency of the Coggins test. A veterinarian can advise you when it is necessary.

A current Coggins test is required for competitions and may be necessary to transport horses across state lines. Be prepared to show a horse's test results at state borders or before being allowed to bring it onto show grounds.

TREATMENT

An EIA infection is permanent. Horses that test positive for the disease must be euthanized or kept at least 200 yards (183 m) apart from other equines for the rest of their lives. They must also be branded to indicate that they are carriers of the disease. Carriers will have an intermittent fever, weight loss, and hind limb incoordination.

PREVENTION

Take precautions to help prevent the spread of EIA. Use syringes only once, and never share them between horses. Demand that any professional caring for your horse sterilize all instruments before using them. Board your horse only at stables that require proof of negative EIA status before admitting horses to their facilities. Check the EIA status of any horse you are considering purchasing.

261

Bending

IF YOU ARE WELL VERSED in horse training, then you already know how important bending is for your horse. If you know how to ride your horse but don't know a lot about what goes into training, then this is a great opportunity to learn.

Bending is when the horse forms an arc with his body, either to the right or the left. If you could see the horse from above, you'd notice that his body looks like a crescent moon when he is bending.

Horses must be taught to bend under saddle, with the help of the rider. This is one of the first things horses learn when they are being trained. If you have a young, green horse, repeated bending is vital to keep him supple and relaxed when being ridden. Even if your horse is a seasoned mount, it's a good idea to practice bending with him to keep him flexible.

You can practice bending with your horse in a few different ways. You can practice doing circles that are 60 feet (20 m) in diameter with your horse, where bending to the inside comes naturally as he makes the circle. If your horse is not well trained, he may try to drop his shoulder into the circle, or dive into it.

It's your job as the rider to get him to bend, which you can do by using your legs and your hands. If you don't know how to bend your horse, take a lesson from a trainer so you learn how it's done.

Another way to practice bending on your horse is to use barrels. At the walk, ask your horse to go around a barrel. He will need to arc his body to do this, bending toward the barrel. This is a good exercise for green horses who like to dive to the inside of a circle. The barrel gives him a guide for how to arc his body.

You can also encourage your horse to bend as you are riding straight. Tip his nose to the inside so you can see his eye, but ask him to move straight with your legs and your outside rein. This will teach him to soften one side of his body to the pressure of the rein.

If you practice bending with your horse on a regular basis, you'll notice he is more responsive to your legs and to the bridle. He will probably be more relaxed when you ride him and may even become more obedient.

Shire

THE SHIRE HAS BEEN KNOWN throughout England for centuries, but its home was the Midlands: the counties of Lincoln, Derby, Cambridge, Norfolk, Nottingham, Leicester, and Huntington. In medieval times it was called the Great Horse. These horses, with their reputation for strength, steadfastness, and courage, carried armored knights into battle. Later, their talents were turned to the more peaceful pursuits of agriculture and industry, and they were called by such names as the Leicestershire Cart Horse, the Old England Black Horse, and the Lincolnshire Giant. Today, they're simply called the Shire, shorthand for the counties that produced them.

Shires were used to pull carts to deliver ale from breweries to pubs, which was a task they first performed in the eighteenth century. Most Shires have been replaced by trucks these days, but some of them can still be seen performing their historical function at British breweries as well as at the Coors Visitor Center (formerly the Bass Museum) in Burton Upon Trent.

Although the Shire is a British breed, its development was aided by crosses to various Belgian and Dutch horses, including the Friesian. Robert Bakewell is widely credited with improving the breed in the eighteenth century—for a time it was known as the Bakewell Black—and making it the horse it is today.

This English draft breed is the tallest of all the pulling horses, with some stallions standing 18 hands or more. Shires stand a minimum of 16.2 hands with the average being 17.1 hands. The Shire is built to work, with a long, slightly arched neck; short, strong, muscular back; long, sweeping hindquarters that are wide and muscular; and long legs with dense bones. The long, lean head is topped with sharp and sensitive ears.

Large, alert eyes gaze out with a mild expression. Preferred colors are black, brown, bay, gray, or the rare chestnut/sorrel. In any color, excessive white markings and roaning are undesirable. Feathering down the back of the legs is fine, straight, and silky. Mares are slightly smaller than stallions, with a feminine appearance and plenty of room to carry a foal.

Shires will never again be used as a primary form of transportation, as they were in their nineteenth-century heyday, when more than a million Shires made the wheels of industry turn, but Shire horsepower is still appreciated in some areas of farming, commerce, and leisure.

Shire

Lead-Line Class

HORSES AREN'T JUST FOR teenaged girls, cowboys, and middle-aged women. Tiny tots enjoy horses, too. The lead-line class, seen in both English and Western shows, was created for young children who want to be part of the action.

Lead-line classes feature a well-behaved horse or pony all decked out in her best show apparel. Children aged seven and under compete in the class in their show clothes.

A person over the age of fifteen leads the horse by a rope at the walk as the judge observes the equitation of the little rider, who holds the reins as if he or she is riding alone.

In many classes, ribbons are given to all the riders so as not to disappoint the young entrants. Judges often express how difficult it is to officiate lead-line classes because of the cuteness factor of the exhibitors.

Mr. Ed

"A HORSE IS A HORSE, of course, of course." So begins the theme song to *Mr. Ed*, one of the most popular U.S. television shows of the 1960s.

Starring a palomino gelding named Bamboo Harvester, *Mr. Ed* featured a talking horse who would only speak in front of his owner, Wilbur Post. The horse would get Wilbur into all kinds of trouble with his misbehaviors and refusal to verify Wilbur's claims that he had a talking horse.

Bamboo Harvester was a skilled trick horse who could do things like open doors, answer the phone, and write with a pencil. He also wiggled his upper lip to appear as if he was talking. This was achieved by trainer Les Hilton, who ran a nylon thread under the horse's top lip. When the thread was jiggled, Ed's lip wiggled.

Mr. Ed is probably the most famous equine television star to ever grace the small screen. He won the coveted PATSY award, given to animal actors, no fewer than four times between 1962 and 1965.

Pulling Back

IT'S A SCARY SIGHT WHEN 1,000 pounds (455 kg) of horse gets thrown against a halter. Ask anyone who has seen a tied horse pull back, and they will verify this.

Pulling back when tied is a nasty habit that some horses develop usually by accident. The first incident starts when the horse spooks at something while tied, feels claustrophobic because he can't break free, and panics. He throws his weight against the halter and lead rope, and the halter breaks. The horse discovers he is free. Lesson learned: Pull back and you don't have to be tied up anymore.

Some horses are genuinely claustrophobic and just can't handle being tied. In many cases, however, horses have learned that one way to get out of having to stand is to simply lean back and break the halter.

If you have a horse who habitually pulls back, you need the help of a trainer. It takes a lot of effort to train a horse not to pull back, and it's usually too much for the average horse owner to manage.

To keep your horse from developing this unfortunate habit, follow these basic rules of tying.

Always tie with a safety knot. That way, you can untie your horse quickly if he starts to panic. If you use cross ties, make sure they have a safety release.

Be sure to tie your horse to a secure object, preferably one that is meant for securing horses. If your horse pulls back, you don't want the object to come out of the ground.

Pay attention to your horse when he's tied. Anticipate when something in the environment might scare him. React before it happens and untie him quickly. Then if he spooks, you'll be holding onto him instead of having him tied.

If your horse starts to pull back, stand behind him and shout. This will startle him into putting his weight back on his front end.

Use a tie clip that allows the lead rope to slide through it if your horse starts to pull back. Or you can try an elastic lead rope, designed for horses who pull back. You can buy either of these tools on the Internet.

Never tie your horse by the reins. If your horse pulls back, he will break your reins, your bridle, or his jaw.

Horse Cloning

SOME MARES BECOME PREGNANT in a not-so natural way. Cloning has hit the equine world, although not in every field.

Biological cloning is the process of producing genetically identical individuals. Italy produced the first cloned horse in 2003. In the United States, the first cloned horse was produced at Texas A&M University in 2005.

Cloned embryos are produced by placing the DNA-bearing nucleus of a horse's cell into an unfertilized egg that has had its nucleus removed. When the egg develops into an embryo, it is then implanted in a mare's uterus and carried to term. The resulting foal shares the DNA of the horse whose DNA was used to create the embryo. The mares that carry the embryos are screened for health and temperament, and watched closely when delivery is near to ensure that nothing goes wrong. The cloning process is extremely expensive—considerably more than most stud fees.

Cloning is of interest to horse owners who want to preserve or continue the genetic makeup of their performance horses. Equine sports that permit cloned competitors include carriage horse racing, endurance horse racing, cutting, dressage, polo, and show jumping. In dressage, for example, many of the horses are geldings. Cloning is a way to preserve and reproduce the genetic lines of an outstanding horse that otherwise couldn't produce offspring.

Not all horse registries permit cloning. The Jockey Club, which oversees the registration of Thoroughbreds, does not permit the registration of any foal produced by artificial insemination, embryo transfer or transplant, cloning, or any other form of genetic manipulation. The Jockey Club uses DNA testing to ensure that all foals registered were bred naturally. The American Quarter Horse Association also prohibits the registration of clones.

It remains to be seen whether horses created with the reproductive technology will be as healthy as the originals, or if they will be affected by the health problems that have plagued some other cloned animals, such as shortened life span and immune-system problems.

Happy in Bad Weather

IT'S A COLD NIGHT AND YOU ARE WARM and snug by the fire. What about your poor horse? Standing in the wind, rain, snow, and cold can't be pleasant for her. Right?

In truth, horses are much more tolerant of bad weather than humans. Our species is designed to seek shelter and stay out of bad weather. After all, we don't have winter coats to keep us warm and dry. Horses, on the other hand, evolved to live outdoors only. They don't have a denning instinct like dogs, cats, or humans. Nature equipped them to be able to handle bad weather. Hence those thick winter coats that start growing in the early fall.

Nevertheless, you will want to make sure your horse is comfortable when it's cold outside. If you love your horse, you want to feel like she's cozy and warm—even though that is really more of a human impulse.

Generally, horses are fine in cold weather as long as they stay dry. However, hundreds of years of human interference has rendered certain breeds with coats that hardly seem capable of keeping them warm in very cold weather. Horses that have short coats can benefit from being blanketed on cold nights. Older horses, sick horses, and horses that must stand tied during the night should also wear a blanket when the temperature drops. If the rain and snow are in the forecast, these horses should wear a water-resistant blanket.

One of the most unpleasant aspects of bad weather for horses is the lack of exercise they usually get when temperatures are uncomfortable for humans. If it's pouring rain out, the last thing you want to do is take your horse out. A day or two in a stall or small paddock without getting out won't kill your horse, but beyond that, she is going to start to feel pretty cooped up. A twenty-minute hand walk can do wonders for your horse's attitude as well as for her body. Invest in a good raincoat and rain boots, and get out there and get your horse moving even if it's pouring outside.

Some people like to give their horses warm bran mash during cold weather. This is a nice gesture, and horses love it, although it's really more for your own peace of mind than for the horse. Horses survived millions of years in cold weather before humans came along to give them a warm mash on a chilly evening.

Finally, keep your horse happy in bad weather by continuing to care for her even if it's uncomfortable for you to be outside. Feed her a little bit extra on cold days to help her fuel her internal heat engine. Clean her feet every day, just like you would if the weather were nice. Take her for hand walks if it's too lousy outside to ride. And try not to worry about her too much when the weather is bad. Nature is taking care of her.

Oldenburg

THE OLDENBURG MAY SOUND LIKE an old-timey automobile, but in reality it's a German sport horse whose bloodlines date to the seventeenth century. It comes from Germany's Lower Saxony region near the city of Oldenburg, from which it takes its name. The breed descends from the Friesian with contributions as well from Spanish, Neapolitan, Thoroughbred, Hanoverian, and Barb horses.

The great horseman Count Anton Gunther von Oldenburg first brought the breed to prominence in the 1600s. Many small breeding farms in the Oldenburg area produced war horses, and Count Anton traveled the world to acquire fine stallions for his own stud, and for the use of his tenants and other local farmers. His goal was to create a lighter, more refined, but still powerful horse. The Oldenburg horses were well known for their quality, and they were frequently given as gifts to members of royal and noble families, and as donations to generals during the Thirty Years War (1618–1648). One of the earliest depictions of the breed is a painting of Count Anton riding his splendid dapple-gray stallion Kranich, whose long mane and tail swept the ground.

The early Oldenburgs, with their magnificent looks, coal-black color, great power, and willingness to work, were popular carriage horses. As the use of carriages declined, more Thoroughbred and Norman blood was introduced to develop them as all-purpose saddle horses. Today Oldenburgs are found competing in dressage, show-jumping, and three-day eventing. Some people take them back to their origins and use them as driving horses.

An Oldenburg is a large but compact horse with a long, strong neck, a deep chest, powerful hindquarters, and relatively short legs. Large hooves support its weight, which are essential for this heaviest of the German warmbloods. The Oldenburg comes in a variety of colors, but it is most often seen in black, brown, or gray. The Oldenburg has a kind character as well as natural athletic ability. It is an elegant, refined, all-purpose saddle horse.

Oldenburg

Mounted Search and Rescue

WHEN A CHILD OR ADULT BECOMES lost in the wilderness, it often makes the local news. People anxiously watch and wait to see if the missing person will be found.

One of the most effective ways to search for someone who is lost in the wilderness is on horseback. Searching on horseback is faster than searching on foot, and it's often more accurate. Riders have a higher view than searchers on foot, and they can carry more equipment. Horses are also good at alerting their riders to someone in the environment.

Mounted search-and-rescue units operate around the country, usually on a volunteer basis. Always on call, these equestrians leap into action when needed, trailering their horses out to remote areas even in the middle of the night. Volunteers who don't ride are also part of the action, working behind the scenes in coordinating the search.

Horses who participate in search and rescue must be able to travel with speed through rough terrain while carrying equipment. They must also be able to stand tied for long periods of time, wear hobbles (a device that limits the horse's ability to move its legs), be willing to cross streams and bridges, and be ponied or pony another horse. Many other criteria exists for search-and-rescue horses as well, including a willingness to leave and be left by other horses, stand quietly for mounting from either side, and remain under control in a group traveling at all gaits

Search-and-rescue riders also need training, which includes CPR, first aid, and a host of other types of activities related to finding and assisting lost persons.

Hippocampus

IF YOU TOOK ANATOMY in high school, you probably remember the hippocampus. This is the part of the brain that is involved in motivation and emotion. But did you know how the hippocampus got its name?

The word "hippocampus" goes back to Greek mythology. In Latin, the word literally means horse (*hippo*) sea monster (*kampos*). The hippocampus in Greek religion was half-horse, half–sea creature that pulled the chariot of Poseidon, the great god of the ocean. The front end of the hippocampus looked like a horse, while the back end resembled a dolphin.

In biology, the term hippocampus refers to the genus of seahorse, a fish that can be found around the world. Seahorses are called sea-horses because their heads and neck look very much like a horse. The genus name of hippocampus was drawn from the mythical sea monster of Greek fame, because seahorses look like half–horse, half–sea creature.

So how does this relate to the hippocampus of the brain? Turns out this part of the anatomy is shaped like a seahorse. Scientists dubbed it the hippocampus in honor of the horse-shaped fish.

Pacing

IF YOUR HORSE WERE A Standardbred pulling a sulky, you might want him to pace. This is the gait performed by many Standardbred racehorses that involves the legs on both sides of the horse moving at the same time. Standardbreds trained for the track can pace at speeds of around 35 miles an hour (15.6 m/s).

While pacing is a desired gait on the Standardbred track, it's usually not a good thing when a horse is under saddle. The problem with pacing is that it's very uncomfortable for the rider. A two-beat gait is like the trot, the pace is unsettling to sit and difficult to post. It's especially disconcerting for riders of gaited horses who are looking for a smooth four-beat gait and end up with the jarring two-beat pace instead.

Standardbreds aren't the only horses that can pace. Any breed can do it, although it's most often seen among gaited horse breeds. (Icelandic horses do have a desired pace, a gait called the tolt, which is slightly different from the pace seen in other breeds and that is more comfortable to sit.)

Horses pace for a number of reasons. One is that they have trouble rounding their backs, which is necessary to perform a four-beat gait. The horse may also be sore, tense, weak, or afraid. All or even one of these elements can lead to pacing.

The best way to cure pacing is to find out what is causing it, and then treat the problem. Have a vet examine your horse to make sure pain isn't the culprit.

Next comes conditioning. Slowly condition your horse so his muscles are strong enough to hold him in frame where he can do a four-beat gait. Next, consider retraining. A horse that has been given a clean bill of health and is well conditioned but still won't stop pacing needs help from a trainer, specifically one who deals with gaited horses.

273

Craniosacral Therapy

THE CRANIUM IS THE PART of the skull that encases the brain. The sacrum is a bone that lies between the lumbar and coccygeal regions. Craniosacral therapy, then, addresses a horse's problems from head to tail. Originally developed for use in people, it is one of the many alternative therapies now available to horses.

Craniosacral therapy is a hands-on treatment designed to release restricted motion of the bones of the skull, vertebral column, and pelvis, increasing mobility. It uses extremely light finger pressure to optimize body movement, and it is said to help strengthen the central nervous system, relieve stress, and improve disease resistance. Whether or not it actually does those things, the one- to two-hour treatment probably feels good to the equine recipient, who becomes deeply relaxed and calm. That's good for anyone, equine or human.

Craniosacral therapy may also have other benefits. Practitioners say that restrictions in the craniosacral system can affect attitude, ability to learn, hearing, and vision. When horses are treated with this therapy, owners might see improvements in behavior problems or positive changes in demeanor.

Craniosacral restrictions are thought to be caused by the wear and tear of being ridden and handled, the use of bits and saddles, the aches and pains of increasing age, trauma, stress, and minor injuries such as strains and sprains. Eventually, these issues can create imbalances in the body.

Craniosacral therapy has been used successfully to help problems such as head shaking, weaving, cribbing, and temporomandibular joint syndrome. Shortened strides, "hunter bumps," (the lay term for an injured sacroiliac), and back problems are other conditions that may benefit from craniosacral therapy. The touch used is so light and gentle that even horses in pain receive enjoyment from it.

The number of treatments required depends on the individual animal. Improvements are sometimes seen after only one treatment, however.

Practice Mounting

MOUNTING IS THE FIRST THING you tackle when you learn to ride a horse. After all, you can't do much until you at least get on.

Some riders are very adept at mounting, swinging gracefully into the saddle with hardly an effort. Others struggle to hoist their weight up. Some can only mount if they have a mounting block available. Most can only mount from the horse's left side because that is the way they were taught. (The tradition of mounting from the left side goes back to the days of the cavalry when soldiers carried swords on their left sides, making it hard for them to mount from the horse's right.)

It's a good idea to be able to mount without effort, from the ground and from the off, or right, side of the horse. This is especially true if you are a trail rider. You never know what kind of situation you might find yourself in out on the trail. You may not be able to find something to boost yourself up with, and you might not be able to get on from the left side.

The best time to hone your skills in such matters is when you are in safe environment, with a patient and reliable horse. If you have trouble mounting gracefully even from a mounting block, take some time to practice this before you ride.

Much of graceful mounting has to do with upper body strength. With practice, your arm muscles should get stronger, and you'll be able to lift yourself up so you can swing into the saddle. (This is usually more of an issue for women riders, who usually have less upper body strength than men.)

Your purpose when practicing is to be able to swing up and over without pulling on your saddle (and hence the horse), and without landing heavily in the saddle. Practice mounting several times before each ride to make sure you've got it down.

Mounting from the ground can be trickier, especially if you are an older rider. Don't be afraid to use a mounting block whenever you can because it helps you, and it also helps your horse since pulling on the saddle is hard on the horse's back. But try to still be able to mount from the ground if it's necessary. You can use high ground to mount, meaning you can position your horse so that she is on a slightly lower elevation than you are. This will help you get into the saddle with less effort.

Rocky Mountain Horse

THE ROCKY MOUNTAIN HORSE is a gaited breed developed in the Appalachian Mountains of Kentucky in the early twentieth century. Legend has it that a young stallion hailing from the Rocky Mountains was brought to eastern Kentucky at the turn of the twentieth century and put to a group of Kentucky-bred mares with Spanish bloodlines for breeding. The resulting offspring were horses possessing a four-beat gait, exceptional temperament, and a chocolate brown coloring with a flaxen mane and tail. Because of their isolation in the remote Appalachians, the traits of these horses became more clearly defined over time, and the Rocky Mountain Horse was born.

Early in the breed's history, a man named Sam Tuttle purchased his first Rocky Mountain Horse in 1918. He began using this mare for breeding, and she gave birth to a number of foals that Tuttle came to use as trail mounts at the Kentucky Natural Bridge State Park riding concession, where he worked. Among these offspring was a stallion named Ole Tobe. Considered the breed's primary foundation stallion, Ole Tobe can be found in the pedigrees of every Rocky Mountain Horse today.

In large part because of Tuttle's use of the breed in his public riding concession and the exposure these horses received, the Rocky Mountain Horse gained a small following. However, no breed registry existed for the horse, and a lack of record keeping and indiscriminate breeding practices threatened to destroy the breed.

In the mid-1980s, a fancier of the Rocky Mountain Horse set out to save the breed from imminent extinction. In 1986, the Rocky Mountain Horse Association was formed.

One of the first tasks of the association was to become involved in genetic research to help identify the Rocky Mountain Horse as a distinct breed. In 1988, research was conducted to establish the breed's genetic identity. More than 100 foundation horses were studied by an equine geneticist, and five unique markers were discovered. These markers indicate that the breed was isolated for a significant period of time and that its blood remains pure.

The Rocky Mountain Horse has a four-beat lateral gait, which can be either slow or fast. The breed can be found in any solid color, but most horses are a dark chestnut with a flaxen mane and tail.

Rocky Mountain Horses measure anywhere from 14.2 to 16 hands. They are well known for their tractable disposition.

Rocky Mountain Horse

Play Days

CHILDREN WHO RIDE LIVE FOR play days. These are fun events that involve all sorts of exciting games on horseback.

Play days can be put on by 4-H groups, horseback riding camps, boarding and training stables, and riding instructors. Ribbons and prizes are usually the rewards for kids who do well in the games, which take place on their own horses or lesson horses.

Here are a few of the games you might see at a play day.

Egg and spoon race: The object of this game is to perform various maneuvers on horseback while holding an egg on a spoon. Riders go around the arena performing different gaits and maneuvers called out by the judge. The last rider who is still holding the spoon is the winner.

Ride-a-dollar: This popular horseback game is often performed bareback. Riders start at one end of the arena lined up single file. A ring steward (or the judge) puts a dollar bill under the rider's leg, elbow, seat, or calf. Half of the dollar bill is sticking out. The rider must then perform different gaits and maneuvers based on what the ring steward calls out. The last rider with the dollar bill still in place is the winner.

Magazine race: This game is a relay race to see who can best follow directions while also quickly mounting and dismounting. A pile of magazines is placed on the ground at the end of the arena. Riders line up at the other end. The ring steward gives a page number to each rider, along with details on how to hold the page and what gait will be followed.

When the game begins, the first rider for each team dismounts, tears out the correct page number, remounts, and carries it back to the line as instructed. If the rider drops the page, holds it incorrectly, or uses the wrong gait, she must get off the horse and retrieve it. The first team to have all riders finish the relay is the winning team.

Charisma

ONE OF THE GREATEST CHAMPIONS in the world of three-day eventing was a 15.3-hand, dark bay gelding named Charisma. Born in 1972 in New Zealand to a Thoroughbred stallion carrying some Percheron blood and a Thoroughbred mare, Charisma was known for being easy to train from a young age. He demonstrated his jumping prowess early on when, as a yearling, he escaped his pasture by jumping a 4-foot (1.2 m) fence. It was hard to keep this natural jumper confined, and by the time Charisma was four years old, he had bred four mares on his own. He was finally gelded.

In the early 1980s, New Zealand rider Mark Todd made Charisma his mount. The two began a successful eventing career that culminated in two individual Olympic gold medals, one in 1984 and one in 1988, and a bronze team medal, also in 1988.

Charisma was the subject of some intrigue when his owner, Fran Clark, decided to sell the horse out from under Todd. Clark didn't want Todd to have the horse for personal reasons, and instead sold him to another rider. That rider schemed with Todd to transfer ownership to Todd despite Clark's feelings, and Todd ended up owning Charisma in the end.

Charisma, whose nickname was Podge because he loved to eat, was retired in 1988 after his second Olympic victory, and lived to be thirty years old. He was euthanized at Todd's Cambridge, England farm in 2003. Todd wrote a book about his famous horse, simply titled *Charisma*.

Body Language

HUMANS COMMUNICATE PRIMARILY through speech, but horses do their talking—and listening—through body language.

The horse's face is the focal point of its body language, sending messages using the ears, eyes, mouth, and nostrils. Head posture is also a way of expression. Here are some examples.

Aggressive horse: Horses send a message of aggression loud and clear with ears tightly back and nostrils tight. Bared teeth may also accompany this expression. Horses often lunge toward the object of their aggression.

Scared horse: Horses who are frightened express themselves by showing the whites of their eyes and by tensing up their bodies. The head usually goes up in the air, and if the object of the fear is in the distance, the ears are pointed straight up in the air.

Relaxed horse: When a horse is feeling happy, healthy, and safe, his ears are in a neutral position. His eye has a calm look to it, and his muscles are relaxed.

Besides being good at expressing themselves through body language, horses are experts at reading it. They get particularly good at sensing a human's intentions or emotions by reading the person's body language, which can be disconcerting to people who aren't confident around horses. Horses sense this lack of confidence and sometimes take advantage of it.

Whenever you are around your horse, remember that he can read you like a book. Even if you think you are hiding how you really feel, your horse probably knows exactly what you are feeling.

Relaxed

Afraid

Threatening

Alert

Equine Metabolic Syndrome

THE CONDITION CALLED Equine Metabolic Syndrome is a cluster of problems that includes obesity, insulin resistance and laminitis, or founder. It tends to affect horses with certain characteristics: they tend to be overweight or gain weight easily, even when they don't eat much or eat only hay or pasture grass; they have fat deposits at the crest of the neck or at the head of the tail; and they have difficulty regulating the levels of glucose in their blood. Breedings may not take in affected female horses.

Any breed can be affected by EMS, but some breeds appear to be more prone to it. They include some pony breeds, domesticated mustangs, Paso Finos, Peruvian Pasos, Morgans, Arabians, Quarter Horses, European warmbloods and American Saddlebreds. Affected horses generally range from 6 to 20 years of age.

DIAGNOSIS

Diagnosis often begins with a history of laminitis, which often strikes horses in the spring when they are grazing on lush, green pasture grass. Chronic laminitis is indicated by abnormal growth rings on the hoof wall. Blood work may show slightly to moderately elevated levels of blood sugar and triglycerides in some horses with EMS.

An intravenous glucose tolerance test (IVGTT) can measure the effectiveness of insulin in a horse suspected of having EMS. Together, the physical signs of EMS (obesity, fat deposits, and laminitis) and supportive evidence provided by diagnostic tests can provide a definitive diagnosis.

TREATMENT

If EMS is diagnosed, the goal of treatment is weight loss and control over future weight gain. This can be done by reducing caloric intake. Feed only hay—no grain, pellets, or sweet feed—and avoid giving fat-enriched diets to senior horses or high-concentrate diets to young, growing horses. Supplementation with vitamin E and chromium picolinate may benefit horses with high blood levels of insulin.

Implement an exercise program for horses that don't have laminitis or that have recovered from the condition. Appropriate exercise includes walking on a lead rope, exercise on a lunge line, or being turned out in a paddock with no grass. Riding is also encouraged. Horses with laminitis can benefit from non-steroidal antiinflammatory drugs (NSAIDs) for pain management.

Make a Disaster Plan

NATURAL DISASTERS HIT HUMANS HARD, but they often hit horses even harder. Many horse owners are ill-prepared to evacuate their equine companions in the event of a fire or other catastrophe, and the horses ultimately suffer.

If you have horses, plan ahead in case you ever need to evacuate your animals. Spend a few hours figuring out what you will do in the case of an emergency, taking the following points into consideration.

- Have a plan in place to trailer your horses out of the area if you are asked to evacuate. If you don't have a trailer of your own, or you have more horses that you can fit in your trailer, ask a friend if you can count on him or her for help if needed.

- Know where other horse owners and boarding stables are in the surrounding areas so you can be prepared to take your animals to a safe place if evacuated. County fairgrounds and local showgrounds are often made available to horse owners during an emergency. Know where these facilities are located in advance.

- Leave instructions for friends and neighbors on how to evacuate your horses if a disaster strikes when you aren't home.

- Keep your horse's vital records all in one place, in a spot that is easily accessible if you have to evacuate. This should include Coggins tests results, photographs of your horse, and phone numbers of your vet and farrier.

- Have halters and lead ropes available at all times so you or a neighbor or official can evacuate your horse in an emergency. Many horse owners hang halters and lead ropes in their horses' stalls.

- Make sure your horses are good at loading into a trailer. The last thing you need in an emergency is to fight with your horse to get him loaded. Practice loading well before you need to do so in an emergency.

283

Irish Draught

IRISH FARM HORSES OF THE nineteenth century filled multiple roles, from tilling the fields, to pulling carts, to fox hunting on the weekends. That called for a lighter-weight animal than the traditional draft horse, but it was still substantial, making it popular today for its breeding qualities. Irish Draught mares produce excellent hunters when mated with Thoroughbreds, and Irish Draught stallions mated to lighter-weight mares bequeath extra bone and substance to their foals.

The docile but strong Irish Draught dates to the nineteenth century. Despite being economical to keep, living handily in winter on boiled turnips and bran, or meal of that could be spared from the cows, it was fortunate to survive the poverty and famine that plagued Ireland during that time.

Breeders often couldn't afford to register their horses, and thousands of the horses went to slaughterhouses when it became too expensive to keep them. Breed enthusiasts, working with the Irish Horse Board, labored to start a new stud book and save the breed from extinction.

In appearance, the Irish Draught has a big, kind eye and a proud bearing, carrying its head and neck gracefully. It is powerful but not ponderous, and moves freely. Stallions stand 15.3 to 16.3 hands, mares 15.1 to 16.1 hands. The Irish Draught may be any whole color, including gray.

The Irish Draught is a versatile mount for riders of all ages. Its jumping ability, soundness, and stamina make it capable of participating in various levels of jumping, eventing, dressage, hunting, and driving.

Irish Draught

Roping

A WESTERN SPORT BORN IN THE days of the Old West is roping. Now a rodeo event, roping uses a calf and features specially trained horses and very skilled riders.

Ropers compete in a few different classes. In tie-down roping, a horse and rider pursue a calf that comes out of a chute. The rider throws a lasso around the calf's neck and leaps off the horse when the calf is snagged. The trained roping horse holds the rope taut, which immobilizes the calf. The roper then throws the calf down on its side, and ties three of its legs together. The event is timed, and it stems from the cattle work done on ranches to secure calves for branding or medical treatment.

Another event is team roping, or heading and heeling. In this event, there are two horse and rider teams. One rider lassos the calf by the horns, while the other lassos the calf's back feet. Once the calf is secured, the riders face each other and pull their ropes taught to lay the calf on the ground.

In the breakaway roping event, a short lariat is tied to the saddle horse with a string. A flag is also attached. The rider ropes the calf, and at that moment, the horse stops short. The string and flag break from the saddle, signaling the end of the rider's time.

Roping events are popular, but they have drawn criticism from the animal rights movement, which argues that the treatment of calves in these events is inhumane.

The Black Stallion

FOR DECADES, HORSE-LOVING children around the world have enjoyed the exploits of a jet-black Arabian stallion named Shêtân, but most often called the Black, and his adventurous offspring. The creation of Florida author Walter Farley, the Black or his progeny has appeared in twenty-one books in *The Black Stallion* series.

The book that started it all was *The Black Stallion*, published in 1941. The story focuses on the Black, who is shipwrecked on a tropical island after being mistreated by his handlers. Also washed up on the island is Alec, a young boy who was traveling on the same ship. The Black and Alec become close friends, and when the two are ultimately rescued, they go back to the United States. Here the Black becomes a successful racehorse.

The success of *The Black Stallion* led to a number of sequels and prequels, including books about three of the Black's offspring: Satan, Bonfire, and Black Minx.

Black Stallion Literacy Project

Although Walter Farley passed away in 1989, his family has kept his name alive with The Black Stallion Literacy Project, founded in 1999. Established in conjunction with the owners of the Arabian Nights Dinner Theater in Kissimmee, Florida, the project encourages children in grades one to three to read on their own and to learn about horses. Children are also helped to read their favorite book to a horse. Fourth graders are then given their own copy of *The Black Stallion*. They finish the program with a visit to the Arabian Nights Dinner Theater show, which features an array of horses performing in a variety of ways.

Proper Leading

ONE OF THE FIRST THINGS you learn about horse handling is how to lead. Seems simple enough: Just grab the lead rope and walk, and the horse will follow. Of course, that's not all there is to it. Leading safely and correctly is another story.

People who have been around horses all their lives are usually the worst culprits when it comes to unsafe leading. They have become so comfortable around horses, they don't think about what could happen if they are walking directly in front of the horse, are wearing flip-flops instead of boots, or have the excess lead rope wrapped in a coil. But think about these situations and what could occur. If the horse spooks from the behind, she could run the handler over. If she steps on the handler's bare feet, she could break bones. If she bolts and runs off, she could drag the handler by the hand when the coiled lead rope tightens.

When it comes to leading, always do it right. Here is a refresher.

- Stand at your horse's left, between her head and her shoulder.

- With your right hand, grasp the part of the lead rope clipped to the horse's halter about 6 to 10 inches (15 to 25 cm) from the clip.

- With your left hand, hold the remainder of the lead rope in a folded loop.

- When you walk with the horse, make sure the horse stays to your right side, with your body positioned between her head and her shoulder.

Follow these basic tenets, and you'll stay safer when leading your horse.

287

Bowed Tendon

ATHLETIC HORSES FREQUENTLY SUFFER from tendonitis, or bowed tendon. It is a primary reason for the retirement of many horses, in particular racehorses.

With this type of injury, the tendon fibers rupture to varying degrees. Blood vessels also rupture, and fluid can accumulate in the affected area. A bowed tendon usually occurs after a horse has been exercised improperly. Fatigue and poor condition are contributing factors. Horses that are shod improperly, and those with joint malformations, are also prone to tendonitis.

DIAGNOSIS

A bowed tendon injury can be acute (short term) or chronic (long term). Signs of tendonitis are severe lameness and hot, painful, swollen joints. Stall rest is advised for horses with acute tendonitis. Cold packs and non-steroidal anti-inflammatory drugs can help to reduce the inflammation, but injecting corticosteroid drugs into the tendon is not recommended because it can cause infection. Depending on the severity of the injury, support and immobilization may be necessary. Gradually reintroduce exercise.

In horses with chronic tendonitis, the fibrous tissues surrounding the tendon become thickened and scarred. Often, these horses look sound at a walk or trot, but they go lame at a gallop.

TREATMENT

Forelegs are more likely to be affected than hind legs. Tendonitis commonly occurs in the mid-cannon region of the superficial digital flexor tendon. That location has a relatively small cross-sectional area compared to the impact it must withstand when the fetlock is hyperextended at high speeds. Even if the injury heals, it's not unusual for a reinjury to occur.

The prognosis for complete recovery from tendonitis is limited. Researchers are studying the potential of bone marrow injections that contain stem cells and growth factors.

Backing in Hand

IF YOU RIDE REGULARLY, you probably practice backing up your horse, especially if you are a Western rider. But how much do you practice backing your horse in hand?

Start by putting your horse in a halter and lead rope. Find a place where you have a lot of room to maneuver. Ask your horse to back up by facing him, standing slightly to the side. Apply backward steady pressure on the lead rope until your horse drops his nose down. Release the pressure on the rope the moment your horse tucks his chin.

Ask him again by applying pressure to the lead rope once more, waiting until he tucks his chin and shifts his weight backward before you release the pressure. Do it again, keeping the pressure until your horse takes a step backward. Reward him by releasing the pressure, then repeat, asking him to take two steps back. Continue until your horse is backing up several steps. Praise him and tell him what a good horse he is!

Zorse

A HORSE IS A HORSE, of course, of course, but what is a Zorse? If you guessed that it's half zebra, half horse, you're correct. There are also Zebroids or Zebrulas (any hybrid horse with zebra ancestry), Zules (when crossed with donkeys), and Zonies (when crossed with ponies). They are the result of mating between a male zebra and a female horse. Female zebras mated with male horses, may be called Hebras.

The unusual hybrid was first created by geneticist James Cossar Ewart, a professor of natural history at Scotland's University of Edinburgh from 1882 to 1927. He used a zebra stallion and Arabian mares, with one goal being to produce a draft animal that could withstand the heat and diseases of South Africa, and that would be more tractable than a zebra or a mule. Other experiments with the hybrids were made by the U.S. government and reported in science journals in 1929.

Zorses are said to be stronger and faster than horses, resistant to heat, and tireless. They resemble horses more, but they sport stripes on their legs and sometimes on the body or neck.

Although horses, donkeys, and zebras all belong to the genus equus, they are different species. Because Zorses are a hybrid of two different species, they are infertile.

While Zorses have many good qualities, they are not as docile as horses. Their strong, aggressive temperament makes them unsuited to being handled by novice riders.

Zorse (foal)

Draft Horse Competition

THE DRAFT HORSE BREEDS were originally developed to pull heavy loads, which is something they have been doing for centuries. Although we now have motorized vehicles to do this work, draft horses are still valued in some circles for their ability to pull.

Draft horse pulling competitions can be found around the world, and they are designed to test the strength of these mighty equines. Each pull has its own rules. For example, a pull will have two load weight classifications: Light Weight and Heavy Weight. Each team of working horses (usually a team of two, but sometimes one) is given two chances to pull a weighted sled 20 feet (6.1 m).

In the Heavy Weight division, the sled weight might begin at 3,400 pounds (1,542 kg) and increase by 2,000-pound (907 kg) increments, and may go as high at 10,000 pounds (4,535 kg) before a winning team is declared.

Horses pull these loads willingly and are not whipped or harmed in anyway in an attempt to get them to pull. To ensure the safety of the horses, most pulling clubs have rules on the humane treatment of horses.

Rex: Silver Screen Star

Equine movie stars have been around since the film industry first came into being. A popular subject for movies, horses have proven themselves to be box office winners.

One early equine movie star was a black Morgan stallion named Rex, whose career spanned the 1920s and '30s. According to Petrine Mitchum, author of *Hollywood Hoofbeats*, Rex was a difficult horse to train. Before Rex began his career as an actor, he was relegated to an isolated stall because he was difficult to handle, and a trainer had mysteriously died while alone with Rex. When trainer Chick Morrison discovered the horse, he immediately recognized Rex's charisma. He convinced Clarence "Fat" Jones, a supplier of movie horses, to purchase him.

Rex was wild in person and on camera, and audiences loved it. Rex starred in several films, including *King of the Wild Horses*, *Guardians of the Wild*, and *Wild Beauty*.

Rex's wild nature made him a temperamental star who quit when pushed too hard for obedience. For scenes that required close-up shots with people and dogs, a horse named Brownie usually served as stand-in. Rex did learn to work at liberty, but he couldn't always be trusted. He once ran away from a set in Nevada and was found 17 miles (27 km) away.

Rex was eventually retired to a ranch in Arizona, where he died in the early 1940s.

Kicking

Nature equipped the horse with a few different means of protection. Speed and agility are among the horse's top weapons of self-defense. Kicking is another.

Most horses kick because they are afraid. A startled horse may kick first and ask questions later. If you happen to be the one who startled him, look out.

Horses also kick to get rid of something—or someone—who is bothering them. Dogs seem to get kicked a lot because they don't know to keep their distance. People get kicked, too, if they are doing something around the horse's flanks or rear end that the horse doesn't like.

Follow these basic rules of safety:

- Don't approach a horse directly from behind. Instead, come from a side angle.

- Speak to the horse whenever approaching one from the rear. Letting the horse know you are there will keep him from startling.

- Yell "quit!" at the top of your lungs if a horse turns her rump to you with ears pinned, threatening to kick. Don't run away because this will show the horse you are afraid, and the behavior will be repeated.

- If your horse kicks at you often, call in a professional trainer for help.

Hyperkalemic Periodic Paralysis

POTASSIUM IS AN ELECTROLYTE that is essential for healthy functioning of the body, but in the case of hyperkalemic periodic paralysis (HYPP), it is too much of a good thing. This inherited disease of the muscle is caused by a genetic defect. Horses with HYPP are predisposed to intermittent episodes of muscle tremors or paralysis caused by too much potassium in the blood. That condition is known as hyperkalemia, and it has the effect of causing a horse's muscles to contract abnormally.

DIAGNOSIS

This occurs because of a mutation in the sodium channel gene. The job of the sodium channels is to control muscle fiber contraction. Horses with this particular gene defect experience involuntary muscle contractions when blood potassium levels fluctuate. For example, this may happen when horses that haven't eaten consume a feed such as alfalfa, which contains high levels of potassium.

When affected horses are managed properly, they generally don't have any problems, but stress—ranging from such causes as changes in diet to exercise restriction related to illness—or increased blood levels of potassium can cause signs of muscle dysfunction: shaking or trembling, weakness, or collapse.

During an attack, some horses may also display loud breathing noises caused by paralysis of upper airway muscles. In severe cases, the horse may die suddenly from heart failure or respiratory muscle paralysis.Sometimes attacks of HYPP are mistaken for other conditions. They can resemble tying up syndrome, seizures, respiratory problems, choking, and even colic if the horse is down on the ground and reluctant to stand.

TREATMENT

Diet, exercise, and stress reduction are all important in the management of HYPP.

Horses with HYPP should eat several times daily. Feed them timothy or Bermuda grass hay, or grains such as oats, corn, wheat, barley, and beet pulp. Avoid feeds that are high in potassium, including alfalfa hay, brome hay, canola oil, soybean meal or oil, and sugar and beet molasses. Make any dietary changes slowly so the horse's digestive system has time to adjust. (See Day 187 for more information on changing a horse's diet.)

Regular exercise or free time in a paddock or pasture helps to reduce stress. This is especially true if the horse is normally confined to a stall. If you must transport your horse, stop every two hours for a break and replenish his water.

If your horse ever needs general anesthesia, be sure to remind your veterinarian that he has HYPP. The veterinarian can then take steps to avoid or be prepared for an episode of paralysis, which may be triggered by anesthesia.

There is no cure for HYPP. Horses that have it can pass the gene to offspring, even if they themselves show few or no signs of the disease. There is a DNA test for HYPP, and it is recommended that all descendants of Impressive be tested for the disease.

The Father of HYPP

HYPP has been identified only in descendants of a Quarter Horse named Impressive. Most genetic mutations do not survive, but this one accidentally became widespread because Quarter Horse breeders wanted to produce horses with heavy musculature. They unwittingly bred widely to Impressive, hence the other name for this condition, Impressive Syndrome.

Grow Your Horse's Carrots

ONE OF THE MOST LOVING THINGS you can do for your horse is to grow her carrots. Home-grown carrots are healthier and less expensive than store bought ones, and they taste better, too.

If you are new to gardening, you'll need to pay a visit to your local nursery to buy some basic supplies.

Soil: Unless you live on property that is located on very rich soil, chances are you will need to add something to improve the dirt already in your yard. Adding packaged garden soil, potting mix, growing mix, or earthworm castings will improve the quality of your existing soil and result in better plants. If you opt for packaged soil, look for an organic mix. Organic garden soil or potting mixes are void of synthetic chemicals and other non-natural additives—ingredients you want to stay away from when growing healthy carrots for your horse.

Tools: You'll need some basic gardening tools to get the job done, including a metal rake, a hoe, a spading fork, and a trowel. If your garden will be located out of reach of a garden hose, you'll need a watering can. Also, consider purchasing a pad to kneel on when you are gardening.

Keep in mind that you don't need to buy expensive tools for your garden. Even the lowest priced tools at a reputable nursery will be of good enough quality to last a long time.

Gardening apparel: Buy a pair of water resistant gardening gloves to protect your hands when you work, as well as gardening clogs for your feet and a wide-brimmed straw hat to shade your face from the sun.

Fertilizer: Your carrots will need to be fertilized on a regular basis to ensure a good crop. Select an organic fertilizer that is designed for use in the vegetable garden. This can be a prepared mix or a natural product such as fish emulsion or blood meal.

Pest control: Keeping your garden free of pests that will destroy your young carrot plants can be a challenge, but you don't want to resort to using chemical pesticides or herbicides. Instead, buy insecticidal soap, which is a much safer product for killing bugs. Once your plants are mature, you can also buy beneficial insects for your garden, such as ladybugs and praying mantis.

Carrots grow best in the spring, summer, and fall, so start your seeds in the spring. Plant them in a part of the garden that drains well. Place the seeds 3/8 inch (9 mm) into the soil and space them at least 15 inches (38 cm) apart. Cover the seedlings with straw or organic mulch. Once the seedlings come up, you can add more mulch around them.

Carrots take about a month to mature. You can keep planting them throughout the growing season, keeping in mind they will die at the first hard frost.

When you feed carrots to your horse, serve them with the green tops still attached. Your horse will love it!

Lusitano

THE IBERIAN PENINSULA HAS produced many fine horses, among them the Andalusian of Spain and the Lusitano of Portugal, first developed for warfare, and in Portugal now used in the bull fighting ring. Both situations call for a horse that must remain calm and move with agility to protect its rider in the face of attack. The two breeds bear a certain similarity and are believed to have a common ancestor. Until 1960, they even shared a registry, and in North America both breeds are registered with the International Andalusian and Lusitano Horse Association.

In appearance, the Lusitano may more closely resemble the original Iberian horse, while the Andalusian, more influenced by the Arab, has something of an Oriental head shape. Portuguese breeders have set up their own stud book, allowing them to more easily and successfully make improvements in the breed.

The Lusitano is characterized by a long, noble head with a convex profile and finely curved nose; large, generous eyes; a powerful arched neck; short-coupled body; broad, powerful loins; and fine, clean legs with dense bones. Most notably, its movement gives a smooth and comfortable ride. The Lusitano usually stands 15.1 to 15.3 hands, but some reach more than 16 hands. Most often gray or bay, the Lusitano may be any true color, including dun and chestnut. Rarely, they come in palomino, buckskin, or cremello, and Lusitanos in those colors are highly sought after. The mane and tail are thick and silky.

This is an intelligent, sensible horse with a kind temperament. The Lusitano bonds strongly with people, no doubt a remnant of its long history of working closely with them on the battlefield and its simulation the bull ring. The Lusitano can be found competing in dressage and show jumping or simply enjoying a trail with her rider.

Lusitano

Trail Trials

TRAIL RIDING IS THE NUMBER ONE pastime of horse owners, so it's no wonder that competitions have been created to help encourage training of good trail horses.

One of these competitions is trail trials. Held by different regional organizations around the United States, trail trials test the willingness, sensibility, and obedience of trail horses.

Trail trials are obstacle course competitions that take place over a several mile (kilometer) trail route. To participate in a trail trial, you need a good, well-trained trail horse, and you need the skills to handle a horse in different trail situations.

At a trail trial, you may be asked to cross water and bridges, step over logs, walk through tunnels, and negotiate hills.

At trail trials, judges often ask riders to perform certain tasks such as opening and closing a gate while mounted, or dragging a tire or a log. Horses must also be led from the ground, be willing to lift their feet quietly when asked, and stand tied without fussing.

Many clubs that offer trail trials sponsor clinics that allow riders to enroll their horses and spend a few hours learning how to perform the required tasks.

Narragansett Pacer

WILD ANIMAL SPECIES AREN'T THE only living things to become extinct. Horse breeds can also go the way of the dinosaur. That is what happened to a horse called the Narragansett Pacer.

The Narragansett Pacer was a U.S. breed that developed in the 1600s, reportedly in Rhode Island. No one knows for sure how the breed was created, although some historians believe it came from a cross between British Hobbie and Galloway horses and Spanish stock. The breed was used as a saddle horse and also for racing by the colonists.

The Narragansett Pacer, which was usually chestnut in color, was known for its very smooth gait, which was most likely a four-beat movement. Although not a flashy horse, the breed's gait was considered very desirable.

As a result, the Narragansett Pacer was crossed to other breeds in the hopes of recreating the pacing gait in larger, more impressive-looking mounts. The consequence of all this out-crossing was the eventual destruction of the breed. Shortly after the Revolutionary War, the Narragansett Pacer became extinct.

Before its demise, the Narragansett Pacer contributed to the development of several U.S. breeds that can still be found today, including the Tennessee Walking Horse, the Saddlebred, and the Standardbred.

Bran Mash

ON DAYS WHEN THE WEATHER IS crisp, doting horse owners like to give their horses hot mash to eat. The theory is that it helps keep the horse warm while giving him a nice treat.

Whether a hot mash really does anything to help keep a horse warm is up for debate, we do know two things about hot mashes: They make horse owners feel good, and horses love to eat them.

Most hot mashes are made from bran. Horse owners like to mix bran with 1/3 bucket of warm water, a few chopped carrots or apples, and a cup of molasses to create a yummy winter treat. Although a bran mash provides very little nutritional value to horses, it's okay to give it to them, but only on occasion.

The truth about bran is that if you feed too much of it, you can cause your horse to develop enteroliths—stones that form in the intestines. Bran can also disrupt your horse's calcium and phosphate ratio, causing metabolic problems. Bran also irritates the lining of a horse's intestines, and it can give him soft stool, although it doesn't necessarily help with constipation.

So is it all right to give your horse a hot bran mash on chilly winter days? Sure, as long as you do it in small amounts and infrequently.

Rain Rot

ALSO CALLED RAIN SCALD OR, more formally, equine dermatophilosis (after *Dermatophilus congolensis*, the cause of the problem), this condition is a bacterial infection on the surface of the skin. It is a common problem for horses during wet winter or spring months, but it can occur in horses turned out during any extended period of rain or wetness.

When the skin is frequently damp, especially if water pools in concave areas, such as over the withers, back, and rump, it creates an ideal environment for bacterial growth. That's how the problem starts.

Other factors also cause damage to the skin, opening it up to infection. These include insect bites, external parasites, poorly fitting tack, and moisture from heavy sweating. The bacteria that cause rain rot can be transmitted from horse to horse by flies, brushes, blankets, or tack, but they cannot infect dry, healthy skin.

DIAGNOSIS

Horses with rain rot lose small tufts of hair as they are being shed out. They look as if their coat or skin has been scalded with drops of water, primarily on the back and sides. This effect occurs when the skin secretes a sticky substance that causes the hairs to clump together, giving them the appearance of paint brush tips. Small scabs eventually form that are painful to the touch but not itchy. Removal of the scabs results in soreness and minor bleeding. A small amount of pus is common, and the skin beneath the scab appears irritated or inflamed.

Other conditions can resemble rain rot. Ringworm, other bacterial infections such as those caused by *Staphylococcus* or *Corynebacterium pseudotuberculosis*, skin allergies, and sarcoids can all cause similar signs. A definite diagnosis can be made by examining the crusts microscopically for the presence of *D. congolensis* or performing a skin biopsy and culturing the sample for bacteria.

TREATMENT

Rain rot is treated by removing the scabs with 0.5 percent betadine or 2 percent chlorhexidine and then drying the skin thoroughly so the bacteria cannot recur. Affected areas are treated topically with chlorhexidine or lime sulfur every day for a week, always ensuring that the skin dries thoroughly afterward. Plenty of time in the sun helps.

If the skin responds, the frequency of application can be reduced until the condition clears up. Severe cases may require treatment with oral or injectable antibiotics.

Avoid placing tack on affected areas until rain rot goes away, and clean tack and grooming tools thoroughly before use to prevent them from reinfecting the horse or any other horses.

Check Saddle Fit

WE WOULD ALL LIKE TO THINK THAT our horses enjoy being ridden. This is more likely to be true if your horse is wearing a saddle that properly fits him.

Some horses are very expressive about their discomfort, going so far as to buck their riders off if the saddles they are wearing are pinching them or creating some other kind of discomfort. Other horses are stoic creatures and give no clue that the saddles they are wearing cause them pain.

Just because your horse hasn't thrown you or become incapacitated doesn't mean that his saddle fits him properly. Spend some time giving your saddle fit the once over just to be sure your horse isn't suffering needlessly.

To do a basic check on your English saddle, follow these guidelines.

- Put the saddle on the horse without a saddle pad and tighten the girth.

- Have a helper sit in the saddle.

- Keeping your hand flat, slide your fingers underneath the pommel. Your fingers should fit comfortably between the horse and saddle. You should be able to fit at least three fingers between the withers and the arch below the pommel.

- Put your fingers in between the top of the horse's shoulder blade and the pommel. Have someone lift the horse's left foreleg off the ground and pull it forward. As the shoulder moves, make sure the saddle does not restrict the movement of the shoulder. Do this on the other side of the horse as well.

- Stand behind the horse. Look through the saddle to see a tunnel of light. If you don't see light, the saddle is too tight.

- To check the length of the saddle, check to see if the seat panel reaches past the main part of the back onto the loins. If it does, it is too long for your horse.

To check your Western saddle, do the following.

- Put the saddle on the horse's back with a Western saddle pad underneath it. Tighten the cinch so it is comfortable.

- Have someone sit in the saddle with his or her feet in the stirrups.

- Fit three fingers between the arch of the pommel and the horse's withers. If you can't, the tree is too wide for your horse.

- Make your hand flat and place your fingers between the saddle and the top of the horse's shoulder. If the fit is so tight that you can't squeeze your fingers in, the tree is too narrow for your horse.

Holsteiner

MONASTERIES HAVE PLAYED A key role in the development of many breeds. The Holsteiner is one of them. It hails from the Schleswig-Holstein region of northern Germany where it dates to the fourteenth century. The Holsteiner was bred by local monks for multiple purposes: first as war horses prized for their strength, courage, and reliability, and then as heavily muscled riding horses, carriage horses, and draft horses that could withstand the cold winter climate. In the wake of the Protestant Reformation, breeding of the horses was taken over by private individuals and the state. When times changed, they modified the horses as needed. For instance, Yorkshire Coach Horses and Cleveland Bays were used to create elegant driving horses for the nineteenth-century equivalent of luxury car drivers.

When the need for carriage horses declined and then disappeared, Holsteiner aficionados modernized the breed for use as a sport horse suited to dressage, eventing, and show jumping.

They crossed with Thoroughbreds, Anglo Arabs, and Selle Francais to add refinement and jumping ability. Their success is indisputable. Holsteiners have carried Olympic riders to gold and silver medals in dressage, show jumping, and three-day eventing, and in 1976 a team of four Holsteiners won the world championship in combined driving.

The medium-framed Holsteiner has a small head with large, intelligent eyes, a strong back and loin, a well-angled shoulder, and an arched neck. It stands 16 to 17 hands and moves fluidly. Bay in color, it has few or no white markings. The overall picture is of a horse that is elegant and expressive, renowned for a kind temperament, intelligence, and willingness to work. All of these characteristics contribute to the Holsteiner's reputation as one of the world's best sport horses, capable of performing equally well in dressage, driving, and show jumping.

Holsteiner

Camas Prairie Stump Race

A TWIST ON THE SPORT OF barrel racing, the camas prairie stump race is a class seen only in Appaloosa Horse Club-sanctioned shows. Named after the traditional Nez Perce Indian tribal sport that involved horses racing (the Nez Perce lived on the Camas Prairie in the Pacific Northwest), the camas prairie stump race is a test of speed and agility.

The event works like this: Two horse and rider teams enter the area at the same time, on two opposite three-barrel courses. The barrels are positioned in a triangular shape.

The horses race from a common starting point to the barrel on their right, turning right around the barrel and racing to the barrel on the left of the starting line.

They then go around the barrel to the left and then race to the barrel farthest from the starting line. After negotiating this barrel by running around it, they race to the finish line, which is located at the same point as the start line. The horse and rider who come out in front of each round remains in the game until only two horses and riders remain to fight it out for first place.

Two horses run reflective patterns at the same time during the Camas Prairie Stump Race.

Equus

HORSES LOVERS INITIALLY REJOICED when they heard a play about horses called *Equus* had opened on Broadway in the early 1970s. Their rejoicing was soon replaced with disgust when they found out the play was about a seventeen-year-old boy who deliberately blinds horses.

Equus became a huge sensation, even though it was disturbing, especially for people who care about horses. Playwright Peter Schaffer came up with the story after hearing about a real incident where a teenaged boy blinded six horses at a stable just outside of London.

The result is a psychological thriller about a disturbed teenager, a psychiatrist in the midst of a career crisis, and a group of innocent, unsuspecting horses.

> The play received the Tony Award for best play in 1975, and it was made into a movie starring Richard Burton.

Bitless Bridles

HORSES HAVE BEEN RIDDEN in bits for hundreds of years, but a recent trend in bitless riding is questioning this age-old method of controlling a horse. All part of the move toward "natural" horsemanship, bitless riding is reported to be more humane for the horse than wearing a bit.

Bitless bridles work by putting pressure on different areas of a horse's head, instead of relying on pressure inside the mouth. Depending on the design of the bridle, pressure is applied to the poll (the area just behind the horse's ears), nose, and/or chin. Bits, on the other hand, put the majority of pressure on the bars of the horse's mouth. Critics say that bits cause pain to horses, no matter how mild the bit is reported to be. They also hamper the horse's ability to eat and drink, which is often an issue for people who spend a long time riding on the trail.

Bitless bridles come in a variety of designs. The most commonly seen are hackamores, which are Western bridles that work by applying pressure to the bride of the horse's nose and the chin, without use of a bit. The bosal is the mildest of these types of bridles, while the mechanical hackamore can be very severe in the wrong hands.

Newer bitless bridles are designed to be mild and to operate with gentle pressure instead of a harsh sensation. Proponents claim that any horse can be ridden in one of these bridles, although a horse must be fairly well trained to be responsive to the most subtle pressure—especially if that horse is normally ridden with a severe bit. Horses that are used to being ridden in harsh bits often need retraining with a bitless bridle before they are completely reliable.

Homeopathy

HOMEOPATHY IS THE USE OF very dilute substances to affect a cure. It involves treating conditions by administering substances that produce clinical signs in healthy horses similar to the signs of the horse being treated. The key phrase is "like cures like." For instance, if a horse has a problem caused by inflammation, a homeopathic veterinarian might prescribe a remedy that used at full strength would cause inflammation. The homeopathic drug is an infinitesimal dose, extremely diluted.

There are well-established ways to use homeopathic remedies. The most important thing to know about homeopathy is that the substance must match the exact signs the horse exhibits. If two horses were examined by a homeopathic veterinarian for the same condition, each might receive a different homeopathic remedy based on its individual signs.

For home use, homeopathic remedies should be limited to acute conditions, such as strains, sprains, bruises, minor cuts and scrapes, bug bites and hives, and abscesses. Anything more serious should be treated by a professional.

Common homeopathic preparations include the following:

- Arnica for bruising, sprains and strains

- Calendula for minor cuts and scrapes or to accelerate healing

- Nux vomica for fright, panic, or indigestion

- Dulcamara 30C or thuja for rain rot or rain scald (two types of fungal infections of the skin)

- Apis 30C for bug bites and stings or hives

Avoid using too many homeopathic remedies at once.

If the problem goes away, discontinue using the remedy. If it does not improve after three or four doses, consult a veterinarian who is experienced in homeopathic medicine. For conditions such as colic, always call a veterinarian first. There could be complications that are not appropriate for treatment by homeopathic remedies.

Homeopathic drugs are created in Food and Drug Administration (FDA)–regulated laboratories and registered with the FDA, just as conventional drugs are. Some are applied topically while others are taken internally.

Ride a New Horse

HORSE OWNERS HAVE A HABIT OF riding only their horses, and not surprisingly. Most people barely have time for their own equines, never mind someone else's. But it's actually important to ride an unfamiliar horse now and then. Here's why.

Boost your confidence. When you ride the same horse all the time, year after year, you get comfortable with that horse and forget what it's like to get on another one. Believe it or not, this can erode your confidence level. You need to feel like you can ride horses besides your own, and the only way to do that is to ride one once in a while.

The more horses you ride, the better rider you will be. Trainers are really good riders for a reason. They spend most of their time riding, and they also ride a lot of different horses. Horses are amazing teachers, and each horse has something to teach us.

Variety is the spice of life! Aside from the practical reasons for riding another horse now and then, you should also do it because it's fun.

Finding another horse to ride besides your own might be a challenge, so here are some ideas for how to do it.

Swap with your friends. If you have friends you ride with, suggest that you swap mounts one day. There are a couple of caveats here: Make sure the horse you agree to ride is safe and appropriately behaved for your skill level. Also, make sure you friend is a decent rider capable of properly handing your horse.

Offer free exercise riding. If you know someone who doesn't have much time to ride, offer to take his or her horse out for exercise every now and then. You'll get experience riding a new horse, and you will be helping out this person (and the horse).

Take lessons. Consider taking a few riding lessons on a school horse. This is your best bet if you have confidence issues riding a strange horse. School horses are usually very safe, and you'll have an instructor there to guide you.

Fell Pony

FELL PONIES ARE AMONG THOSE native English breeds called mountain and moorland ponies. They were bred to be easy keepers in the harsh country of northern England, able to survive and thrive even with poor grazing land and only rough shelter. The name Fell derives from the local word for the surrounding hills.

The Fell Pony is a descendant of dark-colored native ponies and horses from Friesland that were brought to the British Isles when the Romans invaded in 55 BC. When the Romans withdrew, many of the horses remained. Those in the north bred with the native ponies, and among their offspring were the equines that became the Fell Pony.

The Fell Pony has had a varied career, being used as a plowhorse, pack animal, draft horse, and even under saddle. The Industrial Revolution brought an end to its usefulness, and many were sold for slaughter, but enough remained in their original Lakeland home in the hills of Cumbria that they didn't disappear entirely.

Fells bear a striking resemblance to the much larger Friesian, in appearance and also in trotting ability. They were famous for their speed and stamina at a trot, which is a trait that they retain to this day.

In appearance the Fell Pony has a neat head set on a fairly long neck. A large or coarse head and a short, thick neck are undesirable. Muscular quarters and good legs with plenty of bone are hallmarks of the breed. Primarily black but sometimes dark brown, bay, or gray, it rarely has white markings. The mane and tail are long and thick, and straight, silky feather extends up to the knee. Most Fell Ponies average 13.2 hands, but the height limit is 14 hands.

This lively and alert pony is characterized by hardiness, courage, and adaptability. It's sturdy enough to carry an adult, but a docile temperament makes it suited to be a child's mount. In competition it is suited to combined driving. The Fell Pony's advantage in this sport is its great stamina, although it lacks the speed of some other breeds. It is also a creditable jumper. Any rider will find it a comfortable ride, with its easy, steady trot over long distances and surefootedness over rough, rocky, hilly, or marshy terrain.

Fell Pony

Ranch Sorting

On CATTLE RANCHES THROUGHOUT the West, the sorting of cattle takes place on a daily basis. Like many ranching tasks involving horses and cattle, sorting has become a competitive activity.

Ranch sorting is a timed event that can be done by one rider, or by a team of two or three. Eleven head of cattle are placed in a 50- or 60-foot (15.2 or 18.2 m) pen, and they are given numbers from 0 to 9, with one cow left unnumbered. The unnumbered cow is a "trash cow," meaning it is not supposed to be sorted but is included just to make things tougher for the horse and rider.

A second 50- or 60-foot (15.2 or 18.2 m) pen is attached to the one containing the cows, with a 12- to 14-foot (3.7 to 4.3 m) opening between the two pens.

The rider (or riders) goes from the empty pen to the pen containing the cows, and the time begins. The rider or riders must separate the cattle in numerical order and move each cow individually into the adjoining pen. The rider (or team of riders) with the fastest time is the winner.

Ranch sorting events are held throughout the United States, as well as in conjunction with American Quarter Horse Association shows.

Seabiscuit

One of the most well-known racehorses of all time was a little bay stallion named Seabiscuit. A grandson of Man o' War (see Day 269), Seabiscuit began his racing career in 1935, in the midst of the Great Depression. He started out as unimpressive, and he didn't really begin to shine as a racehorse until he went into training with Tom Smith. Within a few years, Seabiscuit had proven himself to be the top money-winning Thoroughbred of all time. He also beat the great War Admiral, sired by Man o' War, in a match race. The horse's popularity was stunning, and he was such a celebrity that when he finally died in 1947, the location of his grave had to be kept a secret.

Seabiscuit's fame was resurrected in 2001 when Laura Hillenbrand wrote the best-selling, nonfiction work *Seabiscuit: An American Legend*. The book took off, earning racing writer and first-time book author Hillenbrand national fame. In 2003, a film was made from the book, starring Jeff Bridges and Tobey Maguire. The movie was nominated for seven Academy Awards, and it gave the sport of horseracing a much-needed shot in the arm.

Training for Harness

HAVE YOU EVER HAD THE URGE TO hitch your horse up to a sleigh so you could trot through the snow? If so, consider training him for harness.

Training a horse for harness is similar to training a horse to be ridden, except the horse must learn to pull something behind him instead of carry a rider on his back. If your horse is already saddle trained, part of his harness training is already started. He won't need to get used to wearing a bit or a pieces of a harness.

You will need to slowly get your horse acclimated to wearing blinkers and teach him how a driving bit feels in his mouth as opposed to a riding bit. Get your horse used to having his tail handled a lot and practice rubbing leather straps on his legs.

You'll need to teach your horse to ground drive, which means you will stand behind him holding long reins that are attached to his bit.

The next steps involve teaching the horse to respond to voice commands and getting him used to pulling something behind him. Many horses are terrified the first time they see a cart, so just getting him used to having the cart near him will be a task. Eventually, you can have a friend walk the cart behind the horse as you lead him around the arena.

It won't be long before you can hitch up the cart and ask your horse to pull it. Keep in mind that this should be done in an arena, and with the help of someone experienced in driving.

Quidding

QUIDDING REFERS TO AN EATING disorder that may be caused by an abnormal space between adjacent cheek teeth. Horses that quid often chew with their mouth open. They take a mouthful of food, chew it partially until it forms a mass, and then drop it from the mouth. Sometimes the horse stops chewing briefly, and then starts again. At other times, the partially chewed food becomes stuck between the teeth and cheek. Quidding is a sign of an oral or dental problem, such as difficulty swallowing or broken teeth.

A horse that's capable of chewing and swallowing properly keeps her lips closed and doesn't let much food fall to the ground. Be concerned if the horse shifts food in her mouth from side to side or frequently drops it.

Horses that are in poor condition or have difficulty keeping on weight may well have a dental problem. (See Day 110 for more on equine dental care.)

Besides being a common cause of severe quidding, painful periodontal disease or a sore mouth can cause related digestive problems. It's not unusual for a horse to bolt her food without chewing in an attempt to avoid irritating the tender area. The result is often indigestion or colic. And food that isn't chewed properly doesn't provide good nutrition. That's why these horses often appear unthrifty.

Widening the space between the teeth so food won't get trapped with a burr attachment on a motorized rasp can help the food move more easily through the mouth. This is a procedure performed by a veterinarian. The horse must be standing and heavily sedated. When this technique is successful, quidding often resolves within a week of treatment.

Caroling on Horseback

IF YOU LIKE TO HEARKEN BACK TO the old days when country folk hitched up their horse to a sleigh and went caroling around the neighborhood during the winter holidays, consider putting together a horseback caroling group.

Caroling on horseback is tremendous fun. Nothing feels more spirited than riding your horse through the community on a brisk December evening, looking at all the holiday lights and singing seasonal favorites to your neighbors.

First, find five or six (or more) riders who would like to go caroling. Next, plan out a route. If you live in an area where you'll have to ride along a road to get from one house to another, be sure to put reflective tape on your horse's tack and legs. If you can, scope out a ride that will keep you as far away from traffic as possible.

Determine a staging area where everyone can gather around dusk. Print out the lyrics for about ten different holiday songs and hand them out to the riders. Tell everyone to decorate their horses in Christmas ornaments and lights. Warn them to get their horses used to wearing these things a few days before the actual caroling.

On the night of the caroling, brief all your riders beforehand as to the route and the order of songs you will sing. Then start out on your ride, going from house to house. When you get to each house, have a rider dismount and knock on the door. When the resident answers, tell them you are here to carol and ask them if they'd like to hear it. They will probably gather the family and watch with happy grins as you sing from atop your horses.

You can also use caroling as a way to collect for a local charity. After you finish singing a few songs, thank the family for listening and tell them you are collecting donations for a charity. Odds are, you'll make some money for a good cause.

When you get back to the staging area, have someone standing by to serve hot chocolate and hot apple cider. With this finishing touch, everyone who participated will remember the event for years to come. And who knows—you may want to make it an annual tradition.

Percheron

THE ANCESTORS OF PERCHERON, the French draft horse, existed long before the keeping of records. They may have been horses dating to the Ice Age or horses the Romans used when they invaded Brittany some 2,000 years ago. Whatever their origin, it is known that at some point mares of the Perche region of France made the acquaintance of Arab stallions, producing offspring that became widely recognized for their substance, soundness, beauty, and style.

First serving as war horses, the horses of Le Perche were in great demand for various other purposes by the seventeenth century. They were, of course, farm horses, and they pulled stage coaches at a pace of 7 to 10 miles an hour (3.1 to 4.5 m/s), their gray and white color keeping them visible at night. In cities, they pulled omnibuses carrying passengers. The military also expressed an interest in them, establishing a stud at Le Pin in the early nineteenth century to develop army mounts. A Percheron named Jean Le Blanc was foaled there in 1823, and all of today's Percherons trace their lines back to him.

Not quite two decades later, in 1839, the first Percherons were imported to the United States. The big gray horses became favorites of farmers and freighters, but the invention of the tractor and the mechanization of farming put an end to their popularity.

A few farmers preserved the breed, and it saw a resurgence in the back-to-the-land movement of the 1960s and beyond. Today the horses perform their traditional work on small farms, and they are an essential part of many hayrides, sleigh rides, and parades. At state and county fairs, they compete in hitching and halter classes.

To look at a Percheron is to see ruggedness and power. They can weigh up to 2,600 pounds (1,179 kg), with the average being 1,900 pounds (862 kg), and stand 15 to 19 hands high, with most between 16.2 and 17.3 hands. The lower thighs are notable for their heavy muscling. Percherons are usually black or gray, but they also come in sorrel, bay, roan, and other colors. The Percheron has large eyes; a broad, full forehead; and a straight face. The head reflects the breed's Arabian heritage, with its strong jaw and refined ears.

The Percheron is strong enough to pull heavy loads, yet graceful enough to pull a carriage with style. It willingly carries a rider, and many are good jumpers. Tractable and an easy keeper, the Percheron has a pleasing disposition that combines pride, awareness, intelligence, and willingness to work. As its history shows, it is versatile, able to adapt to many climates, conditions, and activities.

Percheron

Harness Racing

HARNESS RACING IS AN EXCITING SPORT that harkens back to the days when farmers raced their trotting horses against one another on country roads. Today, harness racing takes place on racetracks, and it is a favorite sport for bettors.

The breed most often used for harness racing is the Standardbred. The breed can race at either the trot or the pace, and horses specialize in one gait or another. Pacers wear special hobbles when they race to ensure they stay in gait. Trotters that break into a gallop during a race must be taken to the outside of the field and slowed down until they go back into a trot.

Trotters and pacers pull sulkies, which are lightweight two-wheeled carts. Sulky drivers carry long whips that they use to tap the horses or make noise by striking the sulky shaft.

Harness racers do not break from a gate like flat-track racers. Instead, they start behind a moving starting gate, which is pulled by a truck. When the horses are all evenly lined up trotting or pacing behind the gate, the driver folds the gate back, and the field is off!

Retired Standardbreds need homes, and a number of rescue organizations have sprung up around North America. These organizations often retrain these horses to work under saddle and find them good homes.

Barbaro

ONE OF THE SADDEST HORSE STORIES is the tale of Barbaro, the courageous bay Thoroughbred stallion who broke his leg when running in the 2006 Preakness Stakes in Maryland.

Barbaro was undefeated on the day he walked to the starting gate at the Preakness, having just won the Kentucky Derby two weeks before. Barbaro was the favorite for the Preakness, and he was expected to win the Triple Crown, a feat that hadn't been accomplished since 1978.

After a false start, Barbaro shattered his right hind leg early into the race. He was taken to the New Bolton Center at the University of Pennsylvania School of Veterinary Medicine, where he underwent surgery the following day.

Barbaro spent the next eight months in the intensive care unit, recovering. During that time, the media reported on his condition daily, and concerned people from all over the world sent gifts to the ailing colt. Get well cards, treat baskets, and good-luck charms adorned his stall at the New Bolton Center.

Despite the fact that Barbaro was a cooperative patient and his injured leg had healed, he had to be euthanized in January 2007. He developed laminitis in his two forelegs as a result of trying to bear his weight on only three legs. Doctors determined that Barbaro could not be saved. His co-owner, Gretchen Jackson, said after Barbaro's passing: "Certainly, grief is the price we all pay for love."

Going Barefoot

HORSES WENT BAREFOOT for millions of years before humans started putting metal shoes on them in the sixth century. Proponents of the contemporary barefoot movement are quick to point this out, noting that wild horses have healthier feet than domestic horses.

Debate rages in the horse community over whether horses need shoes or not. Proponents on both sides, adamant about their beliefs, wage a war of words on the Internet.

Many veterinarians say that barefoot is best if you can go that route. However, they are quick to point out that some horses need the support of shoes. Barefoot advocates respond that some horses seem to need the support of shoes because their feet have been ruined by years of wearing shoes in the first place.

Followers of the barefoot movement subscribe to the belief that if a horse's hoof is trimmed in a manner that is identical to how it would naturally wear in the wild, the horse will have healthy feet. They go so far as to say that chronic conditions such as navicular and even founder can be managed and sometimes even cured through barefoot trimming.

Horse owners should make up their own minds about the barefoot vs. shoes issue by studying the horse's leg and hoof anatomy, and reading the detailed arguments being made by both camps. That's the only way to make an educated decision when it comes to the care of your horse's feet. (See Day 68 for more on healthy hoof care.)

Melanoma

THE OLD GRAY MARE ain't what she used to be, especially if she has spent a lot of her life outdoors in the sunshine. Like people, horses are prone to melanomas, or skin cancer.

These tumors can be solitary, but they often appear in multiples, forming a mass of soft or hard nodules that extend in a line, often up the base of the tail. Sometimes the nodules have a stalk-like attachment. They may also develop beneath the skin and lie hidden by the horse's hair until they become ulcerated and infected.

Melanomas are most common in older horses with coats that turn gray or white with age. They are especially common in Arabians, Lipizzaners, and Percherons that are six years or older. Approximately 80 percent of gray horses older than fifteen years develop melanomas. The good news: According to one study, melanomas in gray horses are less likely to be malignant.

DIAGNOSIS

While melanomas are usually a disease of old age, they may begin developing as early as three to four years of age. Melanomas commonly occur at the perineum, beneath the base of the tail, and on the head, at or near the ears, but they may develop at any area of the body. They are diagnosed through a biopsy and classified as benign or malignant.

Even when melanomas are benign, they can be a nuisance. Depending on their location, they can interfere with a horse's ability to urinate or defecate, mate, or wear a saddle, bridle, or halter.

TREATMENT

Melanomas can be removed surgically or frozen and removed. Chemotherapy may benefit horses with large or inoperable tumors. It was hoped that a drug called cimetidine would help control recurrence of melanomas, but studies have not shown that to be the case.

Crosstraining for Riders

DESPITE WHAT YOUR UNCLE JOE might say, riders are athletes. Yes, the horse does a lot of the work, but not all of it. Your body works hard when you ride, no matter how it looks to people whose feet are on the ground. For this reason, it's a good idea to cross-train. In addition to riding as much as you can, consider taking up one of the following activities to help strengthen your body for riding.

Pilates: Pilates improves flexibility and strength without building bulk. Pilates also incorporates mental conditioning, which can help with coordinating your brain and your body.

Weight lifting: Riders can benefit from lifting weights, especially if the emphasis is on repeti-

tion rather than increasing weight. The muscles needed for riding can be built using this method.

Yoga: To avoid being sore after you ride, you need to be flexible and limber. Yoga is a great way to accomplish this. It is an excellent way to relax. It also helps with balance and muscle strength, which is valuable when riding.

If you work at becoming an all-around athlete, riding will be easier for you. You'll have more strength, flexibility, and mental adeptness. Your body will stay fit, enabling you to be riding into your senior years.

Florida Cracker

ALTHOUGH IT MAY SOUND LIKE A snack to have with fruit and cheese, the Florida Cracker is a unique American horse. This rare breed, originally developed in the American South, is struggling to survive.

The Florida Cracker—so named after Southern cowboys of the nineteenth century known for their whip cracking skills—traces its heritage to Spanish horses brought to the New World by the conquistadors. Because of its geographic isolation and free-roaming lifestyle, the Florida Cracker evolved by natural selection to become a hardy and distinctive breed. Closely related to the Spanish Mustang (see Day 8) and Spanish Barb, the Florida Cracker played a large part in Florida's history as a ranching and agricultural state.

A hard-working cow horse, the Florida Cracker was used to work vast herds of cattle. Before this, the horse was integral to the lives of the Seminole Indians.

Eventually, the Florida Cracker was replaced in Florida by the American Quarter Horse. This larger breed was stronger and able to hold roped calves for veterinary treatment, which was a necessity brought on by the cattle screwworm epidemic of the 1930s.

The Florida Cracker is a rare breed, with fewer than 1,000 horses registered with the Florida Cracker Horse Association in Tallahassee, Florida. The American Livestock Breed Conservancy lists this horses as "critical."

Florida Cracker

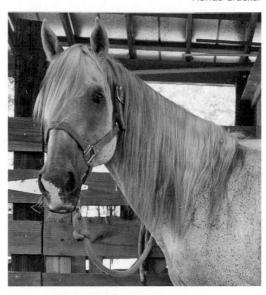

Resources

ASSOCIATIONS AND ORGANIZATIONS

American Academy of Veterinary Acupuncture
www.aava.org

American Cream Draft Horse Association
www.acdha.net

American Hackney Horse Society
www.hackneysociety.com
Photo, Halstead's Viking, page 217,
© Genevieve Kendell-Hayes

American Haflinger Registry
www.haflingerhorse.com

American Heritage Horse Association
www.americanheritagehorse.org

American Humane Association
www.americanhumane.org

American Miniature Horse Association
www.amha.org

American Miniature Horse Registry
www.shetlandminiature.com

American Mule Racing Association
www.muleracing.org

American Quarter Horse Association
www.aqha.com

American Saddlebred Horse Association
www.asha.net

American Veterinary Chiropractic Association
www.animalchiropractic.org

Cream Acres Ranch
www.creamacres.com
Photo, Captain's Barnabus Gold and George,
page 128, Courtesy of Carol L. Pshigoda

English Heritage (White Horse of Uffington)
www.english-heritage.org.uk

Equitours Riding Vacations
www.ridingtours.com

Falabella Miniature Horse Association
www.falabellafmha.com

The Fell Pony Society
www.fellponysociety.org.uk
Photo, Mare and foal, Murthwaite herd, page 305,
Courtesy of the Fell Pony Society

Florida Cracker Horse Association
www.floridacrackerhorses.com
Photo, Robb's Cracker Boy, page 315, Courtesy of
the Florida Cracker Horse Association

Haflinger Association of America
www.haflinger.net

International Federation of Icelandic
Horse Associations
www.feif.org

International Side Saddle Organization
www.sidesaddle.com

Kiger Mesteno Association
www.kigermustangs.org

Missouri Fox Trotting Horse Breed Association
www.mfthba.com

National Reined Cow Horse Association
www.nrcha.com

North American Peruvian Horse Association
www.napha.net
Photo, LEA Poema, page 42, © Barbara Windom

North American Riding for the Handicapped
Association
www.narha.org

North American Trail Ride Conference
www.natrc.org

Okjen Farm
www.okjenfarm.com
Photo, Pico Bello, page 232, courtesy of Okjen Farm

Pony of the Americas Club
www.poac.org

Professional Rodeo Cowboys Association
www.prorodeo.com

Ride and Tie Association
www.rideandtie.org

Rocky Mountain Horse Association
www.rmhorse.com

Spanish Jennet Horse Society
www.spanishjennet.org

Steens Mountain Kiger Registry
www.kigers.com/smkr

Sun and Star Farm
www.sunandstarfarm.com
Photo, page 70, Courtesy of Sun and Star Farm

Swedish Warmblood Association of
North America
www.swanaoffice.org

Tregoyd Cleveland Bays
www.tregoyd-cleveland-horses.com
Photo, page 281, Courtesy of Tregoyd
Cleveland Bays

United States Peruvian Horse Association
www.uspha.net

Thomas Walker Photography
Photo, page 107, Courtesy of Thomas Walker

White Stallion Productions, Inc.
"The Lipizzaner Stallion Show"
www.lipizzaner.com
Photo, Pluto Virtuoso, page 146, Courtesy of
White Stallion Productions

Wild Horse and Burro Program
www.wildhorseandburro.blm.gov

BOOKS

Centered Riding
Sally Swift
Trafalgar Square (1985)

*Hollywood Hoofbeats: Trails Blazed Across
the Silver Screen*
Petrine Mitchum and Audrey Pavia
BowTie Press, Inc. (2005)

Horses for Dummies, 2nd Ed.
Audrey Pavia
Wiley Publishing (2005)

The Illustrated Guide to Holistic Care for Horses
Denise Bean-Raymond
Quarry Books (2009)

The Original Book of Horse Treats
June Evers
Horse Hollow Press (1994)

317

Credits

All photos by Tom Sapp except as noted:

Courtesy of the Acme Design Company, 43

Arco images/agefotostock.com, 300

© blickwinkel/Alamy, 206

fotolia.com, 22; 58; 91; 134; 224; 258; 263; 311

iStockphoto.com, 36; 53; 63; 75; 97; 113; 117; 140;
165; 270; 295

Alain Julien/gettyimages.com, 289

© Juniors Bildarchiv/agefotostock.com, 28; 85;
178; 277; 284

© Juniors Bildarchiv/Alamy, 202

© Jorgen Larsson/agefotostock.com, 251

Mark Newman/gettyimages.com, 211

RFcompany/agefotostock.com, 158

Shutterstockimages.com, 16; 191

© Lynne Stone/agefotostock.com, 102

© WILDLIFE GmbH/Alamy, 184

Index

Acknowledgments

I would like to thank my editor, Rochelle Bourgault, and my agent, Grace Freedson, for including me in this wonderful project. I must also thank my husband, Randy, for being so understanding as I toiled many nights at the computer. And of course thanks to my horses, Milagro and Red, for their constant inspiration.

About the Author

AUDREY PAVIA is a former editor of *Horse Illustrated* magazine and an award-winning freelance writer specializing in equine subjects. She is the author of eight other horse books, and has authored hundreds of articles on various equine topics in a number of horse publications.

Audrey has been involved with horses since the age of nine, has owned and cared for horses throughout her life, and has trained in both Western and English disciplines. She currently resides in Norco, California (Horse Town, USA), with her husband, Randy, and animals of all kinds, including a Spanish Mustang named Milagro and a Quarter Horse named Red.

About the Photographer

TOM SAPP'S passion for taking photos led him to the Hallmark Institute of Photography. His expertise lies in photojournalism, wedding, fine art, digital, and portrait photography. He has been televised internationally on TLC, featured on theknot.com, and published in many publications including *Forbes* and *BusinessWeek* as one of the top regional photographers. Tom is based in Wilmington, North Carolina. See more of his work at www.tomsapp.com.